BIBLICAL ESSAYS IN HONOR OF
DANIEL J. HARRINGTON, SJ,
AND RICHARD J. CLIFFORD, SJ

BIBLICAL ESSAYS IN HONOR OF
Daniel J. Harrington, SJ, AND Richard J. Clifford, SJ

Opportunity for No Little Instruction

EDITED BY CHRISTOPHER G. FRECHETTE, CHRISTOPHER R. MATTHEWS, AND THOMAS D. STEGMAN, SJ

Paulist Press
New York / Mahwah, NJ

Cover image: Gasson Hall, courtesy of Boston College
Cover design by Sharyn Banks
Book design by Lynn Else

Library of Congress Cataloging-in-Publication Data

Biblical essays in honor of Daniel J. Harrington, SJ, and Richard J. Clifford, SJ : opportunity for no little instruction / edited by Thomas D. Stegman, SJ, Christopher Frechette, and Christopher R. Matthews.
    pages cm
    ISBN 978-0-8091-4898-1 (pbk. : alk. paper) — ISBN 978-1-58768-422-7 (ebook)
    1. Bible—Criticism, interpretation, etc. I. Harrington, Daniel J. honoree. II. Clifford, Richard J. honoree. III. Stegman, Thomas editor. IV. Frechette, Christopher G. editor. V. Matthews, Christopher R. editor.
    BS511.3.B535 2014
    221.6—dc23

                                                                            2014006509

ISBN 978-0-8091-4898-1 (paperback)
ISBN 978-1-58768-422-7 (e-book)

Published by Paulist Press
997 Macarthur Boulevard
Mahwah, New Jersey 07430

www.paulistpress.com

Printed and bound in the
United States of America

Contents

Contents

Contents

IV. Early Reception of New Testament Texts

Foreword

BOSTON COLLEGE

OFFICE OF THE PRESIDENT

On June 1, 2008, the Weston Jesuit School of Theology re-affiliated with Boston College and became an integral component of BC's newly established School of Theology and Ministry. This partnership has benefited students and faculty of both institutions as well as the wider Catholic community. Now officially known as the Ecclesiastical Faculty at Boston College, the former Weston Jesuit has additional personnel and financial resources to continue its mission of preparing priests, religious, and lay men and women for ministry in the Catholic Church for decades to come. Jesuits have moved from Cambridge to new quarters more appropriate for their community life and worship, and the number and involvement of Jesuits at Boston College has been enhanced.

The essays in this volume pay tribute to the teaching, scholarship, and pastoral impact of two remarkable Jesuits who began their academic careers at Weston Jesuit and who are greatly respected at Boston College and beyond. Fathers Richard Clifford and Daniel Harrington have each been engaged in the study of Scripture for more than four decades and have made an immense contribution to Christianity and Catholic life through their teaching, writing, and preaching. They have shared their intellectual gifts and insights in impressive fashion with generations of students and believers, an invaluable legacy of faith and scholarship. I am deeply grateful for their commitment, wisdom, and example, and I thank them for their critical roles in the re-affiliation of Weston Jesuit with Boston College.

William P. Leahy, S.J.
President

BOTOLPH HOUSE, 140 COMMONWEALTH AVENUE, CHESTNUT HILL, MASSACHUSETTS 02467-3934
617-552-3250

Editors' Preface

The interpretation of texts is always a challenge—even more so with religious texts that are thousands of years old—because the interpreter is confronted with the particularity and complexity of the human contexts in which they were written, edited, and employed. Richard J. Clifford, SJ, and Daniel J. Harrington, SJ, have proven themselves masters of interpreting biblical texts by applying their formidable scholarly skills to elucidate this particularity and complexity for specialist and nonspecialist audiences alike. In this volume, we have invited a number of distinguished authors to honor Dick and Dan by focusing on one dimension of the scriptural texts prominent in the scholarly work of both: how the writers and editors of ancient Jewish and Christian texts, extrabiblical as well as biblical, drew upon textual and other cultural traditions available to them in order to craft new texts that addressed their own situations.

Dick's and Dan's lives and careers have intersected in major ways. Both are members of the New England Province of the Society of Jesus, having entered the Jesuits in the 1950s—Dick in 1953, Dan in 1958. As young Jesuit students in their formative years, Dick and Dan took their language studies to a higher level by reading together, on their own initiative, the entire Hebrew Bible and Greek New Testament. They found themselves together as doctoral students at Harvard University for the rigorous training that would inform their subsequent teaching and writing careers, graduating in 1970. From 1972 until the present, they have been faculty colleagues, first at Weston Jesuit School of Theology in Cambridge, Massachusetts, and then, after WJST was reaffiliated with Boston College in the summer of 2008, at Boston College's School of Theology and Ministry in

Brighton, Massachusetts. Their assignments in centers of study geared toward professional ministry have meant that their teaching and, to a certain extent, their research and writing have been undertaken with an eye toward pastoral concerns and ministerial contexts. Both have served the Society of Jesus, the church, and the professional guild in exemplary fashion. In the latter instance, both have held the office of president of the Catholic Biblical Association—Dan in 1985–86, and Dick in 1991–92. Both are beloved teachers, renowned for their expertise and skilled pedagogy, and among their personal characteristics, for their friendliness and unassuming humility.

A full picture of Dick's and Dan's scholarly and professional accomplishments would require a lengthy treatise.[1] Some broad brushstrokes will have to suffice. Dan made an early impressive mark with his contribution (along with Jacques Cazeaux, Pierre Bogaert, and Charles Perrot) to the two-volume critical edition of Pseudo-Philo's *Biblical Antiquities* in the prestigious Sources chrétiennes series. He later teamed with his *Doctorvater* John Strugnell to publish the Dead Sea Scrolls text 4QInstruction in the Discoveries in the Judaean Desert series. Dan is the editor of the highly respected eighteen-volume Sacra Pagina series, the first full-scale multivolume Roman Catholic commentary on the New Testament in English. His own commentary on the Gospel of Matthew served as the archetype of the series. This volume is also representative of two of Dan's scholarly passions—the importance of understanding and appreciating the Jewish world from which Christianity and the documents of the New Testament arose, and his commitment to Jewish-Christian relations. Throughout Dan's career, one constant has been his work with *New Testament Abstracts*, an indispensable research tool for scholars. He contributed his first abstract in 1962 and has served as editor since 1972.

Dick too made an early scholarly splash when Harvard University Press published his dissertation on the theme of the cosmic mountain in the ancient Near East. His commentary on Second Isaiah, written in the mid-1980s, is an important study on the literary

---

1. For a complete listing of Dan's publications, see http://hdl.handle.net/2345/3348; and of Dick's publications, see http://hdl.handle.net /2345/3663.

and rhetorical qualities of a most difficult text. More recently, Dick's work has focused on Wisdom literature. He published a commentary on Proverbs in the distinguished Old Testament Library series, as well as a two-volume commentary on the Psalms. From 1976 to 1979, he was the general editor of *Catholic Biblical Quarterly*. In addition to his publications, Dick has taken on important administrative roles. He generously said "yes" to the Society of Jesus' request in 2007 that he become President of Weston Jesuit School of Theology at a critically important juncture in the school's history. Then from 2008 to 2010 he served as the founding Dean of the Boston College School of Theology and Ministry. As a result of his leadership, the school began its new incarnation well-positioned to continue its role in helping to form learned ministers.

We have taken advantage of the fact that Dick's and Dan's scholarly interests intersect in the Wisdom literature to subtitle this volume with a phrase from the prologue of the Book of Sirach: *Opportunity for No Little Instruction*. Their teaching and scholarship have provided ample "opportunity" for students and peers to plumb the depths of the Sacred Page. As mentioned at the outset, they have been at the forefront of appreciating how Jewish and Christian authors drew on and reinterpreted various texts and traditions—both from Israel and from the broader context of the ancient Near East. Such interest is evident in Dick's early work with creation myths and in his suggestions for the ongoing influence of creation and exodus motifs throughout Scripture, including the New Testament. Dan has done much work in the "rewritten narratives" of biblical traditions in the intertestamental period, in addition to highlighting the importance and relevance of the Jewish world in which the New Testament texts were born. It is this shared focus on the use and reappropriation of texts and traditions that links the essays that follow.

The volume begins with a set of four essays, each of which focuses on one of the following aspects associated with the portrayal of God: sexuality, violence, justice, and mercy. Mark Smith asks whether gender and sexuality can be correlated with a divine "essence" based on biblical evidence. Discussing the impact upon biblical texts of notions about the female deities Anat, Astarte, and Asherah—known from Ugaritic and Canaanite sources—he addresses how both male and female images for God are employed side by side in the Bible. Jon Levenson recognizes that divine sanction for violence is implied in the horrifying closing of Ps 137, but argues against removing the text from religious usage on ethical grounds. Levenson employs intertextual biblical evidence to argue that, in its ancient context, this text constituted a plea for justice. C. L. Seow demonstrates the manner in which the author of Job 40:15–24 adapts a variety of traditions to create the character of Behemoth. He discusses this fabulous creature as a manifestation of God's justice beyond what Job can fathom. Gary Anderson demonstrates that the image of God forgiving debts in the Lord's Prayer expresses mercy. Understood over against the Aramaic idiom by which sin is expressed as debt, seeking forgiveness of debt evokes the image of the compassionate lender who cancels a debt out of mercy.

The second set of essays engages biblical and extrabiblical Jewish literature of the late Second Temple period. John Collins observes the influence of Canaanite traditions about the gods El and Baal in the portrayal of God and an exalted angelic being, the "son of man" of Dan 7. He argues that the Gospel writers likely associated this tradition with Jesus in the wake of belief in Jesus' resurrection. Carol Newsom takes issue with those, Collins among them, who emphasize the importance of the Canaanite traditions for interpreting Dan 7. Newsom contends that it makes better sense to assess Dan 7 in terms of how it may adapt type scenes and schemata more contemporary with the writing of Daniel. Read side by side, the essays of Collins and Newsom demonstrate that even accomplished scholars may interpret the same text differently. John Endres investigates the presence of creation traditions in the second-century BCE book of *Jubilees*. He argues that *Jubilees* adapts creation traditions from Genesis for its own theological ends, and that it emphasizes the identification of God as Creator in relationship to the Mosaic covenant. Christopher Frechette interprets the function of the Song of the Three Jews (Dan 3:24–90) within the narrative of Dan 3. He interprets blessing God as a formal greeting analogous to a military salute and argues that the nonhuman elements called upon in the Song to bless God were all understood to be angels, a point that is emphasized in the Greek versions by their allusion to the tradition of creation preserved in *Jub.* 2. Eileen Schuller's essay on prose prayers in Pseudo-Philo's *Biblical Antiquities* takes up a text and a theme that have been neglected by scholars. In addition to drawing up a list of such prayers and to noting similarities with biblical prose prayers, she points to ways in which Pseudo-Philo adapts and transforms traditional usage.

In the third section, each of the seven essays assesses how New Testament authors employ texts and traditions. Thomas Stegman analyzes Paul's citations of and allusions to various scriptural texts in 2 Cor 8—9 in his discourse on the collection for the church in Jerusalem. Stegman focuses on the ways Paul adapts the texts and draws on their literary contexts in order to give richer theological texture to his exhortation to generosity. John Donahue sets forth the pervasive influence of Isaiah on the Gospel of Mark. He contends that Mark employs the Isaian pattern of judgment followed by deliverance; indeed, this pattern is key to interpreting Jesus' use of Isa 6:9–10—where the prophet speaks of the hardness of the people's hearts and their failure to hear and perceive God's ways—in Mark 4:11–12. Christopher Matthews takes up Luke's use of this same Isaian text in Paul's words to a group of Jews in Rome in the climactic scene of Acts (28:23–28). After sampling standard scholarly opinion on the passage, Matthews suggests that a binary opposition of "Christianity" and "Judaism" is anachronistic for Luke's time, and that Luke may view his own Christ-oriented community to still be within the bounds of Judaism.

Donald Senior offers a study of Matthew's context and use of sources and interpretive traditions. He demonstrates Matthew's creativity and pastoral skill in composing his story of Jesus that spoke to the circumstances and needs of a primarily Jewish-Christian community. Harold Attridge analyzes the language of "flesh" and "spirit" in John's Gospel. In contrast to the Dead Sea Scrolls and Paul's letters, which closely associate flesh with sin, John offers a more positive assessment of "flesh" in light of the Spirit's transformative power.

Pheme Perkins turns to the Scrolls and to other intertestamental writings to shed light on John's references to Moses. Perkins's study reveals a rich, nuanced use of Moses traditions and motifs that has ramifications for understanding John's Christology as well as some of the Gospel's polemical features. Adela Yarbro Collins shows how, in the Book of Revelation, John the prophet and seer adapts imagery and language from Daniel and from intertestamental literature to set forth his portrait of the risen Jesus. She also looks at how John employs prophetic denunciations and indictments to speak to the situation of Christian communities reeling from violence perpetrated by Rome.

The two essays of the final section both address the life of the canonical Scriptures in early Christianity. The first recognizes some continued adaptation of certain New Testament texts in particular manuscripts. The second emphasizes the generative effect that New Testament traditions had on early Christian writings. Eldon Epp advocates a new emphasis for textual criticism in which variant readings of a given passage of the New Testament are valued as evidence for the early reception history of the text. Carolyn Osiek discusses the way in which the New Testament traditions of Christ's passion influenced accounts of martyrdom in subsequent centuries. She shows how writers tended to stylize the martyr in terms characteristic of the accounts of Christ's passion.

We are delighted to present this volume in tribute to Dan Harrington and Dick Clifford, our beloved and distinguished colleagues. And we are confident that readers will find in these essays "opportunity for no little instruction."

* * *

On February 7, 2014, a few months after this manuscript was submitted to press, Dan Harrington passed away following a lengthy bout with prostate cancer. Dan was able to read a "protocopy" of this book before he died. He was humbled to be so honored, and expressed his deep gratitude to all the contributors.

Abbreviations

BIBLIOGRAPHICAL

AB	Anchor Bible
ABD	*Anchor Bible Dictionary.* Edited by D. N. Freedman. 6 vols. New York, 1992
AGJU	Arbeiten zur Geschichte des antiken Judentums und des Urchristentums
ANTC	Abingdon New Testament Commentaries
AOAT	Alter Orient und Altes Testament
AOTC	Abingdon Old Testament Commentaries
AthR	*Anglican Theological Review*
AYB	Anchor Yale Bible
BASOR	*Bulletin of the American Schools of Oriental Research*
BDAG	W. Bauer, F. W. Danker, W. F. Arndt, and F. W. Gingrich. *Greek-English Lexicon of the New Testament and Other Early Christian Literature.* 3rd ed. Chicago: University of Chicago Press, 2000
BETL	Bibliotheca ephemeridum theologicarum lovaniensium
Bib	*Biblica*
BJS	Brown Judaic Studies
BNTC	Black's New Testament Commentaries
BTB	*Biblical Theology Bulletin*
BZAW	Beihefte zur Zeitschrift für die alttestamentliche Wissenschaft
BZNW	Beihefte zur Zeitschrift für die neutestamentliche Wissenschaft
CAD	*The Assyrian Dictionary of the Oriental Institute of the University of Chicago.* Edited by I. Gelb et al. 21 vols.

	Chicago: Oriental Institute of the University of Chicago, 1956–2010
CAT	Commentaire de l'Ancien Testament
CBQ	*Catholic Biblical Quarterly*
CBQMS	Catholic Biblical Quarterly Monograph Series
CCSS	Catholic Commentary on Sacred Scripture
ConBOT	Coniectanea biblica: Old Testament Series
CP	*Classical Philology*
CSCO	Corpus scriptorum christianorum orientalium. Edited by I. B. Chabot et al. Paris, 1903–
CSHJ	Chicago Studies in the History of Judaism
CTU	*The Cuneiform Alphabetic Texts from Ugarit, Ras Ibn Hani, and Other Places.* Edited by M. Dietrich, O. Loretz, and J. Sanmartín. Münster, 1995
DDD²	*Dictionary of Deities and Demons in the Bible.* 2nd ed. Edited by K. van der Toorn, B. Becking, and P. W. van der Horst. Leiden, 1999
DJD	Discoveries in the Judaean Desert
DSD	*Dead Sea Discoveries*
EDEJ	*Eerdman's Dictionary of Early Judaism.* Edited by J. J. Collins and D. C. Harlow. Grand Rapids: Eerdmans, 2010
EdF	Erträge der Forschung
EKKNT	Evangelisch-katholischer Kommentar zum Neuen Testament
ErIsr	Eretz-Israel
ESEC	Emory Studies in Early Christianity
ETL	*Ephemerides theologicae lovanienses*
FAT	Forschungen zum Alten Testament
FRLANT	Forschungen zur Religion und Literatur des Alten und Neuen Testaments
HAR	*Hebrew Annual Review*
HDR	Harvard Dissertations in Religion
Her.	*Quis Rerum Divinarum Heres Sit*
HNT	Handbuch zum Neuen Testament

HSM	Harvard Semitic Monographs
HSS	Harvard Semitic Studies
HTR	*Harvard Theological Review*
HTS	Harvard Theological Studies
HvTSt	*Hervormde teologiese studies*
ICC	International Critical Commentary
Int	*Interpretation*
IRT	Issues in Religion and Theology
JBL	*Journal of Biblical Literature*
JECS	*Journal of Early Christian Studies*
JJS	*Journal of Jewish Studies*
JNES	*Journal of Near Eastern Studies*
JQR	*Jewish Quarterly Review*
JRS	*Journal of Roman Studies*
JSJ	*Journal for the Study of Judaism in the Persian, Hellenistic, and Roman Periods*
JSJSup	Supplements to the Journal for the Study of Judaism
JSNTSup	Journal for the Study of the New Testament: Supplement Series
JSOT	*Journal for the Study of the Old Testament*
JSOTSup	Journal for the Study of the Old Testament: Supplement Series
JSP	*Journal for the Study of the Pseudepigrapha*
JSPSup	Journal for the Study of the Pseudepigrapha: Supplement Series
JTI	*Journal of Theological Interpretation*
JTS	*Journal of Theological Studies*
KAI	*Kanaanäische und aramäische Inschriften.* H. Donner and W. Röllig. 2nd ed. Wiesbaden, 1966–69
KAT	Kommentar zum Alten Testament
KHC	Kurzer Hand-Commentar zum Alten Testament
KTU	*Die keilalphabetischen Texte aus Ugarit.* Edited by M. Dietrich, O. Loretz, and J. Sanmartín. AOAT 24/1. Neukirchen-Vluyn, 1976. 2nd enlarged ed. of *CTU: The Cuneiform Alphabetic Texts from Ugarit, Ras Ibn Hani,*

	and Other Places. Edited by M. Dietrich, O. Loretz, and J. Sanmartín. Münster, 1995
LTQ	*Lexington Theological Quarterly*
Neot	*Neotestamentica*
NIB	*The New Interpreter's Bible*
NovT	*Novum Testamentum*
NovTSup	Novum Testamentum Supplements
NTL	New Testament Library
NTS	*New Testament Studies*
NTT	*Norsk Teologisk Tidsskrift*
NTTS	New Testament Tools and Studies
NTTSD	New Testament Tools, Studies, and Documents
OBT	Overtures to Biblical Theology
OED	*Oxford English Dictionary*
OTL	Old Testament Library
OTP	*Old Testament Pseudepigrapha.* Edited by J. H. Charlesworth. 2 vols. New York, 1983.
OtSt	*Oudtestamentische Studiën*
PCNT	Paideia: Commentaries on the New Testament
PVTG	Pseudepigrapha Veteris Testamenti Graece
RB	*Revue biblique*
RS	Ras Shamra
SBLDS	Society of Biblical Literature Dissertation Series
SBLEJL	Society of Biblical Literature Early Judaism and Its Literature
SBLMS	Society of Biblical Literature Monograph Series
SBLRBS	Society of Biblical Literature Resources for Biblical Study
SBLSCS	Society of Biblical Literature Septuagint and Cognate Studies
SBLTCS	Society of Biblical Literature Text-Critical Studies
SBT	Studies in Biblical Theology
SC	Sources chrétiennes. Paris: Cerf, 1943–
ScrAeth	Scriptores Aethiopici
Sem	*Semitica*

SJ	Studia judaica
SNTSMS	Society for New Testament Studies Monograph Series
SP	Sacra Pagina
STDJ	*Studies on the Texts of the Desert of Judah*
TDNT	*Theological Dictionary of the New Testament.* Edited by G. Kittel and G. Friedrich. Translated by G. W. Bromiley. 10 vols. Grand Rapids, 1964–76
TS	*Theological Studies*
TSAJ	Texts and Studies in Ancient Judaism
TTZ	*Trierer theologische Zeitschrift*
UBS	*The Greek New Testament*, United Bible Societies, 4th ed.
VC	*Vigiliae christianae*
VT	*Vetus Testamentum*
WBC	Word Biblical Commentary
WUNT	Wissenschaftliche Untersuchungen zum Neuen Testament
ZAW	*Zeitschrift für die alttestamentliche Wissenschaft*
ZNW	*Zeitschrift für die neutestamentliche Wissenschaft und die Kunde der älteren Kirche*
ZTK	*Zeitschrift für Theologie und Kirche*

ANCIENT BIBLICAL VERSIONS

LXX	Septuagint
MT	Masoretic Text
OG	Old Greek (version of the Septuagint)
Syr.	Syriac
TH	Theodotian (version of the Septuagint)
Vulg.	Vulgate

MODERN BIBLICAL TRANSLATIONS

NABRE	New American Bible Revised Edition
NETS	New English Translation of the Septuagint
NJPS	New Jewish Publication Society of America Tanakh
NRSV	New Revised Standard Version

GENERAL

BCE	Before the Common Era
CE	Common Era
ch./chs.	chapter/chapters
Gk.	Greek
Heb.	Hebrew, literally

I

PORTRAYALS OF GOD

1

The Sexuality of God in the Hebrew Bible

Mark S. Smith
(NEW YORK UNIVERSITY)

INTRODUCTION

I am honored to be invited to contribute to this volume for my teachers, Richard J. Clifford and Daniel J. Harrington. From my student days till today, these two Jesuits have been models for me in their scholarship and their character. Their love for the Scriptures and the church shines through in their writings, teaching, and personal interactions.

The male and female metaphors for God in the Bible constitute an important subject, as questions of God's gender and sexuality have come to the forefront of American religious life. Gender issues have become critical concerns in society, and they have been splitting some churches in North America right down the middle. The Bible has been central to this discussion, because it has been used to justify a male notion of God.

To discuss divine gender and sexuality in the Bible, it is necessary both to represent accurately the ancient evidence and to be sensitive to the modern context. The Bible is not a socially perfect document. The goal is not to make the Bible support modern views. The question is how to explore what the Bible says about God in a manner that recognizes this gap between our present and the biblical past, while discerning a disclosure of the biblical God that can still speak and perhaps even inspire today. I am not sure that this goal can be reached when it comes to the area of gender and sexuality. I say this because biblical metaphor for God involving gender and sexuality is terrifically problematic. Is it a marker of some aspect of God or of the "essence" of God? And if it is a marker of the divine "essence," what view of gender and sexuality is so inscribed into Divine Being? As theologians have noted, these questions are not easily answered,[1] and perhaps our efforts to address them may not get us to intellectually satisfying answers. Instead, the process of pursuing the task itself may teach us about the difficulty of knowing God.

A male understanding of God is the case in much of the Bible. However, this is hardly the whole story, as the Bible contains female images for God as well. In addition, part of the story involves the impact that different goddesses in the ancient Near East made on female imagery for the divine in the Bible. This essay explores gender representations of God in the Hebrew Bible, as well as goddesses contemporary with the biblical authors.

GENDERED IMAGES FOR GOD IN THE BIBLE

When it comes to Israel's Bible, the texts clearly use gendered language for God. When we look at the gendered metaphor of God as divine parent in the Bible, it is clearly weighted—and freighted— to the male.[2] God is imaged as father in many passages: Deut 32:6;

---

1. Janet Martin Soskice, *The Kindness of God: Metaphor, Gender, and Religious Language* (Oxford: Oxford University Press, 2007), 45.

2. See the older survey of Phyllis Trible, *God and the Rhetoric of Sexuality* (OBT; Philadelphia: Fortress, 1978), 31–71. Compassion in the ancient Near East is not always a female attribute (see Ps 103:13), as argued by Trible, *God and the Rhetoric of Sexuality*, 34; and Mayer Gruber, *The Motherhood of God and Other Studies* (South Florida Studies in the History of Judaism 57; Atlanta: Scholars Press, 1992), 6–7 on Isa 49:13; Jer 31:20; Hos 2:19 and 23. Trible's arguments relating a woman's *rehem*, "womb," and divine *raḥămîm*, "compassion," suffer from the "root fallacy," on which see James Barr, *The Semantics of Biblical Language* (Oxford: Oxford University Press, 1961), 100–6.

Isa 63:16; 64:7 [E 8]; Jer 3:4, 19; 31:9; Mal 1:6; 2:10; Wis 14:3; Sir 23:1, 4; cf. Exod 4:22; Jer 1:8; and Hos 11:1. God also appears as the husband of Israel (Hos 2 and Jer 2; see also Ezek 16 and 23).[3] Feminist scholars of the Bible have rightly questioned the normative character of biblical passages such as Ezek 16 and 23, which are so laden with male images of God and female language symbolic of human idolatry.[4] Another central male image for the divine involves God as a great king (e.g., Pss 93; 97; 99).[5] The verbs for kingship used in these psalms include the royal functions of ruling and notions of might applied to the deity. By contrast, there is no comparable language of queen for God (cf. the Queen of Heaven criticized in Jer 7 and 44).

God is also imaged as a mother, for example in Deut 32:18: "The rock who bore you, you neglected, and you forgot God who gave you birth."[6] Isaiah 42:13–14 combines male and female imagery in expressing God's acting for Israel: "Yahweh will go forth like a hero. Like a warrior he will stir up (his) rage. He will shout; indeed he will roar. He will prevail over his enemies. 'For a long time I kept quiet; I was silent; I restrained myself. Now I will scream like a woman in labor. I will inhale, and I will exhale simultaneously."[7] Female language of God as midwife is used in Ps 22:9–10: "You drew me from the womb, made me secure at my mother's breast. I became your

---

3. See Michael David Coogan, *God and Sex: What the Bible Really Says* (New York: Twelve, 2010), 186.

4. See Julia M. O'Brien, *Challenging Prophetic Metaphor: Theology and Ideology in the Prophets* (Louisville: Westminster John Knox, 2008); and Corrine Carvalho, "The Beauty of the Bloody God: The Divine Warrior in Prophetic Literature," in *Aesthetics of Violence in the Prophets* (ed. C. Franke and J. M. O'Brien; Library of Hebrew Bible/Old Testament Studies 515; New York: T & T Clark, 2010), 131–52.

5. For a good survey, see Marc Zvi Brettler, *God Is King: Understanding an Israelite Metaphor* (JSOTSup 76; Sheffield, UK: Sheffield Academic Press, 1989).

6. Trible, *God and the Rhetoric of Sexuality*, 62–64; and Soskice, *Kindness of God*, 2, 79, 181–82. The first verb might be taken as the paternal role of "begetting," but it applies more often to mothers (ca. 208 times versus 22 times for males), and in this passage it is in parallel with a maternal role, as noted by Jeffrey Tigay, *Deuteronomy: The JPS Torah Commentary* (Philadelphia: Jewish Publication Society, 1996), 307 and 404n99.

7. All translations of biblical and extrabiblical texts are by the author.

charge at birth; from my mother's womb you have been my God." There are also passages referring to God in a manner that transcends gender. Genesis 1:27 represents the human person, both male and female, as the image of God, suggesting that God is neither male nor female. Ezekiel 1:26 envisions God's body in human terms, "something that seemed like a human form." In this case, too, God is beyond the category of human gender.

The gender metaphor in these passages focuses on Israel's relationship with God. The question remains: How much of this gendered language was thought to be expressive of who God is? Scholars have commented that the Bible offers no clear statement about God's motherhood in the same manner found for God's fatherhood. As seen in the passages mentioned above, the biblical picture is asymmetrical, with the male metaphor more dominant. How did this sexual asymmetry come to be? What was the situation in Israel that this picture of God's sexuality may be addressing? Is there a larger background that might give some perspective on the situation? It is possible to identify the larger cultural context in ancient Israel for female metaphorical language for God. Important to the cultural context of gender language for God are three goddesses.

THREE GODDESSES AND THEIR IMPACT IN ISRAEL

Early Israel was home to a number of gods and goddesses. The best known goddess may be Asherah, poorly attested in the Bible, but known in Ugaritic and Canaanite sources as the wife of the head god El and mother of many deities. Two other goddesses are also known in Israel's Bible. These are Anat and Astarte. Both are younger hunters and warriors. They are also known from texts outside of the Bible.

Let me begin with Anat. She was a warrior goddess, especially well known from a passage from the Ugaritic texts describing her battling human soldiers from seashore to sunrise (i.e., from "east to west"):

And look! Anat fights in the valley,
Battl[es] between the two towns.
She fought the people of the se[a]-shore,
Struck the populace of the su[nr]ise.
Under her, like balls, were hea[ds],
Above her, like grasshoppers, hands,
Like locusts, heaps of warrior-hands.
She fixed heads to her back,
Fastened hands on her waist.
Knee-deep she glea[n]ed warrior-blood,
Neck-deep in the gor[e] of soldiers.[8]

This passage shows Anat as a "blood and guts" warrior.

But Anat seems to disappear from Israel. Her name survives in the Bible only in the names of people and places, such as Shamgar Ben-Anat (Judg 3:31 and 5:6). However, her imagery apparently survives in the unusual blood and guts battle of Yнwн in Isa 34; 59; and 63. In Isa 63:3, God describes his warfare against Edom on analogy with trodding out the grapes harvested in the fall vintage; the grapes evoke a picture of crushed heads with their blood. These images are echoed in our culture, in the "Battle Hymn of the Republic" composed by Julia Ward Howe (1819–1910):

Mine eyes have seen the glory
of the coming of the Lord;
He is trampling out the vintage
where the grapes of wrath are stored.

In Ugaritic and perhaps early Israel, Anat was quite the divine action hero, but this changed over time. Apart from the rare occurrences of her name and the literary association of bloody battle, she largely faded from ancient Israel. As far as we know, Anat was never a symbol of idolatry in ancient Israel, but her imagery seems to have lived on.

---

8. See Mark S. Smith, "Anat's Warfare Cannibalism and the Biblical Ḥerem," in *The Pitcher Is Broken: Memorial Essays in Honor of Gösta W. Ahlström* (ed. L. K. Handy and S. Holloway; JSOTSup 190; Sheffield, UK: JSOT Press, 1995), 368–86.

Like Anat, Astarte is a warrior, as seen in the following lines from a hymn:[9]

The name of Astarte let my voice sing,
May I praise the name of the lion.
O name, may you be victorious over…
May you/she shut the jaw of El's attackers.
A great panther is Astarte,
A great panther that pounces.

In contrast to Anat, Astarte is criticized in the Bible. As Ashtoret, she is denounced as an idolatrous import from Phoenicia (1 Kgs 11:5). In the plural form Ashtarot, her name is synonymous with the worship of goddesses in general (Judg 2:13). In Jer 7 and 44, some form of Astarte, perhaps one combined or identified with Ishtar, may be the goddess named only as the "Queen of Heaven." In the Bible, Astarte is the female epitome of idolatry.

The story with Asherah is quite different. She is part of the biblical story of idolatry, but her name also becomes part of the story of the monotheistic god. Asherah's husband was the god El, and the two are known from both extrabiblical and biblical texts. Mostly in the Bible, El is identified as a name for YHWH, for example, El Shadday, translated "God Almighty," in Exod 6:2–3. The evidence for Asherah as a goddess in early Israel is cryptic, but Asherah seems to be known in early Israel, as seen in the title "Breasts and Womb" in Gen 49:25–26.

The next chapter in the story of Asherah involves a number of inscriptions from ancient Israel, especially ones that came from a site in the south of Israel called Kuntillet 'Ajrud. Visitors seem to have left wishes of blessings for other people, including invocations of blessing by the main god of Israel along with "his asherah":

---

9. See Dennis Pardee, "A New Ugaritic Song to 'Athartu (RIH 98/02)," in *Ugarit at Seventy-Five* (ed. K. Lawson Younger Jr.; Winona Lake, IN: Eisenbrauns, 2007), 27–39; and idem, "Deux tablettes ougaritiques de la main d'un meme scribe, trouvées sur deux sites distinct: RS 19.039 et RIH 98/02," *Semitica et Classica* 1 (2008): 9–38, esp. 11–13. Note also Theodore J. Lewis, "Athtartu's Incantations and the Use of Divine Names as Weapons," *JNES* 70 (2011): 207–27.

"May they be sated…be granted (?) by [Y]HWH of Teman and
  by [his] asherah";
"I (hereby) bless you by YHWH of Samaria and by his asherah";
"I (hereby) bless you by [Y]HWH of Teman and by his asherah";
"…by YHWH of the Teman and by his asherah."[10]

If the word in the blessing formulas in the Kuntillet ʻAjrud inscriptions
has "his" in it, normally in Hebrew the word is not a name but an
object, and just such an object (the asherah tree-symbol) is condemned in the Bible. This symbol became a way of talking about
YHWH's blessing.[11] Whatever the asherah is, it is his, not hers.

The final chapter in our story of Asherah/asherah involves the
adaptation of the symbol of the asherah into biblical thought but without the notion of a goddess. We can see this transformation in the
imagery of personified Wisdom in the Book of Proverbs. In Prov 3,
Wisdom is described as "a tree of life," much like the asherah tree-
symbol. More than this, Prov 3:18 makes what I think is a clever wordplay on the word *asherah*.[12] Wisdom is described: "She is a tree of life
to those who take hold of her, whoever takes hold of her is happy."
The verse shows the symbolism of the female Wisdom as a tree of life,
much as the asherah is a symbol of blessing. The word *happy* (Heb.
ʼašrê) sounds like a pun on the name of the asherah-symbol. This sym-

---

10. For these inscriptions, see Zeev Meshel, *Kuntillet ʻAjrud (Horvat Teman): An Iron Age II Religious Site on the Judah-Sinai Border* (Jerusalem: Israel Exploration Society, 2012). See also F. W. Dobbs-Allsopp et al., eds., *Hebrew Inscriptions: Texts from the Biblical Period of the Monarchy with Concordance* (New Haven: Yale University Press, 2005), 277–79.

11. Shmuel Ahituv, *Echoes from the Biblical Past: Hebrew and Cognate Inscriptions from the Biblical Period* (Jerusalem: Carta, 2008), 221–24; Frank Moore Cross, "The Phoenician Ostracon from Acco, the Ekron Inscriptions and אשרתה," in *Ephraim Stern Volume* (ed. J. Aviram et al.; ErIsr 29; Jerusalem: Israel Exploration Society, 2009), 20*–22*; Mark S. Smith, "The Blessing God and Goddess: A Longitudinal View from Ugarit to ʻYahweh and…his asherah' at Kuntillet ʻAjrud," in *Enigmas and Images: Studies in Honor of Tryggve N. D. Mettinger* (ed. G. Eidevall and B. Scheuer; ConBOT 58; Winona Lake, IN: Eisenbrauns, 2011), 213–26; and Shmuel Ahitub, Esther Eshel, and Zeʼev Meshel, "The Inscriptions," in Meshel, *Kuntillet ʻAjrud*, 127, 130–32, 138n36.

12. I owe this point to the late biblical scholar Anthony Ceresko.

bol has been transmuted into a metaphor for divine wisdom; in this context, it does not denote the goddess's self or her "essence." The divine male and female became considered male alone, with imagery of the female expressive of one side of that divinity, namely its wisdom. In short, whatever the "ontology" of the goddess was, in Prov 3 it has "moved indoors," inside the Godhead, with the reformed female imagery serving to express the Godhead in the world (cf. Wis 7:25–26). Maleness may be the general understanding of the Godhead for ancient Israel, but this Godhead includes wisdom represented in female terms. The result continues to haunt Christian tradition.[13] While God transcends categories of gender, male language for the deity is regularly reified in our church thinking, backed by our creedal tradition ("I believe in God, the Father Almighty…"). Overall, the biblical tradition raises questions for modern Christians. Is this the end of the matter when it comes to gender imagery for God?

To begin to answer this question, it may help to note that gender language for God in ancient Israel was a moving target. It may also be useful to view the issue in historical and cultural terms. As we have seen, male and female language for gods and goddesses was traditional in early Israel. Traditional language for these older gods and goddesses, including its gendered formulations, did not immediately stop with the emergence of monotheism in Israel. The female imagery for God seems to have accelerated, once goddesses were no longer—or at least considered less—an issue in ancient Israel. As Elizabeth Bloch-Smith has brilliantly suggested,[14] this loss of goddesses in Israel may correlate with the relative proliferation of female imagery for God in a sixth-century work such as Second Isaiah (Isa 40–55).[15] This author apparently was trying out a strategy for understanding Israel's chief

---

13. Soskice, *Kindness of God*, 85.

14. Elizabeth Bloch-Smith, personal communication.

15. Isa 42:14; 46:3–4; and 49:15; cf. 45:10–11; 66:9, 13. See Gruber, *Motherhood of God*; Sarah Dille, *Mixing Metaphors: God as Mother and Father in Deutero-Isaiah* (London: T & T Clark, 2004); and Hanne Løland, *Silent or Salient Gender: The Interpretation of Gendered God-Language in the Hebrew Bible Exemplified in Isaiah 42, 46, and 49* (FAT 2/32; Tübingen: Mohr Siebeck, 2008).

deity, which may not have been an option in earlier periods of Israel's history when goddesses were still part of the religious landscape. The new female language renews the story about an old God. Innovations on the part of Second Isaiah and other authors of this period show that YHWH could be understood in terms of male and female gendered metaphors together. Other passages show God transcending the categories of sexuality (e.g., Gen 1:27 and Ezek 1:26, as noted previously; see also Job 38:28–29). The Bible itself points to the limitations of gender language for understanding God. We may take a cue from this situation in the Bible and recognize our own limitations in this regard.

DIVINE SEXUALITY AND THE ONE GOD

As the preceding section notes, the question of divine gender and sexuality was intrinsic to the development of monotheism. The development of a single God potentially affected prior notions of divine being that had been at home in Israel's earlier polytheistic context. Gender and sexuality constituted a basic construction of the "essence" of deities in earlier Israelite polytheism, but this was not necessarily the case for Israel's monotheistic worldview. In the arena of gender and sexuality, divine oneness issued in what might seem to be misshapen discourse about God. In Tikva Frymer-Kensky's terms, God is represented as male but not acting in male sexual terms. Or, God is male, less in terms of divine "essence" and more in terms of "imagery, concepts, roles and functions."[16] In other words, some passages in biblical literature seem to show that there is no male essence to God, even as God continued to be conceived of as male. This maleness may have conveyed the superior role of God, because male language conveyed that superiority. So, in general for ancient Israelites, did male

---

16. Cf. Beate Pongratz-Leisten, "When the Gods are Speaking: Toward Defining the Interface between Polytheism and Monotheism," in *Propheten in Mari, Assyrien und Israel* (ed. M. Köckert and M. Nissinen; Göttingen: Vandenhoeck & Ruprecht, 2003), 163.

language for God convey essence or roles or both? Was it—for them—a matter of essence or not?

Contemporary linguistic theory on gender may help us in exploring these questions. In recent work on this topic, there has been a profound shift in approach, characterized by Ann Weatherall in these terms:

> Traditionally in gender and language research, like elsewhere in the social sciences, language was viewed as a mirror; it reflected the shared essences about women and men. Language was also thought to reflect society's beliefs and values about women and men. Now language about women and men and the way men and women speak can be understood as part of the same discursive process, the social construction of gender. Sex/gender no longer has to be viewed as something that we are. Rather it is something that we do, an interactional accomplishment that we achieve over and over again, in different ways, throughout the course of our lives.[17]

Weatherall also characterizes the social construction of sex/gender through language in these terms: "Gender is not an essence, but a form of activity....Gender is a routine and joint accomplishment of situated conversational activity."[18] In this view, gender and sexuality are not simply what people are; they are what people do in relation to other persons.

This distinction between gender as "essence" and gender as social "activity" provides perspective. Rather than deciding between gender as "essence" and gender as "activity," the situation in ancient Israel seems to suggest a both/and approach. To use Weatherall's terms of sexuality/gender as "essence" versus "activity," the traditional male gender of the national God in ancient Israel seems to have been conceived of as essence, reinforced by male metaphor in various forms of textual "activity" about God. Yet this was not the end of the biblical

---

17. Ann Weatherall, *Gender, Language and Discourse* (New York: Routledge, 2002), 156.

18. Ibid., 121.

story when it came to God. Israel's textual "activity" changed, with female gender discourse for this national male god increasing in the seventh and sixth centuries and later. This suggests awareness that the male essence of YHWH was far from absolute. The later "activity" (to use Weatherall's term) in works such as Second Isaiah suggests that male language is not a complete way to discuss God. The older, traditional "essence" of God as male gives way to a broader sense of God as transcending one gender or any gender. God can be imaged as father and mother or as male or female—or as neither (Ezek 1:27).

I think the scholarly discussion misses the point: there is no single norm that can be derived from the Bible without flattening out the complexity of its gendered discourse for God. As we have seen, God may be represented as male in most passages, but several passages complicate this picture with either female imagery or representation of God as beyond gender. So we should not, to paraphrase Deut 32:18, "forget God who gave us birth." If Second Isaiah in its time tried to tell a new story about an old God by reference to female-gendered language, then the church today may also try to tell a new story about God without forgetting the biblical God who gave us birth.[19]

THE TRINITY AND GENDER IN BIBLICAL PERSPECTIVE

There are implications for the church's gender language for God. There is no doubt that the language of the Trinity—Father, Son, and Holy Spirit—tends to reify maleness. More fundamentally, it also embodies the central importance of fatherhood, sonhood, and spirithood, and not simply maleness, according to the *Catechism of the Catholic Church* (67 par. 255).[20] The *Catechism* also states: "God's

---

19. Gendered language for God in the Bible is further relativized by theriomorphic imagery for God (e.g., Num 23:22 and 24:8) and by inanimate metaphor for God (e.g., as "rock" in Deut 32).

20. *Catechism of the Catholic Church* (2nd ed.; Vatican City: Libreria Editrice Vaticana; Washington: United States Catholic Conference, 2000). See Soskice, *Kindness of God*, 119–20. Sandra Schneiders (*Women and the Word: The Gender of*

parental tenderness can also be expressed by the image of motherhood [citing Isa 66:3, Ps 131:2]....God transcends the human distinction between the sexes. He [!] is neither man nor woman: he [!] is God. He also transcends human fatherhood and motherhood" (66 par. 252; 67 par. 255).[21] I have added two exclamation points to this quote in order to highlight the male pronouns in this formulation—it is hard for the church statements to get away from the maleness of God.

Some scholars appeal to the Spirit as the "feminine" side or dimension of the Trinity. In this view, the spirit in Hebrew expresses femaleness as a mediating force and in terms of its grammatical gender.[22] However, this approach to the Spirit has been strongly criticized.[23] The divine Spirit in Israel's Bible is not marked for gender like the Father and the Son. While grammatically feminine, the divine spirit's actions and imagery in the Bible are seldom presented, if at all, in the Old Testament in ways that would be considered female. Moreover, *spirit* in New Testament Greek is neuter in grammatical gender (*to pneuma*), and the New Testament shows little imagery that is distinctly female or male for the Spirit. In short, spirit is the dimension of the Godhead that is most unmarked for gender or sexuality. *Spirit* arguably challenges the notion of sexuality in the Trinity, since *spirit* is barely female in gender or imagery, if at all. It stands apart from—and perhaps beyond—sexuality.

The biblical background of the words *Father* and *Son* also needs scrutiny. These terms stress the special relationship between the two divine persons, not their maleness as such. The idea of the relationship of the Father and the Son can be traced back to the royal psalms. The patron-god is the father of the king, who is his son: "You are my son; this

---

God in the New Testament and the Spirituality of Women [New York: Paulist Press, 1986]) discusses multiple gendered metaphors for God from both the Old Testament and the New Testament in arguing against allowing metaphors for God as male to become absolutized.

21. See also the essays in Volker Henning Drecoll, ed., *Trinität* (Tübingen: Mohr Siebeck, 2011).

22. E.g., Elisabeth Schüssler Fiorenza, *The Power of the Word: Scripture and the Rhetoric of Empire* (Minneapolis: Fortress, 2007), 221.

23. Soskice, *Kindness of God*, 112–14.

day I have begotten you" (Ps 2:7). Father and son form a particular expression of the relationship between the divine patron and the human king. When the Gospel of John speaks of the Father and the Son together, it often stresses their relationship and not their maleness.[24]

So what is the language of the Trinity expressing about God? Theologians of our times have struggled with this question. In the phrase of Najeeb Awad, the Trinity may be understood as a "reciprocal *koinonia*" (partnership or communion).[25] For Janet Martin Soskice, "to be" for the Trinitarian God is "to be related."[26] Soskice concludes her discussion of the Trinity:

> The doctrine of the Trinity tells us nothing about how men and women should relate to one another as males and females. It does not show that all men should be like the "father" and all women should model themselves on a feminized Spirit. But it does let us glimpse what it is, most truly to be: "to-be" most fully is "to-be-related" in difference.[27]

Central to the Trinity are relationality and relationship in love, and not some sort of divine male essence or ontology. This is the relational model Augustine uses (*De Trinitate* 8.12.14) for understanding the Trinity: "You see the Trinity when you see the eternal love, for the three are the one loving, the beloved, and their love."[28] This trinitarian love is also a matter of God's love relationship with the world, expressed in traditional theological language in terms of the procession of the Son from the Father and the Spirit from the Father and the Son.

---

24. John 1:18; 5:19–23; 6:40, 45–46; 8:19, 38, 54; 10:25, 38; 12:26, 49; 14:10–13, 23–24, 26–28, 31; 15:8–10, 15, 23–24; and 16:10, 15, 23, 26–27; see also John 3:16–17, 35–36; 5:17; and 20:17.

25. Najeeb Awad, *God without a Face? On the Personal Individuation of the Holy Spirit* (Tübingen: Mohr Siebeck, 2011).

26. Soskice, *Kindness of God*, 123.

27. Ibid., 124.

28. See Laurel L. Schneider, *Beyond Monotheism: A Theology of Multiplicity* (London: Routledge, 2008), 124.

As a Catholic Christian, I affirm the language of Father, Son, and Spirit as a creedal matter. For Christians to sever our link to this language would be to deny who we are as Christians. But I can also regard this traditional language with a critical sensibility. I can understand not only that a full account of the biblical texts suggests no simple male God, but also that Christian tradition can grow in wisdom based on its continual—and critical—return to Scripture. There is no need or basis for regarding the specific gender quality of the image as a matter of divine essence. Nor is there any reason not to acknowledge the problem that it poses for the faith, especially for liturgy (such as the gender language for God in the lectionary's Bible readings). For these reasons, one should champion inclusive language in modern liturgy,[29] and arguably much more.

CONCLUSION

Our times are fractured by sexual and gender politics. When it comes to gender language for God, it is not hard to see why. Even as theologians explore the issues,[30] voices on different sides of the questions are adamant, and there is little sense that the discussion is moving forward. I am afraid that I cannot arrive at a point today that is satisfying to me as a committed Roman Catholic and as a Roman Catholic committed to justice for women and men in the church and beyond. The writing of this story is ongoing, and perhaps it will end

---

29. So Brevard S. Childs, *Old Testament Theology in a Canonical Context* (Philadelphia: Fortress, 1985), 40. Cf. Christopher Seitz, *Word without End: The Old Testament as Abiding Theological Witness* (Grand Rapids: Eerdmans, 1998), 292–99.

30. Kune Biezeveld sees theological possibilities for working out issues of divine gender and sexuality in the context of Christian monotheism in "One Unique God for All Parts of Life: Reconsidering an Exclusive Tradition," in *The Boundaries of Monotheism: Interdisciplinary Explorations into the Foundations of Western Monotheism* (ed. A.-M. Korte and M. de Haardt; Studies in Theology and Religion 13; Leiden: Brill, 2009), 154–73. By contrast, for Schneider (*Beyond Monotheism*) monotheism is inherently incapable of handling the diversity of divinity. For various approaches to gendered language for God in the Bible, see also Løland, *Silent or Salient Gender*; O'Brien, *Challenging Prophetic Metaphor*; and Dille, *Mixing Metaphors*.

only with the *eschaton*. That the ending is not yet written may be the best news at the moment.

One possibility discussed by Soskice involves what she calls the "mobility" of gendered symbolic language.[31] The language may be fixed in creedal stone, but our sensibility about this male language for God need not be. Many fields of study offer new insights into personhood, sexuality, and language. These fields, undertaken by thinking and believing people willing to struggle with these questions, give me hope that we as a church might arrive at a more intelligible and credible understanding of God. For the moment, for this moment, there is not only a problem, but also an opportunity to reconsider not only what the question of sexual imagery and gender language for God discloses about God's transcendence, but also what it hides. At the moment, with the church's work on gender and God seemingly at an impasse, one may sense God hiding the divine face from the church. That, it seems to me, may be the revelation about God and sexuality for our times.

---

31. Soskice, *Kindness of God*, 81–83.

2

The Horrifying Closing of Psalm 137, or, The Limitations of Ethical Reading

Jon D. Levenson
(HARVARD DIVINITY SCHOOL)

I

My subject is one of the most powerful and memorable of the psalms:

> [1]By the rivers of Babylon,
>   there we sat,
>   sat and wept,
>   as we remembered Zion.
> [2]There on the poplars
>   We hung up our lyres,
>   [3]for our captors asked us there for songs,
>   our tormentors, for amusement,
>   "Sing us one of the songs of Zion."
> [4]How can we sing a song of the LORD
>   on alien soil?
> [5]If I forget you, O Jerusalem,
>   let my right hand wither;
>   [6]let my tongue stick to my palate
>   if I cease to think of you,
>   if I do not keep Jerusalem in memory
>   even at my happiest hour.

⁷Remember, O LORD, against the Edomites
    the day of Jerusalem's fall;
    how they cried, "Strip her, strip her
    to her very foundations!"
⁸Fair Babylon, you predator,
    a blessing on him who repays you in kind
    what you have inflicted on us;
    ⁹a blessing on him who seizes your babies
    and dashes them against the rocks!

                            (Ps 137)[1]

No translation can succeed fully in capturing the exquisite literary effects of the Hebrew diction, and a quick look at commentaries produced over the past several decades easily turns up substantive disagreements about the meanings of certain words. It is also the case that even a careful initial reading of Ps 137 cannot do justice to the highly intricate structures that scholars have uncovered in it, or thought they have uncovered, in those same years.[2]

Historically, the Jewish liturgy has designated Ps 137 as the psalm recited just before the blessings that follow meals on weekdays. On the other days—Sabbaths, festivals, or other celebratory occasions—it is Ps 126 that is sung. The counterpoint is obvious: whereas Ps 137 speaks of the misery of exile and foreignness, Ps 126 tells of the surpassing joy of repatriation and restoration, as the people Israel return to Zion, its (and their) fortunes restored by the LORD's astonishing intervention.

Any Jew or Christian who would recite Ps 137 must, however, confront the painful fact that it has, as one of the two highly distin-

---

1. Unless otherwise indicated, all translations from the Hebrew are taken from the Jewish Publication Society *Tanakh* (1985) as it appears in *The Jewish Study Bible* (ed. A. Berlin and M. Z. Brettler; New York: Oxford University Press, 2004). In v. 1, I have changed "thought of" to "remembered" to convey the connection with the other instances of *zākar* in the psalm.

2. See especially David Noel Freedman, "The Structure of Psalm 137," in *Near Eastern Studies in Honor of William Foxwell Albright* (ed. H. Goedicke; Baltimore: Johns Hopkins Press, 1971), 187–205; Pierre Auffret, "Essai sur la structure littéraire du psaume 137," *ZAW* 92 (1980): 346–77; and George Savran, "'How Can We Sing a Song of the LORD?' The Strategy of Lament in Psalm 137," *ZAW* 112 (2000): 43–58.

guished honorees of this volume has aptly put it, "the most horrifying closing line of any psalm."[3] And, in fact, that blessing on anyone who would dash Babylonian babies against the rocks has deterred many from reciting the psalm altogether and even from respecting those who are not so deterred. Athalya Brenner expresses well what is surely the judgment of many. "In the psalm," she writes, "*verbal* revenge against the enemies' babies is called for; this is horrible enough, it is horrible enough that in certain orthodox Judaisms [*sic*] these verses are recited daily."[4] To be sure, Brenner goes on to suggest some extenuation: "How else can the powerless be rid of the poison of anger and hate, the frustrated wish for revenge, if not by giving verbal expression to it?"[5] I wonder, though, whether that horrifying closing rids those who recite the psalm of their poisonous feelings or, instead, intensifies those dangerous affects, keeping them, like the memory of Jerusalem, alive when they might otherwise have faded. If the latter is the case, then the fact that the line is only verbal and not the basis of action, and that it was originally recited by the victims and not the victimizers, provides less extenuation than Brenner seems to think. In any event, outside of Orthodoxy, which is committed (at least in principle) to the maximal retention of traditional liturgy, the tendency of Jews has been to omit the psalm altogether, leaving the festive Ps 126 without a weekday counterpoint.[6]

---

3. Richard J. Clifford, *Psalms 73–150* (AOTC; Nashville: Abingdon, 2003), 275.

4. Athalya Brenner, "'On the Rivers of Babylon' (Psalm 137), or between Victim and Perpetrator," in *Sanctified Aggression: Legacies of Biblical and Post Biblical Vocabularies of Violence* (ed. J. Bekkenkamp and Y. Sherwood; London: T & T Clark, 2003), 87, emphasis original.

5. Ibid. Brenner credits an e-mail message from Toni Craven (dated May 15, 2002) for the idea expressed in the rhetorical question.

6. See, e.g., *Siddur Sim Shalom* (ed. J. Harlow; New York: Rabbinical Assembly/ United Synagogue of America, 1985). On p. 755, this Conservative prayer book specifies Psalm 126 for "Shabbat, Holidays, and other festive occasions," but gives no counterpart for the nonfestive days. The same holds for *Siddur Sim Shalom for Weekdays* (New York: Rabbinical Assembly/United Synagogue of Conservative Judaism, 2005), an adaptation of Harlow's edition (see 230). The most widely used Reform Jewish daily prayer book omits the grace after meals altogether. This is *Gates of Prayer for Weekdays: The New Union Prayerbook* (New York: Central Conference of American Rabbis, 5735/1975). As for Orthodox Jews, my unscientific impression is that large numbers of them simply ignore Psalm 137 and move directly to the grace after meals itself, as Jewish law indeed allows.

To some extent, the near disappearance of Ps 137 from modern Jewish liturgy can be attributed to a general tendency in contemporary religion to stress joyful occasions and to downplay or even omit mournful ones, apparently on the assumption that religious life is best focused on moments of happiness and fulfillment alone, whereas moments of decline, debilitation, and death are best isolated from the liturgical year and dealt with only as they occur in individual cases. Hence, to give a Christian analogy, in contemporary America Easter commands vastly more attention than Good Friday, the saddest day of the Christian liturgical year. In Judaism that doleful honor belongs to the Ninth of Av, the fast day that occurs in midsummer and commemorates the destruction of Jerusalem and especially its temple by the Babylonians in 587 BCE and again by the Romans in 70 CE. Jewish law forbids healthy Jews to eat or drink at all for about twenty-five hours on that occasion; they must sit on the ground or on very low seats, like the mourners they are; and the liturgy, scriptural readings, and teaching that accompany them focus on the destruction itself and kindred catastrophes in Jewish history, with no effort spared to communicate the full measure of the attendant sadness. Interestingly, a minor talmudic tractate specifies our psalm as one of the scriptural readings for the Ninth of Av (*Sop.* 18.4), and it should not surprise us to find that this occasion, too, is largely neglected among non-Orthodox Jews, very unlike Passover for example. Who, after all, would not prefer feasting to fasting?

Mostly, however, the near disappearance of Ps 137 from Jewish liturgy derives from the acute offense its closing line gives. Here, the Protestant biblical scholar Elizabeth Achtemeier provides a good parallel from her own tradition. To be sure, Achtemeier finds worthy material for sermons in the psalm; she suggestively likens the situation of its speakers to Jesus as he was jeered on the cross, to all appearances abandoned by the God in whose name he had claimed to speak.[7] But this makes it all the more significant that she, too, finds the closing

---

7. Elizabeth Rice Achtemeier, *Preaching Hard Texts in the Old Testament* (Peabody, MA: Hendrickson, 1998), 108.

beyond reclaim and goes so far as to doubt that the last two verses have been composed by the same author as the first seven:

> Given the fact that the Psalmist, in v. 7 of our passage, turns retribution over to the Lord, it is difficult to believe that the words of vv. 8–9 come from his lips. Rather, I believe they are responses of others to the Psalmist's words in vv. 4–7, and they speak an entirely different message....There is no trust in God's requital in such expressions.[8]

And Achtemeier is not alone in judging the closing of Ps 137 to be unworthy of public reading. "Some congregations are accustomed to reading verses 1–6 as a responsive reading," she writes. "But I know of no liturgy that has included verses 7–9, with the last hate-filled v. 9, 'Happy shall he be who takes your little ones / and dashes them against the rock.' There is a general feeling that such thoughts should not occur in the Bible."[9]

But occur in the Bible they do, and even if it can be shown that the closing of Ps 137 has been tacked on later—a claim for which there is no real evidence—neither as believers nor as scholars are we free to disregard that line. We must still reckon, rather, with its place in the composition as a whole and in the historical situation to which the poem speaks. Viewed through a lens of ethics, verse 9 is every bit as repulsive as Brenner, Achtemeier, and many others have thought. I take it as obvious that no rational or humane person can justify smashing the enemies' babies against rocks. But to me it is also obvious that viewing Ps 137 through an ethical lens alone condemns us to miss its richness and power, and leaves us only more mystified by the fondness in which the poem has been held in many quarters. One ought not to treat the psalm as a didactic composition focused on teaching people how to act in their daily lives (e.g., by avenging wrongs through deadly violence against the wrongdoers' infants). To do so is to commit a serious category error. The unfortunate result is a severely impoverished

---

8. Ibid., 109.

9. Ibid., 105.

reading, one that makes us wish, like the congregations to which Achtemeier refers, that the horrifying ending of the psalm were not there at all. I hope to show that it is possible to appreciate the literary connections of that closing line, and even aspects of its theology, without weakening the moral condemnation that it rightly evokes. And that is the point of the following discussion—not to justify the horrifying closing but to understand it in its larger context, with special attention to its rich intertextual associations. Doing so will change the meaning of that verse from which we modern Westerners initially recoil, even if it does not and should not make the deed for which the verse calls any less revolting.

II

Psalm 137 is obviously an Israelite response to the destruction of Jerusalem and its temple in 587 BCE when the Neo-Babylonian Empire ended the independence of Israel's sole surviving kingdom, Judah, and captured its last king, Zedekiah. Second Kings describes these events in its dry, matter-of-fact style, but it is not hard to feel the pathos of the scene in which the fleeing Zedekiah is finally apprehended:

> They captured the king and brought him before the king of Babylon at Riblah; and they put him on trial. They slaughtered Zedekiah's sons before his eyes; then Zedekiah's eyes were put out. He was chained in bronze fetters and he was brought to Babylon. (2 Kgs 25:6–7)

The victorious Babylonians not only slaughtered the king's sons. As this report would have it, the slaughter of his sons was also the last thing Zedekiah was to see, though he lived for a time afterward. For the slaughter itself, there was a political reason. These sons, as Zedekiah's potential heirs, represented the possibility that Judah might recover its independence, and they its throne, at some point in the future. But the way in which the Babylonian captors carried out their

execution of the sons, in front of their father, who was himself about
to be blinded, bespeaks a sadism that goes beyond the hard demands
of an amoral Realpolitik. Although the author does not address the
issue directly, his narrative raises the question of how such an atrocity
can be righted. Something more than simply the repatriation of the
Judahites to their homeland, something more than simply the restoration of Zion and Jerusalem after their devastation, is called for.

In biblical tradition, the suffering of the Judahite children at the
time of the Babylonian conquest plays a prominent role, as one would
expect, given the sympathy the image of the afflicted child universally
evokes. Consider these verses from Lamentations:

> [11]My eyes are spent with tears,
> My heart is in tumult,
> My being melts away
> Over the ruin of my poor people,
> As babes and sucklings languish
> In the squares of the city.
> [12]They keep asking their mothers,
> "Where is bread and wine?"
> As they languish like battle-wounded
> In the squares of the town,
> As their life runs out
> In their mothers' bosoms.

(Lam 2:11–12)

> See, O LORD, and behold,
> To whom You have done this!
> Alas, women eat their own fruit,
> Their new-born babes!
> Alas, priest and prophet are slain
> In the Sanctuary of the Lord!

(Lam 2:20)

The tongue of the suckling cleaves
To its palate for thirst.
Little children beg for bread;
None gives them a morsel.

(Lam 4:4)

With their own hands, tenderhearted women
Have cooked their children;
Such became their fare,
In the disaster of my poor people.

(Lam 4:10)

It bears mention that the expression translated as "my poor people" in the first and last examples (*bat-ʿammî*) can be more literally, if perhaps misleadingly, rendered as "the daughter of my people" or "the young woman, my people." It functions very much like "Fair Zion" (*bat-ṣîôn*), used several times in Lamentations,[10] which can be more literally translated as "Daughter Zion," "the daughter of Zion," or "the young woman, Zion," or like "Fair Maiden Judah" (*bĕtûlat bat-yĕhûdâ*) and "Fair Maiden Zion" (*bĕtûlat bat-ṣîôn*), which are preceded in Hebrew by a noun that means "virgin" (Lam 1:15; 2:13). In these texts, the personification of the people as a young woman reinforces the reader's sense of the people's vulnerability and mistreatment, and thus of the unspeakable savagery of their tormentors as well. The inability of the mothers to meet the elemental needs of their own children in the four passages given above—and all the more so the starving mothers' resort to using their own children as food in Lam 4:10—only sharpens the same painful sense in the increasingly shocked reader.

When the author of Ps 137 speaks of remembering Zion, as he

---

10. E.g., Lam 1:6 and 2:1.

does fully four times (vv. 1, 5, 6, 7), he is speaking not of Zion in its glory, when a psalmist could describe it as the "joy of all the earth" (Ps 48:3), or at least not only of that; he is also recalling scenes like these, scenes of helpless women violated and of children, even babies, starved to death. And, in my judgment, when he pledges to "keep Jerusalem in memory / even at [his] happiest hour"—or, to translate the same verse more literally, to "elevate Jerusalem above [his] highest joy" (v. 6)—he is thinking of Jerusalem as the site not of the greatest happiness on earth but of the greatest anguish; the memory of unrectified atrocities tempers even his most intense moments of joy. This, incidentally, is how verse 6 has come to be used in many traditional Jewish weddings. It is sung at the very end of the ceremony, when the groom smashes a glass with his foot to recall, even at this most joyous of occasions, the devastation of Jerusalem that underlies the moving poem that is Ps 137. As a midrash puts it, in this world, neither God nor Israel can be altogether happy. The rejoicing comes in the World-to-Come, when the wounds of this world have been healed and tragedies like the destruction of Jerusalem have been altogether reversed.[11]

III

The savage devastation of Jerusalem by the Neo-Babylonian Empire followed a meeting around 593 in which the kings of five Levantine vassals of the Babylonians converged upon Jerusalem to discuss the possibility of breaking free of the imperial yoke. In the kingdom of Judah itself, the proposed uprising was controversial. The prophet Jeremiah delivered oracles against it, quoting the LORD as announcing that he had foredoomed the rebellion. "I herewith deliver all these lands to My servant, King Nebuchadnezzar of Babylon," the prophet proclaimed. "All nations shall serve him, his son and his grandson—until the turn of his own land comes, when many nations and great kings shall subjugate him" (Jer 27:6–7). On the other side

---

11. *Pesiq. Rab Kah.* 26.3.

stood various prophets who were predicting in the name of the self-same God that the Babylonian yoke would be broken much sooner and that the previous king, Zedekiah's nephew Jeconiah (or, Jehoiachin), would return from captivity in Babylon, to which he had been taken in 597.[12] The party to which Jeremiah belonged seems to have won out; the rebellion, which they continued to oppose, would not take place until 587, when Jerusalem would be sacked and burned, and a larger and more consequential deportation enacted.

It is surely relevant to Ps 137 that among the five monarchs inaugurating the discussions in Jerusalem in 593 was the king of Edom (Jer 27:3). In the case of the rebellion that, unlike this one, actually took place about six years later, we hear nothing about a regional alliance to end the subjugation to Babylonia and cannot assume that the Edomites were members of such an alliance. The evidence of the single-chaptered book known as Obadiah, which concentrates on the future demise of Edom, would suggest, however, that such an alliance existed and that the Edomites betrayed their own allies.[13] For Obad 7 speaks of Edom's own confederates' duping her and defeating her, suggesting that this is precisely what Edom had done to Israel. In any event, quite apart from Ps 137:7, we find a number of texts that relate unambiguously that Edom took the Babylonian side in 587 BCE and even went so far as to join in the assault on Jerusalem. Here again is Lamentations, envisaging a scenario in which defeated Zion and triumphant Edom change places:

> 21Rejoice and exult, Fair Edom,
> Who dwell in the land of Uz!
> To you, too, the cup shall pass,
> You shall get drunk and expose your nakedness.
> 22Your iniquity, Fair Zion, is expiated;
> He will exile you no longer.

---

12. Jer 27:9—28:17. See also the account of Jeremiah's letter to the first set of exiles (those exiled with Jeconiah in 597) in ch. 29.

13. See also Amos 1:9, 11; as noted in Ulrich Kellermann, "Psalm 137," *ZAW* 90 (1978): 58.

Your iniquity, Fair Edom, He will note;
He will uncover your sins.

(Lam 4:21–22)

Similarly, the oracle in Jer 49:7–22 (closely related to Obadiah) not
only predicts the downfall of Edom, but also like Lam 4:21, it uses the
language of the cup in reference to Edom's impending, horrific—and
eminently deserved—demise (v. 12). Putting this together with Obad
7, it is reasonable to think that when Edom's allies dupe and defeat the
Edomites, the latter will experience just what Israel experienced at
their hand: the cup will pass from Fair Zion to Fair Edom.

It is in Obadiah alone that the full measure of Edomite perfidy
and, correlatively, the full measure of Israelite rage at the betrayal
appear most pointedly. The tradition that the ancestors of the two
nations, Esau and Jacob respectively, were brothers and—according to
Genesis, twins to boot (25:19–26)—adds special anger to the prophet's
fury:

> 10For the outrage to your brother Jacob,
> Disgrace shall engulf you,
> And you shall perish forever.
> 11On that day when you stood aloof,
> When aliens carried off his goods,
> When foreigners entered his gates
> And cast lots for Jerusalem,
> You were as one of them.
>
> 12How could you gaze with glee
> On your brother that day,
> On his day of calamity!
> How could you gloat,
> Over the people of Judah
> On that day of ruin!
> How could you loudly jeer
> On a day of anguish!

28

13How could you enter the gate of My people
On its day of disaster,
Gaze in glee with the others
On its misfortune
On its day of disaster,
And lay hands on its wealth
On its day of disaster!
14How could you stand at the passes
To cut down its fugitives!
How could you betray those who fled
On that day of anguish!
15As you did, so shall it be done to you;
Your conduct shall be requited.

(Obad 10–15)

Here again we see the tables turned, as the deed redounds upon the head of the doer. Indeed, that is precisely the metaphor of the last clause in verse 15, literally, "Your recompense will return onto your head (*gĕmūlĕkâ yāšûb bĕrō'šekā*)." Interestingly, the word *gĕmūl*, only very inadequately rendered as "recompense," appears also in Ps 137, along with its cognate verb:

Fair Babylon, you predator,
a blessing on him who repays you in kind
what you have inflicted (*gĕmūlēk šeggāmalt*) on us.

(Ps 137:8)

In both cases—and, as we shall see in more detail, they are obviously related in more than just the historical situation to which they speak—what the author envisions is a reversal of fates: the victim and the victimizer change places, and the victimizer learns what it is like to experience the wrong he has committed. In the language of Obadiah, "Liberators [or, deliverers] shall march up on Mount Zion to wreak judgment on Mount Esau; and dominion shall be the LORD's" (v. 21). In the language of Ps 137, the unbearably painful "day of Jerusalem's

29

fall" (v. 7) will be reversed, as those who brought the city of the LORD's palace and presence to ruins receive what they gave, and Zion and its God are at long last vindicated.

IV

It is common among scholars who discuss Ps 137 either to classify the sentiments of its two closing verses as vengeance or revenge, or to go to some lengths to exonerate them of that charge, often with the argument that the issue at hand is God's control of history rather than a primitive urge to get even.[14] There is some truth in this argument, but the matter is subtler and more complex than any simple dichotomy of divine and human action, or of justice and revenge, allows.

In a famous essay published about six decades ago, Klaus Koch argued that the term "retribution" is profoundly misleading when applied to the Hebrew Bible. "In our day, the consideration of retribution has been characterized in such a juridical fashion that it is thought to be reward or punishment *according to a previously established norm*," he wrote.[15] Yet for the most part, when punishment is mentioned in the Hebrew Bible, there is no reference to any norm or law that has been broken. Koch's observation is most accurate in regard to Wisdom literature like Proverbs, where, as he points out, "there is not a single word about any norm, any legal code,"[16] but he finds the principle to apply to other corpora as well, including the prophets and the psalms. In all the cases he examines, the key point is "that actions have built-in consequences....The one who does something will passively experience the consequences of what was actively

---

14. As in Hans-Joachim Kraus, *Psalms 60–150: A Commentary* (Minneapolis: Augsburg, 1989), 504: "The petition for revenge is a petition that appeals to [the LORD's] power to control history. Cf. also Rev. 18:20. In the midst of historical life we face the decision whether [the LORD] is God or the great powers shall triumph."

15. Klaus Koch, "Is There a Doctrine of Retribution in the Old Testament?" in *Theodicy in the Old Testament* (ed. J. L. Crenshaw; IRT 4; Philadelphia: Fortress, 1983), 59, emphasis original. The essay was originally published in *ZTK* 52 (1955): 1–42.

16. Koch, "Doctrine of Retribution," in Crenshaw, *Theodicy*, 59.

set in motion."[17] Even when, unlike the case in Proverbs, there is talk of God's dramatic intervention, Koch maintains that God facilitates and expedites the process by which the agent experiences the consequences of his action, but God does not interrupt or override it.

Whether Koch's observations apply as generally and as tightly as he thinks is not a question we need to sort out here.[18] The point of relevance, rather, is that the anti-Edomite literature that we have been examining is exceptionally rich in the vocabulary that Koch finds to be indicative of the theology he is tracing. On the use of the verb *hēšîb*, "to bring back," for example, he writes, "It would seem it is assumed that, for a time, an action can distance itself from the person who did it, but then [the LORD] retrieves it so that it can take full effect upon the person who initiated it."[19] It is hard not to see the same dynamic in the prediction in Obad 15 that we have examined above: "Your conduct shall be requited" or, more literally, "Your recompense will return onto your head (*gĕmūlĕkâ yāšûb bĕrō 'šekā*)."

Another case is the verb *šillēm*, meaning "to complete, fill out, make whole, make restitution, compensate, restore," and the like, which Koch brings to bear in consideration of a passage in Proverbs in which God's name is invoked:

> 21If your enemy is hungry, give him bread to eat;
> If he is thirsty, give him water to drink.
> 22You will be heaping live coals on his head,
> And the LORD will reward you (*yĕšallem-lāk*).

(Prov 25:21–22)

Noting that *šillēm* "is never used to describe the specific job of a judge," Koch argues that "Prov. 25:21–22 is not speaking about [the LORD] granting a 'reward' by providing someone with something that

---

17. Ibid., 66. The specific context is Hos 4:4–6.

18. See the discussion and qualification of Koch in Patrick D. Miller Jr., *Sin and Judgment in the Prophets: A Stylistic and Theological Analysis* (SBLMS 27; Chico, CA: Scholars Press, 1982).

19. Koch, "Doctrine of Retribution," in Crenshaw, *Theodicy*, 64.

would not automatically result from the interplay of that person's nature and action. Rather...this text presumes that an action and its consequences have to have an inherent relation to one another, linked hand in hand as it were."[20] In Ps 137 the same verb appears in the anti-Babylonian beatitude-cum-imprecation, "A blessing on him who repays you in kind (*yĕšallem-lāk*) what you have inflicted on us" (v. 8). Given the understanding of divine action that is presupposed in both these texts, it would be unwise to accept Achtemeier's argument that because verses 8–9, unlike verse 7, do not "turn retribution over to the LORD," they evidence "no trust in God's requital" and must derive from another source — a vengeful one, at that.[21] Similarly, it would be a mistake to think, as John Ahn does, that it must be the LORD who is beatified with the *'ašrê* constructions ("a blessing on") in verses 8–9.[22] Rather, it is more likely that those blessed in verses 8–9 are simply doing what the LORD characteristically does, completing what Koch calls *"the correspondence between actions and consequences."* As he points out, writing specifically about the Book of Psalms, "where [the correspondence] actually takes effect, it *is the result of God's faithfulness at work.*"[23] The invocation of God in verse 7 and the beatitudes-cum-imprecations in verses 8–9 are in continuity; they are not at odds here because divine action and human action are not at odds here.

Should we classify what is called for in Ps 137:7–9 as vengeance? Obviously the speaker of these verses harbors a deep resentment for the sadistic treatment his people have endured and very much wants to get even with their captors and tormentors, and in that sense terms like *vengeance* and *revenge* are surely appropriate. If, however, Koch's thinking about "the correspondence between actions and consequences" is correct and applies here, there is something dangerously simplistic about using such terms to describe these verses. For the assumption underlying that usage is that the horrifying fate of the

---

20. Ibid., 60.

21. Achtemeier, *Preaching*, 109.

22. John Ahn, "Psalm 137: Complex Communal Laments," *JBL* 127 (2008): 289.

23. Koch, "Doctrine of Retribution," in Crenshaw, *Theodicy*, 73, emphasis original.

Edomites and Babylonians originates in the Israelite speaker's curse: if he had forgiven them and not sought revenge, the process of evildoing would have come to an end. But if the consequences of their crimes are already implicit in the crimes themselves—if the actions and the consequences are part of a single entity that develops over time until it reaches completion—then the Edomites and the Babylonians have already decreed their own fate, the former through their fratricidal perfidy and the latter through their savagery and sadism. They will not go scot-free under any circumstances. The only question remaining, rather, is the point at which the process will have reached completion—the point at which the deed redounds upon the head of the doer. Until then, the toxin is still present, and its victims (Jerusalem and the people who love it) are still suffering. Until the deed is completed, it is alive and, in this case, dangerous.

"But why the children?" the modern reader will rightly ask. "Surely they have no culpability for the destruction of Jerusalem and the agony the Israelites endured in Babylonia!" Here again, it is dangerous in the extreme to interpret a given act without regard to the background assumptions of those who call for it and to its meaning in their cultural world. In the case of ancient Israel and the ancient Near East in general, identity was vastly less individualistic than it is in the modern West, or, to put the same point positively, it was vastly more corporate and communal. More specifically, identity was more familial: the borders between the individual and the family/clan/tribe/nation were more porous, and thus an individual's identity extended beyond his or her own personal death.[24] If we bear this key difference in mind, we can quickly clear up many puzzles that biblical texts pose. How, for example, can the promise that Abraham or Jacob will possess the land be valid when they died before it was fulfilled? How can Aaron be said to receive tithes that are given only when he is long dead? How can we deem Job's life to have been fully restored when the children born to him in the last chapter of the book are not the

---

24. For a fuller discussion, see Jon D. Levenson, *Resurrection and the Restoration of Israel: The Ultimate Victory of the God of Life* (New Haven: Yale University Press, 2006), 108–22.

same as those who died in the first?[25] In all these cases, the identity of the subject himself (Abraham, Jacob, Aaron, or Job) includes his descendants; the latter are not altogether separate and distinct individuals. And, in fact, it is this interconnection of identities that accounts for the fact that individuals can inherit promises they did not deserve or receive, and can also and equally inherit the consequences of deeds that they never individually performed.

This familial or intergenerational concept of identity is one of the features of the Hebrew Bible that is most foreign to modern Westerners, and it accounts for much of the contemporary sense that the Hebrew Bible is a source of oppression and injustice. In fact, given the concept of justice assumed by those who make that criticism, the critique is quite warranted (concepts of justice are always tied to notions of identity). Already in antiquity, both the Jewish and the Christian traditions mitigated this offending aspect of their common biblical legacy, but they did not altogether nullify it or adopt an atomistic, one-generational concept of human identity. The people Israel and the church both endure through time and claim to inherit promises and judgments made to earlier generations, and in that sense those traditions continue a worldview very different from the more individualistic worldview of the modern West. To say that the horrifying closing of Ps 137 had a different resonance in the ancient Near Eastern world in which it originated, as indeed it did, in no way evades the moral offense that it gives. Before we condemn, however, we must first understand.

In this connection, it also bears mention that in the world from which our psalm came, cruelty to children in warfare was commonplace, as disgusting and embarrassing as that fact may be to those of us who regard the Hebrew Bible as Sacred Scripture and not simply as an artifact of an ancient culture now happily superseded. Thus, to give one example among many, the prophet Elisha predicts that an Aramean king attacking Israel will "put their young men to the sword, dash their little ones in pieces, and rip open their pregnant women" (2 Kgs 8:12). The prophet makes his prediction weeping, but it cannot be assumed,

---

25. Ibid., 109, 115, for a discussion of these examples.

as we might wish, that he weeps at the thought of the violence that God has shown him rather than at the thought that it was Israel in particular whom the brutal Aramean king would so savagely devastate.

Even granting all this, the closing of our psalm (Ps 137:9) is indeed horrifying; it seems likely that the poet wanted to end with the most potent expression of his rage that he could find, deliberately leaving a bitter taste in his readers' mouths. Within the larger structure of biblical literature, however, the closing, though shocking, does not come altogether out of the blue. To the reader who knows 2 Kings, the slaughter of Zedekiah's sons before his own eyes (25:6–7) will rightly come to mind here, and the use in the previous two verses (Ps 137:8–9) of the terms *běnê 'ědôm* and *bat-bābel*, which can be literally rendered as "sons/children of Edom" and "daughter of Babylon," respectively, also brings the idea of young people into the increasingly gruesome picture, as the focus moves horrifyingly from children to babies.

V

Graham S. Ogden has argued that the oracles against Edom in Obadiah and Jer 49:7–22 constitute "two prophetic responses" to the last three verses of Ps 137.[26] Minimally, one would have to concede that the degree of lexical overlap among the three texts is striking and speaks against coincidence. For example, *haššědûdâ* ("predator"), used of Babylon in Ps 137:8, correlates with *šôdědê laylâ* ("marauders by night") in Obad 5. As Ogden observes, "Whereas Psalm 137 applied the root to Babylon, in Obadiah it describes the one who will implement a similar judgment on Edom."[27] He notes as well the use of *šuddad zar'ô* ("his offspring is ravaged") in Jer 49:10, again with reference to Edom.[28] Similarly, he connects the prominence of the term

---

26. Graham S. Ogden, "Prophetic Oracles against Foreign Nations and Psalms of Communal Lament: The Relationship of Psalm 137 to Jeremiah 49:7–22 and Obadiah," *JSOT* 24 (1982): 89–97, at 95.

27. Ibid., 92–93. Whether *haššědûdâ* in the psalm should be retained or revocalized, as several scholars recommend (but others oppose), is not germane to the immediate point.

28. Ibid., 93.

yôm ("day") in Obad 11–14 to Ps 137:7. "The day of [Jacob's] calamity" in Obadiah is "the day of Jerusalem's fall" in the psalm; both texts are directed against the Edomites. That Obadiah and Jer 49:7–22 are related texts would seem obvious, but that both seem to echo the psalm (or, less likely, that the psalm is echoing them) in these and other cases that Ogden identifies is surely suggestive.

Particularly germane to the closing verse of Ps 137 is the expression *šōkĕnî bĕhagwê-sela'* ("you who dwell in the clefts of the rock") in Obad 3 and Jer 49:16.[29] The word for "rock" here (*sela'*) is the same as the term for the "rocks" against which the horrifying closing of Ps 137:9 wishes to see the Babylonian babies dashed. Applied to Edom, as it is in the two prophetic texts, the term has a rich resonance. Ogden points out that it is "synonymous with Edom itself," and Adele Berlin (among others) notes the appearance of Sela as the name of an Edomite stronghold in 2 Kgs 14:7.[30] Putting all this together, the "rocks" against which the psalmist wishes to see the enemy's babies dashed are the Edomites' own stronghold, which they once thought impregnable. They will, the prophets aver, learn otherwise.

Here a problem arises. In Ps 137:9, the enemy whose babies are ideally to be dashed against the rocks are Babylonian, whereas the oracles in Obadiah and Jer 49:7–22 are directed against the Edomites, and it was the latter, of course, to whom Sela belonged. Ogden's solution is to see the *bat-bābel* ("Fair Babylon," but literally "Daughter of Babylon") of verse 8 as meaning "the ally or confederate of Babylon," but the parallels he cites are not persuasive.[31] Others have suggested that verse 8 is an interpolation, so that the babies of verse 9 are those of the Edomites of verse 7, but this, too, is unpersuasive.[32] It is more

---

29. In Jeremiah the term occurs without the *maqēph* and with the definite article on *sela'*. The JPS for some reason translates the word as "in clefts" in Jer 49:16 but "in the clefts" in Obad 3. Neither the Hebrew nor the English variation is significant.

30. Ogden, "Prophetic Oracles," 91; Adele Berlin, "Psalms and the Literature of Exile: Psalms 137, 44, 69, and 78," in *The Book of Psalms: Composition and Reception* (ed. P. W. Flint and P. D. Miller Jr.; Leiden: Brill, 2005), 69. Kellermann ("Psalm 137," 47) had made the same point.

31. Ogden, "Prophetic Oracles," 91.

32. See Erich Zenger, "Psalm 137," in F.-L. Hossfeld and E. Zenger, *Psalms 3: A*

likely that the poet was conflating the Babylonian suzerains and their Edomite confederates.[33] After all, the two acted in concert in the destruction of Jerusalem, and the authors of all three poetic texts seem to regard Edom as the cat's paw of Babylon. However much precision we may expect from historians composing their narratives in prose — and even with them the precision is not what modern historians would wish — surely we should expect less from an author writing a highly evocative poem like our psalm. To whoever composed Ps 137, the difference between Babylonians and Edomites was immaterial.

In the anti-Edomite oracles of Obadiah and Jeremiah, it is clear that the ultimate cause of the recompense for the hideous devastation of Jerusalem comes from God himself, dramatically manifesting in historical events both his passion for justice and his commitment to the people Israel. Long after both *Babylon* and *Edom* had ceased to denote meaningful political entities, their names continued to refer to those world powers who oppose God's will and act with violence and hubris against his special people. A fine example can be found in a chapter in the New Testament that gleefully envisages the violent overthrow of Babylon, now a cipher for Rome. "Rejoice over her, O heaven, you saints and apostles and prophets!" reads a characteristic verse. "For God has given judgment for you against her" (Rev 18:20, NRSV).

In rabbinic sources, Edom became a name first for the Roman Empire and then for Christendom, Roman or otherwise. The expectation that God would eventually emerge triumphant over his and his people's archetypal foe led on occasion to a reinterpretation of Ps 137 that makes the Deity himself a speaker in it, as in this midrash:

Commentary on Psalms 101–150 (trans. L. Maloney; Hermeneia; Minneapolis: Fortress, 2011), 519.

33. Yair Zakovitch ("Poetry Creates Historiography," in *"A Wise and Discerning Mind": Essays in Honor of Burke O. Long* [ed. S. M. Olyan and R. C. Culley; BJS 325; Providence: Brown University, 2000], 317) argues that "the psalmist identifies Edom and Babylon, since Edom was already a symbol for Israel's worst enemies." Zakovitch is commenting on the influence of the psalm on the Chronicler's rewriting of 2 Kgs 14:7 in 2 Chr 25:11–12 (316–17). On this, see also Kellermann, "Psalm 137," 47. It is interesting that the Chronicler gives no indication that the Edomites thrown from the summit of Sela/the rocky cliff were babies. Is this because the Chronicler already found the closing of the psalm horrifying?

"If I forget (*'eškāḥēk*) you, O Jerusalem, / let my right hand wither (*tiškaḥ*)" (Ps 137:5). Bar Kappara said: "My appointed time is in your hand, and your appointed time is in My hand." *My appointed time is in your hand*: [beware lest] your heart grow haughty and you forget (*wešākaḥtā*) the LORD your God" (Deut 8:14). *And your appointed time is in My hand*: "If I forget (*'eškāḥēk*) you, O Jerusalem, / let my right hand wither (*tiškaḥ*)" (Ps 137:5). (*Pesiq. Rab Kah.* 17.5)

In this interpretation, ascribed to a sage of the late second/early third century CE, the final redemption of God and the final redemption of Jerusalem are connected. Jerusalem must take special precautions not to forget her God, and he—here identified as the speaker of the vow of Ps 137:5—will not forget her. Human and divine remembering, like human and divine action, are bound up in a nexus of intense mutuality. It is likely that underlying this interpretation is the notion that God's right hand (signifying his redemptive power) is in chains while the Jews languish in exile and Jerusalem has not yet been restored.[34] A kindred movement takes place in the Targum to the psalms. There it is the angel Michael who speaks verse 7 and Gabriel who speaks verses 8–9.[35] In both cases, the effect is to place the sentiments of those offending verses into a larger perspective in which the primary issue is God's fidelity to Jerusalem and the Jewish people, and his commitment to dealing out justice to those who have wronged them and defied him. This does not make the closing of Ps 137 any

---

34. *Pesikta de-Rab Kahana: R. Kahana's Compilation of Discourses for Sabbaths and Festal Days* (trans. W. G. [Gershon Zev] Braude and I. J. Kapstein; Philadelphia: Jewish Publication Society of America, 1975), 309n18. See also Robert Kirschner, "Two Responses to Epochal Change: Augustine and the Rabbis on Ps. 137 (136)," VC 44 (1990): 249.

35. http://cal1.cn.huc.edu/showsubtexts.php?subtext=81002&cset=Hebrew (accessed May 20, 2013). The text is from *Hagiographa Chaldaice* (ed. P. de Lagarde; Osnabrück: O. Zeller, 1967), with variants from Luis Díez Merino, *Targum de Salmos: edición príncipe del Ms. Villa-Amil n. 5 de Alfonso de Zamora* (Madrid: Consejo Superior de Investigaciones Científicas, Instituto "Francisco Suárez," 1982). I thank my colleague, Prof. D. Andrew Teeter, for pointing me to this bibliography.

less horrifying as human behavior. It does suggest, however, that if we interpret that last verse only within the parameters of human behavior, we condemn ourselves to missing its larger import.

VI

To those who receive the psalm within the ongoing Jewish or Christian traditions, the notion of taking its closing as a guide to behavior ought to seem downright strange. Dashing the enemy's babies against rocks? The Torah itself decrees, "Parents shall not be put to death for children, nor children be put to death for parents: a person shall be put to death only for his own crime" (Deut 24:16). The rabbinic tradition takes this as normative law (*halakah*), and it is not hard to find analogous—and equally uncompromising—Christian counsels against the summary execution of minors.

This adds further weight to the argument that Ps 137 should not be seen primarily through a lens defined by ethics. Viewed through that lens, its closing can only be indefensible. Those who grant hermeneutical primacy to the ethical dimension will inevitably wish to remove the poem from their liturgies, and as we saw in our first section, many Jews and Christians have done just that. Judging the whole psalm and the entirety of the theology underlying it by its horrifying closing is a conversation stopper: it puts an immediate end to the interpretive process. Such a move is not a communally neutral option; it invalidates the use of the text in communities of interpretation for which the text is part of Sacred Scripture. A better course is that richly exemplified by the honorees of this volume, Professors Richard Clifford and Daniel Harrington, who have instead continued the process of confronting the Scriptures (including the problematic ones), adding immeasurably to our understanding both of the ancient texts themselves and their proper use in ongoing religious communities.

I hope to have shown here that however understandably those who have sought to remove Ps 137 from their liturgies have acted, their perspective is too narrow. It is possible to feel both horror at the closing of the poem and appreciation of the profound theological and spiritual message that the psalm as a whole, including its horrifying closing line, continues to communicate to the faithful.

3

Revisiting Behemoth

C. L. Seow
(PRINCETON THEOLOGICAL SEMINARY)

Ever since Samuel Bochart's *Hierozoicon* of 1663,[1] an overwhelming majority of modern scholars have identified Behemoth in the Book of Job with the hippopotamus. In 1978, however, John Gammie offered a novel interpretation of the Behemoth passage (Job 40:15–24).[2] Picking up on Samuel Terrien's passing remark that Behemoth and Leviathan are "caricatures of human endeavor,"[3] Gammie argued that the two beasts are in fact caricatures of Job, both proud creatures that God will nevertheless subdue. Along with the implicit rebuke, however, Gammie also discerns an edifying word for Job, indeed a challenge for him to emulate the beast who continues to "trust" even in the face of adversity (v. 23).

Gammie's thesis that Behemoth and Leviathan somehow represent Job resonates with Jerome Engseth, who sees these creatures "as examples of might and renewal with which Job can identify."[4] Samuel

---

1. Samuel Bochart, *Hierozoicon sive bipertitum opus de animalibus Sacrae Scripturae* (2 vols.; London: Roycroft, 1663), 2:754–69.

2. John G. Gammie, "Behemoth and Leviathan: On the Didactic and Theological Significance of Job 40:15–41:26," in *Israelite Wisdom* (ed. J. G. Gammie; Missoula, MT: Scholars Press, 1978), 221–22.

3. Samuel Terrien, *Job: Poet of Existence* (Indianapolis: Bobbs-Merrill, 1957), 237.

4. Jerome M. Engseth, "The Role of Behemoth and Leviathan in the Book of Job," in *Church Divinity, 1987: National Student Essay Competition in Divinity* (ed. J. H. Morgan; Church Divinity Monograph Series 7; Bristol, IN: Wyndham Hall, 1987), 120.

Balentine has likewise followed suit, contending that "Behemoth repre-sents the one true analogue for humankind that God has placed in the created order."[5] For Balentine, "Behemoth and Job are in some sense twins"; when Job "looks at Behemoth, he somehow sees himself."[6] John Walton adopts a similar interpretation in his recent commentary.[7]

In view of this recent trend, it seems timely to revisit the passage and reconsider its significance in the book. I will argue that Behemoth is no mundane beast. Rather, he is exalted as a preeminent creature, indeed, a creature surpassing human beings who, contrary to a com-mon perception found elsewhere in biblical traditions, are not the epitome of creation.

CONTEXT

At the climax of the Book of Job, YHWH responds to Job in two speeches (38:1 — 39:30; 40:6 — 41:34 [40:6 — 41:26]).[8] The beginning of the second speech recalls the first: 40:6–8 is reminiscent of 38:1–3, with 40:6 repeating 38:1 and 40:7 repeating 38:3 verbatim. The key differ-ences are in 38:2 and 40:8. The former indicates that the topic in ques-tion in the first speech is God's 'ēṣâ, "plan" (commonly translated as "counsel"), while the latter signals that the issue in the second speech is God's mišpāṭ, "justice/right."[9] In the first speech, God accuses Job of obfuscating God's "plan." In the second, God charges that Job is dis-missing divine "right." Job's insistence on his innocence leads to the

5. Samuel E. Balentine, "'What Are Human Beings That You Make So Much of Them?' Divine Disclosure from the Whirlwind: 'Look at Behemoth,'" in *God in the Fray* (ed. T. Linafelt and T. K. Beal; Minneapolis: Fortress, 1998), 270.

6. Samuel E. Balentine, *Job* (Smyth & Helwys Bible Commentary 10; Macon, GA: Smyth & Helwys, 2006), 684.

7. John H. Walton with Kelly L. Vizcaino, *Job* (NIV Application Commentary; Grand Rapids: Zondervan, 2012), 408–9.

8. Biblical references are given according to the Masoretic versification; where this differs from most English translations, references to the latter are provided in paren-theses or brackets.

9. Veronika Kubina, *Das Gottesreden im Buche Hiob* (Freiburgische theologische Studien 115; Freiburg: Herder, 1979), 115–23.

conclusion that God is unjust. God argues, however, that Job does not need to insist on God being wrong in order for him to be right.

The term *mišpāṭ* has a range of meanings at home in Israelite jurisprudence and governance. Most of its twenty-two occurrences in the Book of Job are forensic: "justice,"[10] "judgment" (9:32; 14:3; 22:4; 29:14; 34:23), "case" (13:18; 23:4), and "right" (27:2; 31:13; 34:4, 5, 6; 36:6). Job, who is addressed here, has called divine justice into question (9:19; 19:9), and has insisted on his right to justice (27:2). Yet what God implicitly defends in this speech is not *mišpāṭ* in the sense of the legal and moral justifiability of action. Rather, God is asserting God's right in the governance of the world, that is, divine right as the Creator.[11] This prerogative is what Job has dismissed—not *mišpāṭ* as delimited by mortals, but the *mišpāṭ* of the sovereign Creator of all that exists. Job sees the issue in legal and moral terms, but YHWH places it on a cosmic plane, in terms of God's right to govern as God sees fit.

Job's outlook has been too limited, for it is but human. This point is suggested by the rhetorical question in 40:9. Job neither has an "arm" like God's, nor does he thunder like God. The divine "arm" is a common figure in the Bible for God's power as the divine warrior destroying the forces that threaten order in human history, as in the cosmos. In particular, the "arm" of God is mentioned in the context of the governance of the cosmos through God's victory over the chaos monsters (Ps 89:11 [v. 10]; Isa 51:9). Importantly, the arm of YHWH that governs the monsters results in the establishment of *mišpāṭ* as the foundation of divine kingship in the world (Ps 89:15 [v. 14]). The arm of YHWH brings people under YHWH's jurisdiction (*yišpōṭû*, Isa 51:5).

In ancient Canaanite myth, the subjugation of the chaos monsters by the storm god Baal leads to the establishment of Baal's kingship. Following his cosmogonic battle against these monsters, Baal enters his newly built palace and thunders (*CTU* 1.4.VII.27–31). So the mention of God's thunder (v. 9b) after the allusion to God's arm

---

10. Job 8:3; 9:19; 19:9; 32:9; 34:12, 17; 35:2; 36:17; and 37:23.

11. Exod 15:16; Deut 4:34; 26:8; 33:27; Isa 30:30; 33:2; 40:10; 51:9; Ezek 20:33–34; Ps 89:11, 14 (vv. 10, 13). Sylvia H. Scholnick, "The Meaning of *Mišpat* in the Book of Job," *JBL* 101 (1982): 521–29.

(v. 9a) is entirely in accord with the mythic pattern. At issue here is divine kingship that is beyond Job. The rhetorical question makes clear that Job is not like God.[12]

God then tells Job to go ahead and put on "pride and loftiness" and "splendor and sublimity" (v. 10). The first pair appears also in Jer 48:29 and Prov 16:18, in both cases with negative connotations, though the first word, gā'ôn ("pride"), may also be used of divine "majesty" (Exod 15:7; Isa 2:10, 19, 21; 4:2; 24:14). The second pair is more common than the first, and is always associated with kingship, whether human (Pss 21:6 [v. 5]; 45:4 [v. 3]) or divine (Pss 96:6; 104:1; 111:3; 145:5; 1 Chr 16:27). This pair always has positive connotations. Taken together, the couplet mocks Job's pretensions, as if Job in his arrogance fancies himself overseeing mišpāṭ in the world like a divine king.

Job is then challenged to play the role of a divine king who pours out his angry outbursts and brings down the proud and the wicked.[13] He is challenged to carry out what Buber calls "retributive justice" without exception,[14] without missing anyone, for he is to see *every* proud one and to dispense justice to each accordingly. This challenge is ironic, for Job, who is asked to deck himself with "pride and loftiness," is told to bring down every proud one.

Job is to "conceal" (ṭmn) the proud and the wicked together "in the dirt" (v. 13a). The verb ṭmn recalls the inadequate exercise of "retributive justice" on the part of Moses when he, witnessing an Egyptian beating one of his kinsmen, killed the Egyptian and concealed (ṭmn) him in the sand (Exod 2:11–12). More importantly, the expression "to conceal in the dirt" occurs in Isa 2:10 precisely in the context of bringing down the proud (Isa 2:9–11). There, concealment in the ground is not a burial but an attempt to evade the threat of divine retribution — "the dread of YHWH" and his majestic presence (Isa 2:10). The deity

---

12. Contra Balentine (*Job*, 679–82) who argues that Job is in fact being challenged to be like God, thus living up to his being made in the image of God.

13. Job 40:11–12; see Isa 13:9, 13; 14:6; Hos 13:11; Hab 3:8; Pss 7:7 (v. 6); 78:49; 85:4 (v. 3); 90:11.

14. Martin Buber, *The Prophetic Faith* (trans. C. Witton-Davies; New York: Macmillan, 1949), 195; essay originally published in 1941.

mocks Job's capacity for retributive justice, as if Job could subdue "every proud one" and "crush the wicked in their place," and then keep their presence from sight. In Job's imagination, a just world is one where he would no longer have to see the wicked, for they would be hidden in one way or another. If Job could indeed do even that much, then God would acknowledge Job (v. 14). There is obvious irony in that the Hebrew here, for *'ôdĕkā*, ("I will acknowledge you") recurs elsewhere in the Bible, especially in the Psalms, always of an individual praising God, never of God praising anyone.[15]

After beginning with a reference to the divine "arm" (v. 9a), the stanza ends with Job's "right hand" (v. 14b). Beginning with God's thunder (v. 9b), it ends with God's praise of Job (v. 14a). Moreover, the reference to the victorious right hand is reminiscent of doxologies affirming God's victorious power.[16] Yet the point of the stanza is that Job *cannot* accomplish that much, for he does not have an "arm" like God. Job is in no place to exercise divine *mišpāṭ*, the divine right to govern the cosmos. And two superior creatures, Behemoth and Leviathan, prove this point once and for all.

A FABULOUS BEAST

Despite its plural form "beasts" (*bĕhēmôt*), Behemoth in the passage clearly identifies a single creature. The unexpected ending (*-ôt*) has led many scholars to follow the lead of Bochart in speculating that *bĕhēmôt* is a Hebraized form of an Egyptian designation that he hypothesized, *p3-iḥ-mw*, "the water ox" (that is, the hippopotamus), supposedly rendered in Coptic as *p-ehe-mou(t)*.[17] Yet Bochart's knowl-

---

15. Pss 18:50; 30:13; 35:18; 43:4; 52:11; 57:10; 71:22; 86:12; 118:21, 28; 119:7; 138:1; 139:14.

16. Pss 20:7; 44:4; 60:7; 98:1; 103:7; 109:31; 138:7.

17. Bochart, *Hierozoicon*, 5:753–69. For a review of scholarship on this identification, see Eberhard Ruprecht, "Das Nilpferd im Hiobbuch: Beobachtungen zu der sogennanten zweiten Gottesrede," *VT* 21 (1971): 217–18. This view continues to be defended to this day. See John Gray, *The Book of Job* (Text of the Hebrew Bible 1; Sheffield, UK: Sheffield Phoenix, 2010), 492. It is also the etymology accepted by the *OED*.

edge of Egyptian was faulty; the hippopotamus is never called that in Egyptian. In fact, neither *p3-iḥ-mw*, "the water ox," nor even *iḥ-mw*, "water ox," is attested in Egyptian. The same is true of the putative designation in Coptic: it does not exist. In any case, no ancient reader of the text would have understood the term as anything other than the one that occurs elsewhere in the Bible fourteen times, including twice in Job (12:7; 35:11). The plural here is probably meant to suggest a huge and complex creature, the quintessential beast, or even a composite image of terrifying beasts.

Interpreters from antiquity to the present have tried to identify this beast with specific large animals, including the wild ox (thus the rabbis), the elephant (so Aquinas, Calvin), the water buffalo,[18] or, especially common among modern scholars, the hippopotamus.[19] While animals in the natural world may have served as models for the depiction of Behemoth, the purpose of the poem can hardly be to present a zoological taxonomy. Indeed, no natural beast can account for all the details in this portrait. If the poet intends the elephant, it is puzzling that there is no mention of its most distinctive features—its trunk, ears, and tusks. If the poet means the hippopotamus, it is surprising that nothing is said about its most prominent and fearsome trait, its enormous mouth when opened. If it is the wild ox or the buffalo, it is odd to have no reference to its horns. The depiction, then, seems intentionally generic—enough to suit a number of large animals but matching no particular one.

Other exegetes, prompted by the mythological background of Leviathan, argue that Behemoth is also to be identified with a monster in ancient Near Eastern mythology. At the end of the nineteenth

---

18. André Caquot, "Behemoth," *Sem* 45 (1966): 49–64; Bernard Couroyer, "Qui est Béhémoth?" *RB* 82 (1975): 418–43; and idem, "Béhémoth = hippopotami ou buffle?" *RB* 94 (1987): 214–21.

19. The most extensive and detailed defense of this view is David J. A. Clines, *Job 38–42* (WBC 18B; Nashville: Thomas Nelson, 2011), 113–23, 148–55. See also Ruprecht ("Das Nilpferd," 209–31), who further associates the hippopotamus with the Egyptian god Seth, thought to represent primal evil. So also Othmar Keel, *Jahwes Entgegnung an Ijob: Eine Deutung von Ijob 38–41 vor dem Hintergrund der zeitgenössischen Bildkunst* (FRLANT 121; Göttingen: Vandenhoeck & Ruprecht, 1978), 127–41.

century, scholars associated Behemoth and Leviathan with Apsu and Tiamat,[20] or Kingu and Tiamat in Mesopotamian mythology.[21] With the discovery of Ugaritic texts, others have supposed Behemoth to be the equivalent of Mot, deified Death,[22] or "El's calf, Atik,"[23] known also as *Arš* (*CTU* 1.3.III.43–44).[24] However, all these proposals are purely speculative. There are no detailed descriptions of the appearance of any of these monsters anywhere to provide a basis for comparison. The idea that Behemoth might be a mythological creature comes more from its juxtaposition with Leviathan than from the description in the passage itself. This wondrous creature is a product of the poet's imagination, though one shaped in part by knowledge of various large animals in the natural world.

The poet makes the point that this beast is a product of divine creation (v. 15b). This does not mean that Behemoth and Job are equated with one another, for the poet proceeds immediately to Behemoth's herbivorous nature. The monster is not just like humans; he is also like cattle. The point is that all three—human being, Behemoth, and cattle—are products of divine will manifest in creation. The point is not to exalt Job, as Balentine contends, but to decenter him, which is indeed what YHWH has been doing since his first speech. As Robert Gordis aptly states: "The universe is not anthropocentric, but theocentric, with purposes known only to God, and

---

20. So Crawford H. Toy, *Judaism and Christianity: A Sketch of the Progress of Thought from Old Testament to New Testament* (Cambridge, UK: Wilson and Son, 1890), 160–63.

21. Hermann Gunkel, *Schöpfung und Chaos in Urzeit und Endzeit: Eine religionsgeschichtliche Untersuchung über Gen 1 und Ap Joh 12* (Göttingen: Vandenhoeck & Ruprecht, 1895), 61–66.

22. Richard J. Clifford, *Creation Accounts in the Ancient Near East and the Bible* (CBQMS 26; Washington: Catholic Biblical Association of America, 1994), 194–95.

23. So Marvin Pope, *Job* (AB 15; 3rd ed.; Garden City, NY: Doubleday, 1973), 321–23.

24. John Day, *God's Conflict with the Dragon and the Sea: Echoes of a Canaanite Myth in the Old Testament* (Cambridge, UK: Cambridge University Press, 1985), 72–81; cf. Mary K. Wakeman, *God's Battle with the Monster: A Study in Biblical Imagery* (Leiden: Brill, 1973), 122.

which man cannot fathom."[25] Indeed, Behemoth is exalted far above humanity and cattle.

The beast is presented as having wondrous power. He has a mighty body, evident both in its front and back: its loins, that is, both flanks of his back muscles and his belly muscles are strong (v. 16). Some early interpreters thought that this verse has sexual connotations (Gregory the Great, Albertus Magnus, Aquinas). In fact, the term for "power" (*'ōn*) in verse 16b may be associated with virility.[26] As such, this verse leads naturally to the next couplet (v. 17): "His appendage is stiff like cedar; the veins of his thighs are interlocked."

The term *zānāb* normally means "tail." Yet what animal has a tail that is "like cedar," a tree renowned for its sturdiness and height?[27] Certainly elephants, hippopotamuses, and buffaloes do not have tails that are in any way like cedar. One might, therefore, understand "tail" to be a euphemism for the penis, a meaning well attested in postbiblical Hebrew. If so, the verb *ḥpṣ* may have a double meaning, "to be stiff" and "to delight," [28] both allusions to the erect member of the beast that is "stiff" when it "delights."[29] As for the interlocking veins in verse 17b,[30] one can only surmise that the poet is imagining the buttocks of the

---

25. Robert Gordis, "Job and Ecology (and the Significance of Job 40:15)," *HAR* 9 (1985): 198.

26. See Gen 49:3; Deut 21:17; Pss 78:51; 105:36.

27. 2 Kgs 19:23; Isa 2:13; 37:24; Ezek 17:22; 31:3.

28. The normal meaning of *ḥpṣ* is "to desire," but none of the verses seems to understand the verb in this sense. Several ancient versions (OG, Vulg., and Syr.) suggest erection or firmness. Felix Perles (*Analekten zur Textkritik des Alten Testaments* [Munich: Ackermann, 1895], 76) points to this meaning of *ḥpṣ* in Ps 37:23, where we have, "By YHWH the steps of a man are fixed / his ways are firm." Indeed, Hebrew *ḥpṣ* can imply strength or firmness, as it often does in Hebrew in reference to divine or human resolve (e.g., Judg 13:23; 1 Sam 2:25; 18:25; Isa 58:2; Mic 7:18; 1 Chr 28:9).

29. Most modern scholars cite Arabic *ḥafaḍa*, "lower, abase" (Edward William Lane, *An Arabic-English Lexicon* [London: Willams & Norgate, 1863], 773–74), to suggest the meaning "bend." Yet, apart from the discrepant notion of the tail bending like the cedar, a tree renowned for its sturdiness, it must be said that the meaning "bend" (rigidly or otherwise) is simply not attested in the Arabic term.

30. The term *gîd* should be understood here not as "sinew" but "vein," as in postbiblical Hebrew.

beast as he mates, the visible veins thereof showing the full deployment of his virile power.

The point is Behemoth's virility. In the ancient Near East, as in many cultures around the world, sexual prowess is a mark of potency in all senses of the term.[31] This potency is evident as well in the sturdy structure of the beast, conveyed in hyperbolic terms: his limbs and bones are forged of metal (v. 18). The description can hardly be a cipher for human strength. Indeed, the strength of Behemoth's body stands in stark contrast to Job's, whose strength is not stone and whose body is not metal (6:12).

The description reaches a crescendo in verse 19a when Behemoth is affirmed as "the first of God's ways," an allusion to his ancient origin as well as to his preeminence. Interpreters who recognize the temporal sense of "first" note that according to Gen 1:24–25, the singular *běhēmâ* (usually translated "cattle") is indeed the first of the living things that were created. Even if it is to be identified with this mention of *běhēmâ*, Behemoth was nevertheless not an afterthought to God, but rather a creature made at the very beginning of creation, even before humans were made on the sixth day (Gen 1:26–28). Yet the term "first" (*rēʾšît*) may also be qualitative, meaning the preeminent or the best, as in Jer 49:35; Amos 6:6; Prov 3:9; and Dan 11:41.

Most importantly, the first line of the couplet echoes the characterization of Wisdom: "YHWH created me as the first of his way" (Prov 8:22a). This passage in Proverbs argues that Wisdom was primal in that she was present from the beginning, indeed, with God as the world was being created (Prov 8:22–32). Wisdom was essential to the creation of the world from the start. Perhaps the Joban poet is implying by the choice of words that Behemoth is part of divine providence from the very beginning. He is preeminent in creation and over other creatures. The poet here subverts the view that the human being is supreme over all creatures of land, water, and air (Gen 1:26–27; Ps 8). Rather, even on dry land where humans dwell, he is the awesome beast that rules, not humans. While Eliphaz has accused Job of fancying himself being the "first human" (15:7), YHWH now insists that

---

31. See, e.g., 1 Kgs 1:1–4.

Behemoth is much more than that, for Behemoth, like Wisdom, is the first of God's ways, that is, the prime example of God's creation, created before all others.

The second line of the couplet in verse 19 is more problematic. The traditional Hebrew text, the MT, has *hā'ōśô yaggēš ḥarbô*, literally, "Let the one who made him bring near his sword." However, the text as it stands is grammatically suspect,[32] and even more troubling is the sense of the line. The traditional interpretation is that the creator of Behemoth is the only one who is able to bring "his [the deity's] sword" to kill the beast,[33] or at least to threaten and thus control him.[34] Yet nothing in the passage indicates hostility between God and Behemoth. Recognizing this, some modern interpreters assume that the sword in question is not God's but Behemoth's—a metaphor for the sharp horns given to the beast by the deity. It has even been suggested that the Creator alone can grant the beast "his sword," meaning his tusk used like a sickle to cut grass.[35] These views are unconvincing, not least because they overextend the meaning of the Hebrew verb *ngš* ("to come near").

Following a cue from the Old Greek, Johann Hoffman suggests *he'āśû yiggaš ḥārābô*, "the one made that he should approach his dry land."[36] Instead of *hā'ōśô*, the Old Greek version has a passive participle, presumably reflecting Hebrew *he'āśû*, as 41:25. This prompted Gunkel to read *he'āśû yiggōś ḥārābô*, "the one made that he should rule his dry land," assuming *ngś*, which can mean "to oppress" or "to dominate, rule."[37] The problematic element in Hoffman's solution is the

---

32. It includes a definite article on a participle with a suffix.

33. See Pio Fedrizzi (*Giobbe* [La Sacra Bibbia; Turin: Marietti, 1972], 276), who cites Isa 30:32.

34. See Samuel Terrien, *Job* (CAT 13; Neuchatel: Delachaux & Nestlé, 1963), 261–62; and Norman Habel, *The Book of Job* (OTL; Philadelphia: Westminster, 1985), 567.

35. So Bernard Couroyer, "Le 'glaive' de Béhémoth: Job xl,19–20," *RB* 84 (1977): 59–79.

36. Johann G. E. Hoffmann, *Hiob* (Kiel: Haeseler, 1891), 89.

37. Gunkel, *Schöpfung und Chaos*, 62.

pronominal suffix "his"; it is awkward to speak of Behemoth ruling "*his* dry land." Hence many commentators, especially those who identify Behemoth with the hippopotamus, prefer to emend the text to read *ḥăbērāw* ("his companions").[38] Yet, except for the Old Greek, which has a midrashic addition in verse 19b, the other ancient versions corroborate the MT, while no witness supports reading *ḥbrw*.

We might rather surmise that the original text had *ḥrbh*, "dry land," but *ḥrbh* was later incorrectly interpreted as *ḥarbōh*, "his sword" and "standardized" to *ḥarbô*, a much more common form. Hence, we should read *heʿāśû yiggōś ḥărābâ*, and assume the asyndetic relative clause: "The creature (that) dominates the dry land." Then, elaborating this claim of Behemoth's domination of dry land, the poet speaks of the mountains bringing their yield for him (v. 20): "For mountains bring him produce; and all the wild animals play there." The introductory "for" is climactic, corroborating the picture of Behemoth's rule. The reference to mountains is a stumbling block to the identification of Behemoth with the hippopotamus. What does the hippopotamus have to do with mountains? The language is in fact reminiscent of Ps 72:1–2, which speaks of the mountains bringing *shalom* (peace, well-being) to the people as the manifestation of divine *mišpāṭ* through the agency of the earthly king. Here in Job, in a speech defending the deity's *mišpāṭ* (see v. 8), the text refers to the mountains bringing *bûl*, "produce," to Behemoth.

The term *bûl* is related to the name of the month of the autumn harvest in the Canaanite calendar, known in Phoenician inscriptions and in the Bible—a time of bringing in the produce.[39] It is also cognate to *blt* in Old South Arabic, meaning "tribute" (as something brought).[40] The latter is particularly relevant, for it means both "produce" and "trib-

---

38. See, for example, Bernhard Duhm, *Das Buch Hiob erklärt* (KHC 16; Tübingen: Mohr, 1897), 196; Edouard Dhorme, *Le livre de Job* (Paris: Lecoffre, 1926), 567; Georg Fohrer, *Das Buch Hiob* (KAT 16; Gütersloh: Gütersloher Verlagshaus, 1963), 522; and A. de Wilde, *Das Buch Hiob eingeleitet, übersetzt und erklärt* (OtSt 22; Leiden: Brill, 1981), 382.

39. See *KAI* 14:1; 32:1; 38:2; 1 Kgs 6:38.

40. See Joan C. Biella, *Dictionary of Old South Arabic: Sabaean Dialect* (HSS 25; Chico, CA: Scholars Press, 1982), 45; and *CAD* 2[B]:232.

ute" and is used with the verb *našû*, cognate of Hebrew *nś'* ("to bring/lift up"). Importantly, the verb *nś'* is used of arboreal yield,[41] in the conveyance of tribute (2 Sam 8:2, 6) and, indeed, of the offering (lifting up) of tribute in worship (Ps 96:8; Ezek 20:31). Furthermore, "tribute" is indeed what one expects for one who "dominates" (*ngś*), for the verb *ngś* may imply tribute, as in 2 Kgs 23:35 and Dan 11:20.[42]

Therefore, one may discern two levels of meaning in Job 40:20. The first is naturalistic: the mountains yield food for Behemoth. The second is mythic: the personified mountains bring tribute to Behemoth. Here one may compare a Ugaritic parallel where the mountains bring (*ybl*) tribute to triumphant Baal: "Let the mountains bring you much silver / the hills, the most desired gold" (*CTU* 1.4.V.15–16, 31–33).[43]

The laughter of the wild animals is reminiscent of other occurrences of *śḥq* in the book. Poignantly, since the line here (v. 20b) follows the reference to the produce that the mountains bring in tribute, one recalls that Eliphaz had promised that in the Edenic world of Job's restoration, Job would "laugh" at devastation and famine and not fear the wild animals (5:22). The laughter of the wild animals also harks back to the laughter of the various wild creatures in God's strange menagerie: the wild ass (39:7), the ostrich (39:18), and the wild horse (39:22). Behemoth's wild domain is a microcosm of God's wild domain.

---

41. Ezek 17:23; 36:8 (with "mountains" as subject!); Hag 2:19; Joel 2:22.

42. Cf. Old South Arabic *ngś*, "to impose tribute" (Biella, *Dictionary of Old South Arabic*, 293; and Stephen D. Ricks, *Lexicon of Inscriptional Qatabanian* [Studia Pohl NS 14; Rome: Pontificio Istituto Biblico, 1989], 103).

43. Interpreters who follow Delitzsch in taking *bûl* to mean "beasts" are forced to assume that the verb *nś'* is elliptical for *nś' qwl*, "to lift a voice" (so J. V. Kinnier Wilson, "A Return to the Problems of Behemoth and Leviathan," *VT* 25 [1975]: 7; and Harold R. Cohen, *Biblical Hapax Legomena in the Light of Akkadian and Ugaritic* [SBLDS 37; Missoula, MT: Scholars Press, 1978], 51), or they emend to *yś'w* to read *yśt'w*, "[the beasts of the mountains] gaze" (so C. J. Ball, *The Book of Job: A Revised Text and Version* [Oxford: Clarendon, 1922], 442) or *yślyw*, "[the beasts of the mountains] relax" (so Pope, *Job*, 325–26; Gray, *Book of Job*, 491). In so doing, they miss the poetic play, while having also to disregard the adverb *šām* at the end of the second line. What does it mean to say the wild animals laugh "there"? Where is "there"?

The presence of Behemoth in the swamp and the river (vv. 21–23) troubles those who see Behemoth as a land creature, as opposed to Leviathan as an aquatic creature.[44] Those who believe the intent of the passage is to depict a terrifying monster are puzzled by the tranquility of the scene. Hence some assume that these verses are in fact unmarked rhetorical questions (so the Geneva Bible). Would such a terrifying monster as Behemoth really lie under jujube trees (commonly translated as "lotus") or hide among the reeds in swamps? Yet the point of these verses is to show that while the domain of Behemoth is the dry land, he is nevertheless at ease even at the fringes of that realm, even when chaos threatens to drown him. Despite the encroachment of the waters upon dry land, this area that is betwixt and between provides shelter and cover for him. The poet implies that this liminal space is indeed a site of divine providence, for several of the terms here are associated with divine protection: "covert,"[45] "to cover, shelter" (Pss 5:12; 91:4; 148:8), "shelter/protection,"[46] and "to surround" (Pss 32:7, 10; 71:21). Behemoth, created by God (vv. 15, 19), is also provided for by God.

Even away from that in-between realm, in a river that is chaotic, Behemoth remains unfazed: "Even if the river is turbulent (*ya'ăšōq*), he is not alarmed. He is confident, even if the current (*yardēn*) gushes against his mouth" (v. 23).[47] The choice of words may well be intentional on the part of the poet. The verb appears one other time in the

---

44. So the Jewish sages. See Louis Ginzberg, *The Legends of the Jews* (7 vols.; Baltimore: Johns Hopkins University Press, 1998), 1:30; originally published 1909–38.

45. Pss 27:5; 31:21; 32:7; 61:5; 81:8; 91:1; 119:114.

46. Isa 25:4; 51:16; Pss 17:8; 36:8; 63:8; 91:1; 121:5.

47. Although the term *yardēn* can refer to the Jordan river, here it may not in fact be a proper name. The term *Iardanos* appears in the classical world for rivers in Crete and Elis (see Homer, *Odyssey* 3.292; *Illiad* 7.135). The term appears to have ante-dated Old Persian, thus rendering nugatory earlier explanations in terms of Persian *yardan* (year-river), meaning a river flowing in all seasons. See, e.g., Wolfram von Soden, "Zur Herkunft des Flussnamens Jordan," ZAW 57 [1939]: 153–54). Whatever the case, the term originally probably meant "river." Just as Egyptian *itrw* ("river," Hebrew *yĕ'ōr*) came to mean "the river" of Egypt, the Nile, so *yardēn*, "river," came to mean "the river" of the Cis- and Transjordan.

book, where Job accuses God of acting unjustly toward him (10:3). Unlike Job, who responded in frustration and anger before such a challenge, Behemoth does not panic, or, as the Hebrew allows, he is not hasty. This patient Behemoth in fact shows up the impatient Job.

Indeed, Behemoth is "confident" even when the current "gushes against his mouth" (v. 23b), that is, when the river threatens to overwhelm him. Behemoth, though a creature that rules the dry land (v. 19b, see previously), is confident even in the face of a flood and the prospect of drowning. Job knows well such prospects and fears them, for he speaks of caravans that venture into treacherous wadis in search of shortcuts without recognizing the dangers of flash floods, only to regret their misplaced confidence (see 6:20). The verb "gush" (40:23b) suggests the rush of water. It appears earlier in YHWH's speech in reference to the creation of the sea, representing primordial chaos and portrayed as gushing forth from the womb (38:8). Yet in the face of such a threat of overwhelming chaos, Behemoth remains confident (*bṭḥ*), the verb here being parallel to "not alarmed." Interpreters who detect a subliminal message to Job are perhaps right that God is offering Behemoth as an object lesson on how one ought to respond when tragedy strikes and one is in danger of being drowned in chaos. What the poet conveys is not the evil of Behemoth but wonder at a creature so strong that even the threat of watery chaos does not overwhelm him.[48]

The poet then ends with a rhetorical question — "Who can capture him?" — suggesting that one cannot overcome Behemoth (v. 24). Even though there is abundant evidence in texts and iconography of the capture of the hippopotamus, most notably in Egypt,[49] Behemoth clearly cannot be so caught. Thus the poem ends — abruptly, anticlimactically. With the next-to-last verse affirming the supreme confidence of Behemoth in the face of chaos, the reader certainly does not

---

48. Despite the widespread assumption (beginning with OG) that Behemoth, like Leviathan, represents evil, there is not the slightest indication in this passage that the beast is evil, wicked, or even proud. See Pieter van der Lugt, *Rhetorical Criticism and the Poetry of the Book of Job* (OtSt 32; Leiden: Brill, 1985), 405–6.

49. Torgny Säve-Söderbergh, *On Egyptian Representations of Hippopotamus Hunting as Religious Motive* (Horace soederblomiana 3; Uppsala: Gleerup, 1953), passim; and Keel, *Jahwes Entgegnung an Ijob*, 132–39.

expect a question, even a rhetorical one. It is for good reason, therefore, that commentators, already in the medieval period (e.g., Ralbag), proposed that verse 24 be taken with the following section concerning Leviathan. Yet Leviathan is not named until the next verse. In fact, with verse 24, the stanza ends without closure and even resists it. The rhetorical question seems to align Behemoth with the other wondrous creature that is presented next. That is, the last verse of the Behemoth poem anticipates the Leviathan poem. It is as if one monster is now morphing and merging with another. The interrogatory form prompts the reader to wonder, and that wonder leads to a new climax that is yet to come.

CONCLUSION

In the portrayal of Behemoth, the second YHWH discourse reaches its first crescendo. The first speech has already undermined any pretense that creation is anthropocentric. The complex ʿēṣâ, the design of the cosmos, is far more complicated than one might imagine, though it is nevertheless part of the divine will. Now through the exaltation of Behemoth, clearly a creature of God and yet no mundane beast, the poet makes the point that humanity is not the epitome of God's creation either. On the contrary, there are other beings in the world, whether naturalistic or fabulous, before whom humans can only stand in wonder and awe. This is a testimony to the Creator's sovereign freedom, the divine mišpāṭ that Job has overlooked.

4

Forgive Us Our Debts

Gary A. Anderson
(University of Notre Dame)

> God acts mercifully not by doing anything contrary to His justice,
> but by doing something that goes beyond His justice. In the same
> way, if one gives 200 denarii of his own money to someone who is
> owed 100 denarii, then he is acting generously or mercifully and
> not contrary to justice. The same thing holds if someone forgives
> an offense committed against himself. For in forgiving this debt,
> he is in a certain sense making a gift of it; hence, in Ephesians
> 4:32 the Apostle calls forgiveness a "gift": "Make a gift to one
> another, just as Christ has made a gift to you."
> —Thomas Aquinas, *Summa Theologica* I, q. 21 a.3[1]

Anyone who has read the Bible with any care will readily acknowledge
the various metaphors that are used to depict human sin. For most readers, the presumption would be that a standard set of images circulated
in ancient times, and various writers chose from that set for specific
rhetorical purposes. To a degree that is true, but not completely. Sin, I
have argued, has a history, which means that concepts of sin changed
over the course of the Bible's lifetime.[2] The Old Testament, for exam-

---

1. The translation is that of Alred J. Freddoso; see http://www3.nd.edu/~afreddos/
summa-translation/Part%201/st1-ques21.pdf.

2. This essay has been adapted from portions of my book *Sin: A History* (New Haven:
Yale University Press, 2009), and is used here by permission. The interested reader
will find a lengthier exposition of the matter in that volume. I have translated all rabbinic texts; biblical texts have been taken from the NRSV except where noted. The
translation of the "Our Father" is my own.

ple, contains a number of different metaphors for sin, but pride of place goes to the metaphor of sin as a burden. In Jewish sources contemporary with the rise of Christianity, the metaphor of sin as a burden was replaced by that of sin as a debt. This was a rather unexpected event because there is very little evidence in the Hebrew texts of the First Temple period for such an idea. It emerged as a bolt out of the blue.

Perhaps the best way to get an idea of how significant this transformation was is to take a brief tour through the lexicon of Rabbinic Hebrew. Let us consider three representative examples: (1) the payment of a bill, (2) the state of being indebted, and (3) the act of releasing someone from the obligation to repay a debt. What we will see here is a complete interchangeability between commercial and theological terminology. The significance of the latter is only intelligible in light of the former.

> (1) The payment of a bill: The verb *pāra'* normally means "to pay for something," that is, to provide a cash equivalent for what one owes: "I have repaid you (*pāra' t'îka*) [the money I previously owed]."[3] In the reflexive conjugation (known in Hebrew as the *nip'al*) this same verbal root has the literal sense "to collect payment from someone." But because physical punishment is considered a form of currency with which one can repay a debt, the verb can also be translated "to punish." In a rabbinic commentary on the Book of Exodus known as the *Mekhilta deRabbi Ishmael*, we learn that God separated the waters of the Sea of Reeds so that he could lead Israel to safety and "take payment" (*nipra'*) from those bent on destroying Israel.[4] The reflexive form of the verb (*nipra'*) implies that God took payment on the debt that Pharaoh and his accomplices owed him. The wages of sin was death (cf. Rom 6:23).
>
> (2) The state of being indebted: The most common verbal root for conveying the sense of obligation is *ḥāb*, which normally means "to owe." It has a substantivized adjective *ḥayyāb*,

---

3. *B. B. Bathra* 5a.

4. *Mekhilta deR. Ishmael*, ad Exod 14:21.

which means "one who owes," and a noun *ḥôb*, that refers to the item owed, that is, a debt. Because a monetary debt always involves a contract, the term for a creditor is one who is in possession of a debt instrument (*ba'al ḥôb*), that is, the document (*šṭar*) that was signed when the loan was formally issued. The presumption is that as long as the creditor holds this bond, he is entitled to collect what is due him. As a result, when a bond was paid off, special care was taken either to tear the bond in two to mark its cancellation or to return the bond to the borrower who could dispose of it as he chose. But in a larger metaphoric sense, it was thought that the punishment of a sinner by God was nothing other than the act of the divine creditor's collecting payment (in the form of punishment) on what was due: when an individual was about to be punished, R. Isaac said, "The creditor (*ba'al ḥôb*) found the opportunity to collect on his bond (*šṭar*)."[5]

(3) The act of releasing someone from their debt: The verb *māḥal* means "to cancel a bond of indebtedness" in its literal sense, and "to forgive a sin" in its metaphoric sense. For the former, consider this text from the Babylonian Talmud: "If a man provides a bond (*šṭar*) for a loan then pays it off (*pāra'*), he cannot provide this bond again because the security which it contains has been cancelled (*nimḥal*)."[6] For its metaphoric sense compare this text:

> R. Tanhum b. Hanilai said: "No rain shall fall unless the sins of Israel are forgiven (*nimḥălû*) for scripture says, 'O LORD, You were favorable to your land, you restored the fortunes of Jacob. You have borne away the iniquity of your people; you covered all their sins. You withdrew all your wrath; you turned from your hot anger'" (Ps 85:1–3).[7]

---

5. *Gen Rab* 85:2.

6. *B. Gittin* 26b.

7. *B. Taanit* 7b. I have adjusted the NRSV translation to match how R. Tanhuma has read the text.

It is striking that the biblical idiom of sin as a weight ("you have *borne away* the iniquity of your people") has been ignored in favor of sin as a debt. This is very good evidence of how the metaphor of sin as a weight has dropped out of common speech in later Hebrew. Its replacement by the metaphor of debt is practically complete.

JESUS AND THE "OUR FATHER"

In the New Testament period, the metaphor of sin as a debt was ubiquitous. Jesus frequently told stories about debtors and creditors as a way of illustrating the dynamics of sin and forgiveness. Given that he spoke a form of Hebrew close to that of the rabbinic dialect, this is hardly surprising. As Lakoff and Johnson have documented, metaphors determine how we think, act, and tell stories in the everyday world.[8]

Consider, for example, the famous line from the "Our Father" as found in Matthew's Gospel: "Remit us our debts as we remit those who hold debts against us" (6:12). Forgiveness here is imagined as a gracious act of refusing to collect on an obligation. The person praying asks that God act this way while at the same time affirming an intention to do the same. Nearly all scholars would concede that the Greek form of this prayer that we now have in the New Testament only makes sense when we translate it back into its original Semitic environment. "The Matthean use of 'debts' has a Semitic flavor," observes New Testament scholar Raymond Brown,

> for, while in secular Greek "debt" has no religious coloring, in Aramaic *ḥôbâ* is a financial and commercial term that has been caught up into the religious vocabulary.... The idea of remitting (*aphiemi*) debts which appears in our petition is also more Semitic than Greek, for "remission" has a religious sense only in the Greek of the LXX [the

---

8. George Lakoff and Mark Johnson, *Metaphors We Live By* (Chicago: University of Chicago Press, 1980).

Septuagint, or the Greek translation of the Bible], which is under Hebrew influence.[9]

The significance of "debt" language is not limited to the "Our Father." We find our best illustration of this sort of symbolism in the parable of the unforgiving servant (Matt 18:23–35). In this parable, a king wishes to settle his accounts with various servants:

> For this reason the kingdom of heaven may be compared to a king who wished to settle accounts with his slaves. When he began the reckoning, one who owed him ten thousand talents was brought to him; and, as he could not pay, his lord ordered him to be sold, together with his wife and children and all his possessions, and payment to be made. So the slave fell on his knees before him, saying, "Have patience with me, and I will pay you everything." And out of pity for him, the lord of that slave released him and forgave him the debt. But that same slave, as he went out, came upon one of his fellow slaves who owed him a hundred denarii; and seizing him by the throat, he said, "Pay what you owe." Then his fellow slave fell down and pleaded with him, "Have patience with me, and I will pay you." But he refused; then he went and threw him into prison until he would pay the debt. When his fellow slaves saw what had happened, they were greatly distressed, and they went and reported to their lord all that had taken place. Then his lord summoned him and said to him, "You wicked slave! I forgave you all that debt because you pleaded with me. Should you not have had mercy on your fellow slave, as I had mercy on you?" And in anger his lord handed him over to be tortured until he should pay his entire debt.

This parable brings stunning clarity to what Jesus meant when he advised his disciples to pray that their debts be forgiven just as they for-

---

9. Raymond E. Brown, "The Pater Noster as an Eschatological Prayer," *TS* 22 (1961): 175–208; reprinted in idem, *New Testament Essays* (Milwaukee, WI: Bruce, 1965), 217–53. The citation is taken from the reprinted edition, 244.

give the debts of others. According to the logic of the metaphor this prayer employs, we are in danger of becoming debt-slaves when we sin. Should the act go uncorrected, then one will have to "pay" for the "cost" of the misdeed with a "currency" that is generated by physical punishment. Fortunately, God is merciful and will remit the debt we owe if we humbly beseech him.

As Brown concludes, "The king who wishes to settle debts with his servants is obviously God, and the atmosphere is that of judgment. The parable points out that God's forgiveness of the servant has a connection to that servant's forgiveness of his fellow servant. When this brotherly forgiveness fails, he is given to the torturers until he pays his debt."[10] In this fashion, the parable illustrates the underlying logic of the "Our Father," where we see not only a petition from a servant to his master for debt remission ("remit us our debts"), but also a remission made contingent on how the servant acts toward a peer who is indebted to him ("as we remit those debts we hold against others").

Note that Jesus does not compare a sinner to individuals who are struggling under a heavy burden. Stories like the scapegoat in Lev 16 or the injunction that Ezekiel lie on his side while God loaded upon him the sins of Israel (Ezek 4:4–8) simply do not appear in the New Testament. But neither do they occur in rabbinic literature. This is ample testimony to the wholesale replacement of the weight image in favor of debt.

In spite of its appearance in the Our Father, the Jewish conception of sin has been the subject of some rather heated polemics from Christian thinkers. In particular, scholars of the New Testament who have been heavily influenced by a Protestant concept of law have tended to draw a picture of rabbinic Judaism that is quite unflattering. The metaphor of sin as a debt seems to conjure the notion that God sits in heaven with his account books open, and scrutinizes every human action with an eye toward making sure it is properly recorded

---

10. "Pater Noster," 245.

as either a debit or credit. There seems to be little room for the merciful side of the Godhead to emerge. One need not study theology to get an understanding of this exacting or even punitive side of God; a degree in accounting may do just as well.

One of the principal places to see this sort of critical assessment is the multivolume commentary on the New Testament produced by Hermann Strack and Paul Billerbeck.[11] These two German scholars from the early twentieth century went through the New Testament line by line with a view toward comparing those writings with parallels from the rabbinic corpus. This magisterial work, which continues to inform the work of countless New Testament scholars, frequently selected only those rabbinic texts that illustrated the larger theological program of the authors. Scholars were once ignorant of the prejudicial *Tendenz* of this work and used it as though it were an unbiased record of rabbinic thinking. All of this changed in 1977, when E. P. Sanders rocked the world of New Testament studies with a devastating critique of this sort of approach in his much-acclaimed book, *Paul and Palestinian Judaism*.[12] In this work Sanders provided a convenient summary of how Strack and Billerbeck conceived the theological world of rabbinic Judaism:

> God gave Israel the Torah so that they would have the opportunity to earn merit and reward. Individuals have the capability of choosing the good and the entire system of "Pharisaic soteriology" stands or falls with man's capability to fulfill the law. Every fulfillment of a commandment earns for the Israelite a merit (*zekût*) while every transgression earns a debt or guilt (*ḥôbâh*). God keeps a record of both merits and demerits. When a man's merits are more numerous he is considered righteous, but when transgressions outnumber merits he is considered wicked. If the two are balanced, he is an intermediate. Man does not know

---

11. Hermann Strack and Paul Billerbeck, *Kommentar zum Neuen Testament aus Talmud und Midrasch* (6 vols.; Munich: Beck, 1924–61).

12. E. P. Sanders, *Paul and Palestinian Judaism: A Comparison of Patterns of Religion* (Philadelphia: Fortress, 1977).

how his reckoning with God stands; consequently he has no security on earth. The balance of his account may alter at any moment. At the end his destiny is decided on the basis of the account. One with more fulfillments goes to the [Garden of] Eden, one with more transgressions to Gehinnom, while for one in the intermediate position God removes a transgression from the scale so that his fulfillments will weigh more heavily.[13]

This ledger-book approach to theology is presented as both the beginning and the end of rabbinic thought. As Billerbeck himself put it: "The old Jewish religion is thus a religion of the most complete self-redemption (*Selbsterlösung*); it has no room for a redeemer saviour who dies for the sins of the world."[14] There are texts within the rabbinic corpus that appear to support this conception. But at the same time, many other texts reveal that God does not administer his ledger in a mechanical fashion. Rather than playing the role "by the book" and adjusting each debit to a credit, God was willing to overlook various financial obligations in order to save his people. Although creative accounting of this sort in the world of finance has had catastrophic effects, within the spiritual realm, different rules are in play. God is not adverse to "cooking the books" if the end result falls to the favor of the nation Israel he loves so dearly. Indeed, in some midrashic narratives, the element of fairness disappears altogether. In its place appears the virtue of grace, that is, the receipt of unmerited benefits from God. Strikingly, Strack and Billerbeck do not attend to examples like this.

In order to illustrate this other side of rabbinic thinking, I would like to discuss a text from *Pesikta Rabbati*, a relatively late collection of rabbinic homilies that are dedicated to the various festivals of the Jewish liturgical year. In the forty-fifth chapter of this work, we have a homily dedicated to the Day of Atonement. According to rabbinic thought, God judges the sins of Israel on this day and determines what the fate of each and every individual sinner will be for the following

---

13. Ibid., 42–43.

14. As cited in ibid., 43.

year. If God were to be conceived of as a fastidious banker dealing out just punishment for each and every person, one would expect that this would be the occasion when God would gather up the various bonds that were in his possession and begin to demand payment so that he could balance his books for the close of the financial year. Israelites who stood in considerable arrears because of their sins would have reason to tremble in fright. But such expectations are radically overturned by the following interpretation of Ps 32:1–2.

"An instruction of David. Happy are those whose transgression is carried away (něśûy peša‘), whose sin is covered over (kěsûy ḥaṭṭā't)" (Ps 32:1). This is what David means: you have carried away the sins (nāśā' 'āwōn) of your people, all their sins you have covered up.

Once, on the Day of Atonement, Satan came to accuse Israel. He detailed her sins and said, "Lord of the Universe, as there are adulterers among the nations of the world, so there are in Israel. As there are thieves among the nations of the world, so there are in Israel." The Holy One, blessed be He, itemized the merits (zěkûyôt) of Israel. Then what did he do? He took a scale and balanced the sins against the merits. They were weighed together and the scales were equally balanced. Then Satan went to load on further sin and to make that scale sink lower.

What did the Holy One, blessed be He, do? While Satan was looking for sins, the Holy One, blessed be He, took the sins from the scale and hid them under his purple royal robe. When Satan returned, he found no sin, as it is written, "The sin of Israel was searched for, but it is no longer" (Jer 50:20). When Satan saw this he spoke before the Holy One, blessed be He, "Lord of the World, 'you have borne away the iniquity of your people and covered over all their sin'" (Ps 85:2). When David saw this, he said, "Happy are those whose transgression is borne away, whose sin is covered over" (Ps 32:1).

It is important to note that Satan is not the personification of evil we might expect here. He is rather a cipher for the principle of justice.

His claim is that Israel does not deserve forgiveness; her debits out-
weigh her credits. But God will not allow strict accountancy proce-
dures to govern his heart. Even if Satan is correct, he cannot win. God
amends the situation by "bearing away" the sin of Israel. In this case
God does not remove a weight from someone's shoulders, as the biblical expression would require, but rather a bond. With those bonds
safely removed from the scales, the credits of Israel now have the
upper hand, and God can "justly" forgive his people.

The theme of angelic ire at the generosity of God is hardly rare
in rabbinic literature, and Peter Shäfer has collected a massive catalogue to demonstrate this.[15] In some stories the angels are punished; in
others they are deceived. But the crucial point is that, in the end,
God's accounting for human sin is not according to the pattern that
Strack and Billerbeck had laid out. Though God is just, he is also generous. In the epigram to this essay, Thomas Aquinas remarked that
such generosity does not offend against justice. For just as the man
who owes one hundred dollars is free to pay two hundred, so the person who is owed a hundred dollars can refuse to collect anything. For
in forgiving a debt, the creditor is in a certain sense making a gift of it,
and God is always free to make a gift. Of course, there are many rabbinic stories about sinners who are punished for their wrongdoing. But
in order to draw a proper picture of rabbinic theology, these stories
must be balanced with narratives that show God altering the rules so
that mercy can win. Since all the debt is ultimately owed to God, it is
his right to rescind from collecting it. He does not act unjustly when
he offers the debtor such a gift.

It may be objected that the story from *Pesikta Rabbati* is too late
a text to cast light on how the rabbis themselves construed the matter.
Yet the story as we find it in *Pesikta Rabbati* has a very close counterpart in the much earlier Jerusalem Talmud (fifth century CE). In tractate *Peah* of the Jerusalem Talmud, the observation is made that one
who has a preponderance of merits will inherit paradise, while one
who has a preponderance of transgressions will be heir to the fires of

---

15. Peter Shäfer, *Rivalität zwischen Engeln und Menschen: Untersuchungen zur rab-
binischen Engelvorstellung* (Berlin: de Gruyter, 1975).

Gehenna. But what about the person whose merits and debits are of the same weight?

> Said R. Yose b. Hanina, "Consider the description of God's attributes [in Exod 34:6–7]. 'Who takes hold of transgressions [plural] so as to remove them' is not written. But rather, 'Who takes away [a] transgression [singular].' This means that the Holy One [Blessed be He!] will snatch away one bond, so that his good deeds will predominate."
> R. Eleazar cited the verse, "To you, O Lord, belongs a charitable inclination (ḥesed): you indeed repay each individual according to his deeds" (Ps 62:13). Yet if one lacks [sufficient merit], God will provide some of his! This is in accord with the thought of R. Eleazar for he has [also] said in respect to the verse, "God is abounding in charity (rab ḥesed)" (Exod 34:6), that God inclines the scales of justice towards a charitable decision. (y. Peah 5a)

In the first unit, we can see how R. Yose has taken the biblical text in an overly literal way. The noun "transgression" in the phrase "who forgives transgression" is singular, though the sense of the Hebrew is clearly plural. Nevertheless, that "transgression" was stated in the singular struck R. Yose as peculiar. Why would a verse that purports to describe God's mercy say that he will take away only a single transgression? The answer R. Yose provides is that the biblical text has in mind a person whose scales are evenly balanced. In this case God shows mercy by taking away a single bond so that the debits cannot predominate.

R. Eleazar arrives at a similar conclusion but from a different starting point. Psalm 62:13 says that each person is repaid according to his deeds, but it qualifies this affirmation by saying, "To You, O Lord, belongs a charitable inclination." What might this mean? In the mind of R. Eleazar, it means that it is God's right to mete out justice in accordance with human deeds, but that this general affirmation should not be taken as an iron-clad rule. Since God is defined by the principle of charity, he is perfectly free to bestow some of his infinite merit on those who are lacking. Eleazar reaffirms this principle through a citation of one of the merciful attributes of God (Exod 34:6). The fact that God is one who is "abounding in charity" means that God puts his thumb on the scale such that the balance tilts in favor of the human person he so deeply loves. Since the obligation is to him in the first place, he is free to overlook it should he wish.

As the philosopher Paul Ricoeur has argued, there is no way to approach the notion of "sin" apart from the concrete metaphors that are embedded in any given language.[16] Ricoeur did not mean that these metaphors woodenly determined the types of stories that would be told. Rather, metaphors provided the raw material that religious traditions could shape in a variety of different directions. The mistake of Strack and Billerbeck, and a generation of New Testament scholars that followed, was to assume that Jewish thinking about the forgiveness of sins was determined by the rules of strict financial propriety. As we have seen in this essay, the deployment of the motif was complex and subtle. To be sure, God could be depicted as an imperious lending officer who would demand every penny he had coming. But he could just as easily be portrayed as a soft-hearted aunt who was prone to forget the money she had lent a favorite nephew. Everything depends on the literary context in which we find the metaphor. In paraenetic discourse the utility of accounting imagery is obvious. To spur on moral attentiveness, it is appropriate to describe the divine tribunal as committed to a strict accounting of human sin. But on Yom Kippur, the holiest day of the year, when God judges the entire world, the metaphor assumes a different texture. God in these stories is ever ready to bend the rules so that Israel can be forgiven. If the preservation of Israel—God's beloved son—was the "bottom line," any form of "creative accounting" could be justified.

---

16. Paul Ricoeur, *The Symbolism of Evil*, trans. E. Buchanan (Boston: Beacon, 1967).

II

SECOND TEMPLE RECASTINGS OF SCRIPTURE AND TRADITION

5

The Legacy of Canaan in Ancient Israel and Early Christianity

John J. Collins
(YALE DIVINITY SCHOOL)

Some three hundred years ago, the Jesuit order was embroiled in a controversy relating to its mission to China. The Jesuits claimed that Chinese terms could be used to designate the Christian God, and that Confucian ceremonies were merely civil rites that Christians could attend. These claims were rejected by Pope Clement XI in 1715:

> The West calls *Deus* [God] the creator of Heaven and Earth, and everything in the universe. Since the word Deus does not sound right in the Chinese language, the Westerners in China and Chinese converts to Catholicism have used the term "Heavenly Lord" for many years. From now on such terms as "Heaven" and "Shang-ti" should not be used: *Deus* should be addressed as the Lord of Heaven, Earth, and everything in the universe. The tablet that bears the Chinese words "Reverence for Heaven" should not be allowed to hang inside a Catholic church and should be immediately taken down if already there.[1]

---

1. Quoted from Dun J. Li, ed., *China in Transition: 1517–1911* (New York: Van Nostrand Reinhold, 1969), 22–24. On the history of the controversy see George Minimaki, SJ, *The Chinese Rites Controversy from Its Beginnings to Modern Times* (Chicago: Loyola University Press, 1985). The Vatican lifted its restrictions in 1939.

Pope Clement was no biblical scholar. If he had been, or if he had the benefit of the scholarship on the Bible and the ancient Near East that developed in the nineteenth and twentieth centuries, he might have been more tolerant of intercultural translation. The God of the early Christians, let alone the God of the patriarchs, was not originally known as *Deus*. The propagation of the faith in the God of Israel was of necessity an act of translation that searched for appropriate equivalents in newly encountered languages and cultures.[2] In the second century BCE the *Letter of Aristeas*, ostensibly written by a Hellenistic-Egyptian courtier but unmistakably the work of a Jewish writer, speaks thus of the God of the Jews:

> God, the overseer and creator of all things, whom they worship, is He whom all men worship, and we too. Your Majesty, though we address Him differently, as Zeus and Dis; by these names men of old not unsuitably signified that He through whom all creatures receive life and come into being is the guide and lord of all.[3]

In the same spirit, the Jewish philosopher Aristobulus argued that the intention of the Greek poets referred to God, even when they called him Zeus or Dis.[4] But the identification of the God of Israel with the god of other peoples is attested long before the Hellenistic age.

EL AND YHWH

It is well known that one of the Hebrew words for God, *El*, was the proper name of the Canaanite high god long before Israel appeared

---

2. See the study of this phenomenon in antiquity by Mark S. Smith, *God in Translation* (FAT 57; Tübingen: Mohr Siebeck, 2008).

3. *Let. Aris.* 16; trans. Moses Hadas, *Aristeas to Philocrates* (New York: Harper, 1951), 101–3; see my book, *Between Athens and Jerusalem* (rev. ed.; Grand Rapids: Eerdmans, 2000), 192.

4. Carl Holladay, *Fragments from Hellenistic Jewish Authors*. Vol. 3: Aristobulus (Atlanta: Scholars Press, 1995), 172–73; Adela Yarbro Collins, "Aristobulus," in *OTP* 2:841; and Smith, *God in Translation*, 305.

on the stage of history.[5] The corpus of Canaanite texts from Ugarit contains more than five hundred mentions of El. About half of these use the word as the proper name of the king of the gods. He is described as holy and ancient, with grey hair. He is father of other gods, and also of humanity. Whether he was conceived as creator is a matter of dispute; some scholars infer the role of creator from his fatherhood, but the extant texts do not tell of the creation of the world.[6] His authority is supreme. When Baal becomes king, his kingship is conferred on him by El.

In the Hebrew Bible, El is identified with Yʜᴡʜ, the God of Israel. In the words of Mark Smith, "The original god of Israel was El."[7] The name "Israel" alludes to El rather than Yʜᴡʜ. In Exod 6:3 God tells Moses: "I appeared to Abraham, Isaac, and Jacob as El Shadday, but by my name Yʜᴡʜ I did not make myself known to them."[8] El Shadday is one of several variations of the divine name in Genesis. Others include El Olam (Gen 21:33) and El Elyon (Gen 14:18–20.).[9] The latter epithet is associated with pre-Israelite Jebusite Jerusalem in Gen 14, and with the later Jerusalem cult in Ps 46:5.[10] Despite the frequency of polemic against Canaanite worship in the Hebrew Bible, there is no polemic against El.

Nonetheless, some evidence has survived that El and Yʜᴡʜ were once distinguished. Most notable is Deut 32:8–9, where Yʜᴡʜ appears to be one of the sons of El:

---

5. Frank M. Cross, *Canaanite Myth and Hebrew Epic* (Cambridge, MA: Harvard University Press, 1973), 13–43; Mark S. Smith, *The Early History of God: Yahweh and the Other Deities in Ancient Israel* (2nd ed.; Grand Rapids: Eerdmans, 2002), 32–43; Wolfgang Herrmann, "El," *DDD*[2], 274–80; and John Day, *Yahweh and the Gods and Goddesses of Canaan* (Sheffield, UK: Sheffield Academic Press, 2000), 13–41.

6. See the comments of Richard J. Clifford, *Creation Accounts in the Ancient Near East* (CBQMS 26; Washington: Catholic Biblical Association of America, 1994), 118–19; also Herrmann, "El," 275–76.

7. Smith, *Early History of God*, 32.

8. All biblical translations are from the NRSV unless otherwise noted. Here, I have adapted the NRSV translation by substituting "El Shadday" for "God Almighty" and "Yʜᴡʜ" for "the Lᴏʀᴅ."

9. Cross, *Canaanite Myth*, 46–47.

10. Eric E. Elnes and Patrick D. Miller, "Elyon," *DDD*[2], 293–99, esp. 297–98.

> When Elyon gave the nations their inheritance
> when he separated human beings [literally, the sons of *'ādām*]
> he fixed the boundaries of the nations
> according to the number of the sons of El.
> For YHWH's portion is his people,
> Jacob his allotted heritage. (author's trans.)

The Masoretic Text, the traditional text of the Hebrew Bible, reads, "According to the number of the sons of Israel"; but the Septuagint reads, "of the angels of God" (in most manuscripts) or "of the sons of God" (in some). The latter reading is now corroborated by a fragment from Qumran, 4QDeut[j].[11] Mark Smith argues that "in view of the larger context of Deut 32 (especially verses 12, 17, 21, 31, and 39), it is evident that the composer presupposed the monotheistic identification of Yahweh in verse 9 with Elyon in verse 8."[12] But he grants that "the original composer of the text drew on an old polytheistic picture. This polytheistic picture did not belong simply to some prebiblical culture, but in fact was at home in early Israel."[13] We do not know when Deut 32 was written, but evidently the old idea that YHWH, like Baal, was subordinate to El had not entirely died out.

Further evidence of early Israelite polytheism is found in Ps 82: "God (*'ĕlōhîm*) takes his stand in the council of El; in the midst of gods (*'ĕlōhîm*) he judges." Many commentators have assumed that the text originally read, "YHWH takes his stand," and that the reading was changed in the redaction of the Elohistic Psalter (Pss 42—83).[14] At the least, it is likely that the *'ĕlōhîm* who arises is YHWH.[15] He pronounces judgment on the other "sons of Elyon" because they have failed to exe-

---

11. Patrick W. Skehan, "A Fragment of the 'Song of Moses' from Qumran," *BASOR* 136 (1954): 12–15; and Smith, *God in Translation*, 195–96.

12. Smith, *God in Translation*, 211.

13. Ibid., 210.

14. So, e.g., Hans-Joachim Kraus, *Psalms 60–150: A Commentary* (trans. H. Oswald; Minneapolis: Augsburg Fortress, 1989), 154.

15. Erich Zenger, "Psalm 82," in F.-L. Hossfeld and E. Zenger, *Psalms 2: A Commentary on Psalms 51–100* (trans. L. Maloney; Hermeneia; Minneapolis: Fortress, 2005), 329n3.

cute justice, and declares that they will die like human beings.[16] The gods of the nations, then, are demythologized, but the proceedings still take place in "the council of El."[17] The psalm concludes by declaring that *'ĕlōhîm* (=YHWH) will inherit all the nations. Whether or not the psalm is deliberately responding to Deut 32, it says in effect that the allotment of the nations to the various sons of El is now superseded.[18] But it still preserves the council of El as the context in which these things are decided.

YHWH AND BAAL

YHWH has a less irenic relationship with the Canaanite storm god Baal, but here again the God of Israel is partly conceived in terms associated with the Canaanite deity. In the words of Frank Cross, "The language of theophany in early Israel was primarily language drawn from the theophany of Baal."[19] In the Ugaritic myths, Baal is the "rider of the clouds." In the Hebrew Bible, it is YHWH "who rides the heavens mightily, who gloriously rides the clouds."[20] The classic confrontations between YHWH and Baal in the Elijah cycle (1 Kgs 17–18) and the prophecy of Hosea concern the proper identification of the god who provided the grain, the wine, and the oil (Hos 2:8), by bringing rain in season. YHWH, then, combined the roles of the two major Canaanite deities. However, in the biblical tradition, he is identified with El, while Baal remains his rival.

---

16. Zenger, "Psalm 82," 331.

17. E. Theodore Mullen, *The Divine Council in Canaanite and Early Hebrew Literature* (HSM 24; Chico, CA: Scholars Press, 1980).

18. Mark Smith, *The Origins of Biblical Monotheism: Israel's Polytheistic Background and the Ugaritic Texts* (Oxford: Oxford University Press, 2001), 48–49.

19. Cross, *Canaanite Myth*, 156–57; cf. Day, *Yahweh and the Gods*, 68–90.

20. Deut 33:26; trans. Cross, *Canaanite Myth*, 157.

DANIEL 7

We should not be surprised that Canaanite imagery figured prominently in early Israelite depictions of divinity. It is now apparent that Israel emerged from the matrix of Canaan. What is more surprising is that Canaanite imagery persists a millennium later. One of the most intriguing cases of Canaanite imagery in the Hebrew Bible is found in the latest book in that collection, the Book of Daniel, in a passage that dates to the reign of Antiochus IV Epiphanes of Syria in the second century BCE.

Daniel 7 reports, in Aramaic, a vision that Daniel allegedly had in the first year of King Belshazzar of Babylon. In fact, Belshazzar was never actually king of Babylon, and the content of the vision transparently alludes to events in the Hellenistic period. In the vision, he saw "the four winds of heaven stirring up the great sea," and four great beasts coming up out of it. The fourth beast, which has ten horns plus an eleventh upstart horn, is especially fearsome, but then the scene changes. First, Daniel sees an Ancient of Days whose hair is white as wool, enthroned on a fiery throne, surrounded by a court of thousands. Judgment is passed on the beasts, and the fourth one is consigned to the fire. Then "one like a son of man" (i.e., like a human being) comes "with the clouds of heaven" and everlasting kingship is conferred on him. An angel explains to Daniel that the four beasts represent four kingdoms, and that "the holy ones of the Most High" will receive the kingdom. In a final clarification, the angel adds that the kingship will be given to "the people of the holy ones of the Most High."[21]

The broad outline of this vision brings to mind the story of Baal in the Ugaritic texts. As already noted, Baal was the rider of the clouds. One of his adversaries in the Ugaritic myth was Yamm, the Sea. But he prevails and kingship is conferred on him by the venerable, aged El. To be sure, the details of the vision go beyond the ancient myth to fill in details that can serve as allegories for the history of the Hellenistic

---

21. See my commentary, *Daniel: A Commentary on the Book of Daniel* (Hermeneia; Minneapolis: Fortress, 1993), 274–324.

period. But the gestalt of the vision, and the relationship between the protagonists, corresponds to the myth in a way that cannot be dismissed as coincidental.[22]

While the imagery of the turbulent sea is rooted in Canaanite myth, it is also well attested in the Hebrew Bible.[23] Biblical poetry often alludes to a conflict between YHWH and the sea, or sea monsters called Rahab or Leviathan, but the story is never told in detail. In many cases this conflict is associated with creation:

> By his power he stilled the Sea;
> > by his understanding he struck down Rahab.
>
> > > > (Job 26:12)

> You divided the sea by your might;
> you broke the heads of the dragons in the waters.
> You crushed the heads of Leviathan.
>
> > > > (Ps 74:13–14)

In some cases the splitting of the sea serves to assimilate the exodus to creation:

> Was it not you who dried up the sea,
> > the waters of the great deep;
> who made the depths of the sea a way
> > for the redeemed to pass over?
>
> > > > (Isa 51:10)

In other cases, this battle is projected into the future as the eschatological battle that will bring history to its end: "On that day the LORD with his cruel and great and strong sword will punish Leviathan the

---

22. See my essay, "Stirring up the Great Sea: The Religio-Historical Background of Daniel 7," in John J. Collins, *Seers, Sibyls and Sages in Hellenistic-Roman Judaism* (Leiden: Brill, 1997), 139–55.

23. For full treatment see John Day, *God's Conflict with the Dragon and the Sea: Echoes of a Canaanite Myth in the Old Testament* (Cambridge, UK: Cambridge University Press, 1985).

fleeing serpent, Leviathan the twisting serpent, and he will kill the dragon that is in the sea" (Isa 27:1).

It is not especially surprising, then, that a visionary in the second century BCE would draw on this tradition to portray the threat posed to the Judean way of life by foreign rule. What is more surprising is the juxtaposition in the vision of two heavenly, apparently divine, figures—the venerable Ancient of Days and the Rider of the Clouds. In a Canaanite context in the second millennium, such juxtaposition is to be expected. But how should it be understood in a Judean context in the second century BCE?

The Ancient of Days is evidently El, the Most High God. It is he who presides over the judgment and confers the kingship on the Rider of the Clouds. Nearly all scholars assume that in a Jewish text from this period, the Most High God must be identified with YHWH. But in the Hebrew Bible it is also YHWH who is portrayed as the Rider of the Clouds. As John Emerton pointed out in a famous article, "The act of coming with clouds suggests a theophany of Yahweh himself. If Dan vii. 13 does not refer to a divine being, then it is the only exception out of about seventy passages in the O.T."[24] If YHWH is the Ancient of Days, who can this second figure be?

One strand of modern scholarship, prevalent from the late nineteenth through the mid-twentieth century, sought to avoid the problem by supposing that the "one like a son of man" was merely a symbol for the Jewish people, the "people of the Holy Ones of the Most High," who are also said to receive the kingdom.[25] But the heavenly individual is more likely to be the representative of the people than a "mere" symbol for them. Later in the Book of Daniel, we find that Israel is represented on the heavenly level by the archangel Michael, and he has increasingly been recognized as the most likely referent of the "one like a son of man."[26] The Holy Ones, too, are not

---

24. John Emerton, "The Origin of the Son of Man Imagery," *JTS* 9 (1958): 225–42.

25. E.g., Louis F. Hartman and Alexander A. Di Lella, *The Book of Daniel* (AB 23; Garden City, NY: Doubleday, 1978), 85–102.

26. Collins, *Daniel*, 304–10; André Lacocque, *The Book of Daniel* (Atlanta: John Knox, 1979), 133; John E. Goldingay, *Daniel* (WBC 30; Dallas: Word, 1989), 172; and Day, *God's Conflict*, 172.

the pious Jews but the heavenly host, in accordance with the most common usage of "holy ones" in the literature of the time. The Jewish people to be sure is "the people of the holy ones," but the whole point of Daniel's visions is that they are complemented and aided by angelic powers on the heavenly level.

Recently Michael Segal, who is preparing a new commentary on Daniel for the Anchor Yale Bible series, has offered a radically new interpretation of the "one like a son of man."[27] Like Emerton before him, Segal notes that all other references to a figure riding on the clouds in the Hebrew Bible are to YHWH; he recognizes the Canaanite provenance of the motif. Moreover, he points out that in Dan 3:32–33; 4:32; and 6:26–27, YHWH is the one to whom everlasting kingship and dominion are attributed. Consequently, he takes "a somewhat radical theological position: the one like a man can be identified with YHWH himself." He also argues that the plural "Holy Ones" is a plural of majesty, and that this expression also refers to YHWH. The biblical parallels adduced by Segal are unimpeachable, but his proposal faces an obvious objection, which he himself recognizes: "Simply expressed—is it conceivable that there were Jews in this period who believed in the existence of a deity superior to YHWH?" While we may grant that *a priori* arguments should generally be avoided, even Segal recognizes that an interpretation is problematic if it posits a belief that is without parallel in this period. Accordingly, he tries to evade the implications of his radical proposal:

> Due to the unique worldview described here (at least unique to the period to which the composition of Daniel 7 is attributed), it is perhaps however preferable to explain this hierarchy of deities not as the result of an exceptional theological perspective, but rather due to the literary and exegetical dependence of the author of Daniel 7 upon the ancient myths of the division of the world as expressed in

27. Michael Segal, "Reconsidering the Theological Background of Daniel 7 and 4Q246 in Light of Innerbiblical Interpretation" (paper presented at the annual meeting of the Society of Biblical Literature, San Francisco, November 21, 2011). I am grateful to Professor Segal for providing me with a copy of his lecture.

Deuteronomy 32 and Psalm 82. The contours of the description of the eschatological period in this apocalypse are not therefore a direct description of this author's religious worldview, but instead a literary reflection of the foundational passages of biblical cosmogony which were then further developed in the description of the eternal kingdom of YHWH. According to this approach, the author of Daniel 7 intended for his audience to identify and be aware of these earlier source passages, and to understand the new composition against this religioliterary backdrop. The theological hierarchy is therefore not the primary point of this passage, but rather a mythical echo of its sources.

In effect, this would require that the author either did not notice the hierarchical implications of his vision, or that he expected his readers to notice a literary allusion but maintain a critical distinction over against the actual scene portrayed in the text. Either scenario is highly problematic. To my mind, it is far more likely that the author of Daniel attributed to the archangel Michael the role of the subordinate deity, which had been the role of Baal in Canaanite tradition and was apparently that of YHWH in an early stage of Israelite religion.

Segal's suggestion, however, also bears on another vexing question. How did this Canaanite imagery, for which our best evidence dates from the second millennium, become available to a Jewish writer of the Maccabean era? While there is a clear biblical tradition about the turbulent sea, we do not find the Rider of the Clouds subordinated to a higher god in the Hebrew Scriptures. Motifs relating to the Baal myth, including that of the turbulent sea, played a part in the royal cult in Jerusalem. Paul Mosca has pointed to Ps 89 as a crucial link between Canaanite mythology and Dan 7.[28] The psalm celebrates the sovereignty of YHWH in "the assembly of the holy ones," grounded in his rule over the sea and slaying of Rahab. Mosca argues that YHWH is assimilated to El, and that the role of Baal is transferred to the Davidic king. This may be, but even the psalms do not portray anyone

---

28. Paul Mosca, "Ugarit and Daniel 7: A Missing Link," *Bib* 67 (1986): 496–517.

other than Y<small>HWH</small> riding the clouds. And the royal cult was defunct for several hundred years before Daniel was written.

Segal takes a different tack. He suggests that Dan 7 is in large part an interpretation of Deut 32 and Ps 82. In Deut 32 Y<small>HWH</small> is given sovereignty over Israel. In Dan 7 his sovereignty is extended to the rest of the world. Daniel 7 does not replace Deut 32, since the two texts refer to different periods, Deuteronomy to the past and Daniel to the future. In this respect, Dan 7 is also the natural continuation of Ps 82, in which 'ĕlōhîm/Y<small>HWH</small> denies the power of the other "sons of El" in the divine council. Daniel 7 then would be a remythologization of the role of Y<small>HWH</small> in relation to the supposed gods of the nations, a more imaginative depiction of the judgment of the gods in Ps 82.

Even if one grants that there is some allusion to Deut 32 and Ps 82 in Dan 7, however, that allusion by no means accounts for the fullness of the mythological imagery in the latter passage. There is neither sea nor clouds (nor a Rider of the Clouds) in Deut 32 or Ps 82. Dan 7 cannot be explained as exegesis or innerbiblical interpretation. While the transmission of Canaanite myths and motifs remains obscure to us, we cannot evade the fact that the imagery of Dan 7 conforms to that of the Baal cycle to a greater degree than anything in the earlier books of the Hebrew Bible. The Bible preserves only a selection of the religious traditions of Israel and Judah. Old traditions, known to us from the Ugaritic texts, evidently survived in Judaism into the Hellenistic era.

JESUS AND THE SON OF MAN

Daniel Boyarin has argued that what we find in Dan 7 is an "unreconstructed relic of Israel's religious past (if not her present as well)."[29] It calls up "a very ancient strand in Israel's religion, one in which, it would seem, the El-like sky god of justice and the younger rider of the clouds, storm god of war, have not really been merged as they are for

---

29. Daniel Boyarin, *The Jewish Gospels: The Story of the Jewish Christ* (New York: New Press, 2012), 45.

most of the Bible."[30] Boyarin, however, goes further: "I find it plausible that this highly significant passage is a sign of the religious traditions that give rise to the notion of a Father divinity and a Son divinity that we find in the Gospels."[31] Consequently, he sees the theology of the Gospels not as a radical innovation within Israelite religious tradition but as a return to an ancient tradition that had been largely but not entirely suppressed. Boyarin thinks that the author of Daniel tried to suppress this ancient tradition by making it into an allegory for the Jewish people in the time of Antiochus Epiphanes. However, it would be very strange if a vision-ary tried to suppress the very material that was the substance of his vision. Rather, the author of Daniel adapted the ancient myth so that the lesser god is no longer YHWH but an exalted angelic being. This adaptation persists in late Second Temple texts, where the "second god" is variously identified as Michael, Melchizedek, Yaoel, or, in the Parables of Enoch (*1 Enoch* 37–71), simply as "that Son of Man."[32]

This so-called Jewish "binitarianism" provides a crucial context for the development of early Christology, a fact that has often been noted in recent years.[33] Two Jewish apocalypses, the Parables of Enoch and *4 Ezra*, which date from the early and late first century CE, respectively, identify the "one like a son of man" of Daniel's vision as a "messiah." Even apart from this development, the Davidic messiah was tradition-ally regarded as the son of God, as attested in Ps 2 and 2 Sam 7. The fur-ther identification of this figure with the heavenly Son of Man allowed for a more distinctly supernatural, divine messiah, although we cannot be sure how widely this concept of the messiah was shared.[34]

---

30. Ibid., 46.

31. Ibid.

32. See my essay, "Jewish Monotheism and Christian Theology," in *Aspects of Monotheism* (ed. H. Shanks and J. Meinhardt; Washington: Biblical Archaeology Society, 1997), 81–105.

33. See, e.g., Carey C. Newman, James R. Davila, and Gladys S. Lewis, eds., *The Jewish Roots of Christological Monotheism: Papers from the St. Andrews Conference on the Historical Origins of the Worship of Jesus* (JSJSup 63; Leiden: Brill, 1999).

34. See Adela Yarbro Collins and John J. Collins, *King and Messiah as Son of God: Divine, Human, and Angelic Messianic Figures in Biblical and Related Literature* (Grand Rapids: Eerdmans, 2008).

Boyarin argues that this supernatural profile was part of the job description of the messiah before Jesus was born: "The job description—Required: one Christ, will be divine, will be called Son of Man, will be sovereign and savior of the Jews and the world—was there already and Jesus fit (or did not according to other Jews) the bill. The job description was not a put-up job tailored to fit Jesus!"[35] Consequently, he argues that some Jews recognized Jesus already in his lifetime as the Son of Man incarnate. This is why, in his view, the Son of Man has power on earth to forgive sins (Mark 2:5–10) and is lord even of the Sabbath (Mark 2:28). In Daniel and the Parables of Enoch, however, the "Son of Man" does not appear on earth. He is a comfort to the oppressed righteous on earth precisely because he is not subject to the trials of earthly life. He is the heavenly representative of the righteous who guarantees their ultimate victory. Even in the appendix to the Parables in *1 Enoch* 71, Enoch is only identified with the Son of Man when he is taken up to heaven at the end of his life. In *4 Ezra*, the messianic figure who rises from the sea and rides on the clouds takes his stand on Mt. Zion to destroy his enemies in a final battle. But he does not have an earthly career prior to his eschatological manifestation. The idea that the heavenly Son of Man could walk around on earth in the manner of Jesus of Nazareth was a novelty in the Jesus movement. It seems very unlikely that anyone would have identified Jesus as the heavenly Son of Man without the prior belief that he was risen from the dead, ascended to the right hand of the Father, and enthroned as heavenly Messiah. Only then would it have made sense to expect that he would come again on the clouds of heaven, as envisioned in Mark 13 and parallels.[36]

There is no doubt whatever that Dan 7 was a crucial text for the development of early Christology. To a great degree, that development was exegetical. The Gospel writers viewed Daniel's vision as a prophecy and believed that Jesus would fulfill it in his second coming. The Son of Man passages in the Gospels adapt the element of Daniel's

---

35. Boyarin, *Jewish Gospels*, 73.

36. See Adela Yarbro Collins, "Jesus as Son of Man," in Yarbro Collins and Collins, *King and Messiah*, 149–74.

vision that speaks of the one like a son of man coming on the clouds of heaven, and give him a more active role in the judgment than was the case in the original vision. There is little reason to relate the Son of Man passages in the Gospels directly to old traditions derived from Canaanite mythology.

Those traditions, however, do leave their mark in the Book of Revelation. The imagery of Revelation is hybrid, and is drawn from many sources, Jewish and pagan, in the Hellenistic world.[37] The influence of Daniel is patent at many points, for instance, in the beast rising from the sea in Rev 13:1, the "one like a Son of Man" seated on a cloud in Rev 14:14, or the composite vision of the Son of Man whose hair is white as wool or snow in Rev 1:14. The ten horns of the beast on which the Whore of Babylon rides in Rev 17:3 correspond to the horns of the fourth beast in Dan 7. But the beast of Revelation also had seven heads, a detail not found in Daniel's vision. The ancient Ugaritic texts, however, speak of Shilyat of the seven heads, who is associated with Lotan or Leviathan, the primeval dragon smitten by Baal.[38] Moreover, when the first heaven and earth pass away in Rev 21:1, the sea is no more. John of Patmos, it would seem, knew more of the mythical lore of the Canaanite tradition than could be derived from Daniel or the Hebrew Scriptures.

Revelation in the biblical tradition is not dropped in pristine form from heaven, but is woven from the fabric of the religious traditions of the ancient Near East. The Jesuits who went to China were wise to seek continuities with native beliefs rather than to dismiss the pagan world as wholly other.[39]

---

37. See Adela Yarbro Collins, *The Combat Myth in the Book of Revelation* (Missoula, MT: Scholars Press, 1976).

38. Cross, *Canaanite Myth*, 150; and Day, *God's Conflict*, 13–14.

39. It is a pleasure to dedicate this article to two remarkable Jesuits, Richard J. Clifford and Daniel J. Harrington, who befriended me when I first came to the United States in 1969 and have always exemplified the best in the Catholic tradition, both in their scholarship and in their personal integrity.

6

The Reuse of Ugaritic Mythology in Daniel 7
An Optical Illusion?[1]

Carol A. Newsom
(EMORY UNIVERSITY)

The first principle of interpretation, unless the composition is a crazy patchwork…is to allow the document to speak for itself as the product of the writer's mind, and to subordinate extraneous influences, unless they are required to make his thought intelligible.[2]

These words express the frustrated conclusion to James L. Montgomery's discussion of the theory proposed by Gunkel and developed by Heinrich Zimmern, Wilhelm Bousset, and others that the characters and scenario described in Daniel 7 are to be traced back to Mesopotamian mythology, specifically the chaos myth, more or less as it is found in the *Enuma Elish*.[3] Subsequently, the discovery of the Ugaritic tablets from Ras

---

1. I am delighted to dedicate this article to Dan Harrington and Dick Clifford. Dan ("Prof. Harrington") was the person who taught me the biblical Aramaic that has allowed me to study the Book of Daniel. Dick ("Prof. Clifford") was the editor of the *Catholic Biblical Quarterly* who accepted my very first academic publication. Both of these scholars have continued to be important in my intellectual development. I owe them a great debt.

2. James L. Montgomery, *The Book of Daniel* (Edinburgh: T & T Clark, 1927), 323.

3. Hermann Gunkel, *Creation and Chaos in the Primeval Era and the Eschaton* (trans. K. W. Whitney Jr.; Grand Rapids: Eerdmans, 2006), 205–13. See Montgomery, *Book of Daniel*, 321–24, for a survey of early arguments concerning the theory of Babylonian influence.

Shamra, including mythic accounts of Baal's conflict with the sea, shifted scholarly attention. Beginning with comments from Otto Eissfeldt and Aage Bentzen,[4] and developed in more detail by John Emerton,[5] the argument was made that indeed an ancient Near Eastern chaos myth stands behind Dan 7, but it is to be sought in Canaanite traditions rather than Mesopotamian ones. This position has been most forcefully articulated by John Day and John Collins,[6] with significant contributions from other scholars as well. Although objections to the thesis have been raised,[7] it is widely accepted and might appropriately be described as the consensus view.

What is discussed too seldom is the purpose for which the parallels between ancient Near Eastern myth and Dan 7 are investigated. Confusion about the purpose and significance of such comparative work is evident in the debates between proponents and opponents of the thesis concerning Dan 7, as one sees in Montgomery's dismissal of the Babylonian parallels. To be sure, the practice of comparative analysis of religious myths and symbols was in its infancy at that time, and much of what was proposed now looks quite undisciplined. Yet even into the present, the attempt to clarify the nature and purpose of comparative work remains elusive.[8] In this article, I want to suggest

---

4. Otto Eissfeldt, *Baal Zaphon, Zeus Kasios und der Durchzug der Israeliten durchs Meer* (Halle: Max Niemeyer, 1932), 25–27; and Aage Bentzen, *Daniel* (Tübingen: Mohr Siebeck, 1952), 59–61.

5. John A. Emerton, "The Origin of the Son of Man Imagery," *JTS* 9 (1958): 225–42.

6. John Day, *God's Conflict with the Dragon and the Sea* (University of Cambridge Oriental Publications 35; Cambridge, UK: Cambridge University Press, 1985), 151–78; and John J. Collins, *Daniel: A Commentary on the Book of Daniel* (Hermeneia; Minneapolis: Fortress, 1993), 280–94.

7. Maurice Casey, *Son of Man: The Interpretation and Influence of Daniel 7* (London: SPCK, 1979), 35–38; Arthur J. Ferch, *The Son of Man in Daniel 7* (Andrews University Seminary Doctoral Dissertation Series 6; Berrien Springs, MI: Andrews University Press, 1979), 40–107; and Chrys C. Caragounis, *The Son of Man: Vision and Interpretation* (WUNT 38; Tübingen: Mohr-Siebeck, 1986), 36–41.

8. For a helpful discussion of the methodological issues, see Brent Strawn, "Comparative Approaches: History, Theory, and the Image of God," in *Method Matters: Essays on the Interpretation of the Hebrew Bible in Honor of David L. Petersen* (ed. J. M. LeMon and K. H. Richards; SBLRBS 56; Atlanta: Society of Biblical Literature, 2009), 117–42.

that, at least in the case of Dan 7, we need to place the issue of possible religiohistorical parallels in a methodologically broader context. We need to think of comparative analysis as a species of cultural intertextuality and to remember that intertextuality functions in more than one way. It can refer to an *author's* conscious or unconscious use of literary or cultural motifs and patterns that can be identified from other sources—motifs and patterns that a contemporary audience might be expected to recognize as part of their cultural competency. But it can also refer to patterns of resemblance constructed by *noncontemporary readers* whose range of cultural intertexts may be quite different from those of the author and first audience. This kind of intertextuality may not tell us anything about the forces shaping the imagination of the ancient author, though they may be significant for other purposes. In the case of Dan 7, a modern scholar, steeped in the ancient Near Eastern mythology that was newly recovered in the nineteenth and twentieth centuries, is primed to recognize echoes of the Baal myth, and more distantly, the *Enuma Elish*, because those texts loom large in *our* mental set of reference texts. There are, to be sure, genuine points of similarity between Dan 7 and the Baal myth as it is known from Ugarit. The question I want to pose, however, is whether in making this comparison, we are at risk of confusing our modern, scholarly *readers'* intertextuality with a claim of historical *authorial* intertextuality. Does our set of reference texts create a kind of optical illusion that greatly exaggerates the patterns of relationship between the Ugaritic myth and Dan 7?

MYTHIC NARRATIVE PATTERNS AND CULTURAL COMPETENCY

Of the various scholars who have argued for the significance of the parallels between the Baal myth and Dan 7, John Collins has been the most explicit about the nature and significance of the religiohistorical parallels, as he sees them. For Collins, as for Day, the claim is a historical one. The point of identifying and understanding mythic elements in Dan 7 is one of acquiring a cultural competency that was lost when the ancient Near Eastern mythic tradition was lost. Only by recognizing these parallels do we adequately grasp what is going on in the text. As Collins notes, "The parallels are of significance for the sense of the text rather than for the reference."[9] One is not claiming that the Son of Man is a reference to Marduk or Baal but rather that "he functions in a manner similar to the way Marduk or Baal functions in the pagan myths."[10] If, as modern readers, we do not recognize that, then we miss some of the communicative purpose of the composition. Collins rightly argues that the relationship need be neither conscious nor direct.[11] No claim is being made that the author of Dan 7 had direct access to a version of the Baal myth per se, only that the narrative template was culturally present in ways that could shape the composition of a text like Dan 7. Further, Collins distinguishes between the type of comparison involved when one is comparing the whole "pattern of religion" between a biblical text and a myth on the one hand, and the literary reuse of motifs or patterns on the other. In the latter case, appropriation "ordinarily involves tearing motifs or patterns from one context and transferring them to another."[12] The author's literary creativity thus means that there will be discontinuities with the posited sources as well as continuities. But, Collins concludes, "what is significant is whether there are also aspects of the text that are rendered more intelligible when considered in the context of the proposed background."[13]

No one, of course, denies that there are resonant mythic *elements* in Dan 7. But the claim by Collins, Day, and others is somewhat stronger. Their position is that these mythic elements are part of a mythic narrative *pattern*—including characters, epithets, actions, and plot structures distinctive to the Baal myth—and that this pattern signif-

---

9. Collins, *Daniel*, 281.

10. Ibid.

11. Ibid., n41.

12. Ibid., 281.

13. Ibid., 282.

icantly shapes the composition of Dan 7, whether or not the author was fully aware of the force of such a culturally inherited pattern.

The prima facie case does indeed seem strong. In the Baal myth, the Sea is the first of two enemies who threaten Baal, and with him the security of the world. When Baal, who is described as "Rider of the Clouds" (*KTU* 1.2 IV 29),[14] defeats Sea, the craftsman god Kotar-wa-Hassis acknowledges his victory with the words "May you take your eternal kingship, your everlasting dominion" (*KTU* 1.2 IV 10). This acclamation is later echoed by the deity Athtart ("Yamm surely is dead! Baal rei[gns!]" (*KTU* 1.2 IV 32). Other texts make reference to El's having appointed various deities to kingship, though such references to Baal occur only in damaged contexts.[15] Moreover, El is a god who is sometimes said to sit as judge ("El sits with Athtart, El the judge sits with Haddu his shepherd," RS 24.252).[16] And El is represented in the Ugaritic myths as an aged god with the epithet *'ab šnm*, which is commonly understood as "father of years" (*KTU* 1.1 III 24; 1.3 V1; 1.4 IV 24; 1.6 I 36). Thus the pattern involves: a threat from Sea, a battle in which Sea is defeated by Baal, and Baal's kingship being granted by the older God El, who nevertheless remains the ranking deity.

One of the problems faced by scholars who champion the influence of the mythic pattern on the composition of Dan 7, however, is accounting for how the author of this Hellenistic-era text could have known the outlines of a myth attested only in second millennium BCE sources. Attempts have been made to demonstrate the vitality of the Baal Hadad cult down into the Hellenistic and even Roman periods,[17] though no accounts of the myth are known from that era. Others have suggested that the mythic pattern was preserved in Israelite religious thought in the royal Davidic poetry, which makes use of some of

---

14. Translations from the Ugaritic follow Mark S. Smith, *The Ugaritic Baal Cycle*, vol. 1 (Leiden: Brill, 1994); and Mark S. Smith and Wayne T. Pitard, *The Ugaritic Baal Cycle*, vol. 2 (Leiden: Brill, 2009).

15. Day, *God's Conflict*, 162–63.

16. Jean Nougayrol et al., *Ugaritica V* (Paris: Imprimerie Nationale, 1968), 551–53.

17. Rollin Kearns, *Vorfragen zur Christologie* (3 vols.; Tübingen: Mohr Siebeck, 1978–82), 3:3–82.

these motifs and sees in the Davidic line the representative of YHWH's sovereignty on earth. Thus Dan 7 would be the remythologization of this tradition in an apocalyptic context.[18] This is perhaps the most persuasive attempt to describe a vehicle of transmission for elements of the tradition. Collins also holds out the possibility that the author had access to traditions other than those preserved in the Hebrew Bible.[19]

PRIORITIZING TEMPORALLY AND LITERARILY PROXIMATE MATERIAL

While it is certainly not impossible that such a mythic pattern might have survived into the Hellenistic period, what is methodologically problematic about the champions of the mythic pattern approach is that they simply begin with this ancient pattern and then map it onto Dan 7. Such an approach tends toward the circular, as it does not sufficiently distinguish between mere points of correlation and a truly formational force of a mythic pattern. Indeed, as will be seen, some advocates of this theory are so influenced by their starting point that they read elements of the pattern into Dan 7, even when there is no exegetical basis. Authors certainly do create new compositions by means of blending culturally available narrative patterns, schemata, motifs, phrases, and other items in novel ways.[20] Understanding a text is enhanced by identifying these conceptual elements and observing how they have been blended. Methodologically, however, one should begin by analyzing the most temporally and literarily proximate type scenes and schemata that provide the intellectual raw materials used by

---

18. Paul Mosca, "Ugarit and Daniel 7: A Missing Link," *Bib* 67 (1986): 496–517. See further discussion below.

19. Collins, *Daniel*, 294.

20. Mark Turner and Gilles Fauconnier, "A Mechanism of Creativity," *Poetics Today* 20 (1999): 397–418. I explore the usefulness of conceptual blending for tradition-critical work more fully in "Why Nabonidus? Excavating Traditions from Qumran, the Hebrew Bible, and Neo-Babylonian Sources," in *The Dead Sea Scrolls: Transmission of Traditions and Production of Texts* (ed. S. Metso, H. Najman, and E. Schuller; STDJ 92; Leiden: Brill, 2010), 57–79.

the author. Only after those have been accounted for in Dan 7 can one identify other elements and assess whether or not they invite or require the hypothesis of a more distant mythic pattern that shapes the text.

Daniel 7 is constructed primarily from two pieces of traditional material that are indeed temporally and literarily proximate. The first is the schema from chapter 2 of four Gentile kingdoms succeeded by a fifth that manifests God's sovereignty (Dan 2:31–35, 36–45). The second is a court judgment type scene, which is variously attested in the Enoch tradition of the Book of the Watchers (*1 En.* 14.18–23), the Book of the Giants (4Q530), and the Animal Apocalypse (*1 En.* 90.20). The creative work of the author of Dan 7 is primarily to bring these two culturally formed templates together. If the mythic pattern concerning Baal is to be seen as having influence, it will be in the coordination of these elements and in the selection of imagery and symbolic figures.

The theopolitical problem with which Dan 2 and 7 are dealing is the nature, status, and legitimacy of Gentile imperial rule in the period after the Babylonian conquest of 587 BCE. Various texts had attempted to resolve the cognitive dissonance between an affirmation of YHWH's sovereignty and the reality of Gentile rule by the theory of a temporary divine grant of earthly sovereignty to one or another Gentile sovereign. In the MT version of Jeremiah, it is represented as a seventy-year reign by the king of Babylon, after which the reign of his dynasty would be terminated by yet other Gentile nations (Jer 27:5–7). In Isa 45, the sovereignty is to be vested in Cyrus of Persia, though there is no indication of how long his mandate would last. The same idea is formative for the political theology of Dan 1—6, articulated most explicitly in 2:38 and 4:29–34. It is also present in the representation of Cyrus's decree in 2 Chr 36:22–23 and Ezra 1:1–4.[21] This conceptualization appears to have provided a reasonably stable intellectual accommodation during the time of Persian rule, but the sudden and particularly violent impact of Alexander and the Diadochi

---

21. The historicity or lack thereof of this decree does not affect the status of my argument. My point is simply that this is the way in which early Second Temple texts represented Gentile sovereignty in a manner that affirmed the overarching divine sovereignty of YHWH.

rendered such an accommodation unsatisfactory. Thus Dan 2 reformulates the theory of divine delegation of sovereignty as an explicitly limited stage of history that will be brought to an end with the destruction of Gentile imperium and the resumption of direct divine rule. Daniel 7 reiterates this schema with different imagery.[22]

THE SCHEMA OF FOUR GENTILE KINGDOMS

What has to be negotiated in this conceptualization of history is that Gentile sovereignty has to be seen both as YHWH's intention and yet as somehow inherently problematic and so leading to its own termination. Thus, imagistically, both Dan 2 and 7 use a gestalt figure for the totality of Gentile sovereignty that marks it as YHWH's other. Daniel 2 uses the image of a statue, thus marking Gentile sovereignty with the stigma of idolatry, even as Daniel describes Nebuchadnezzar as the "head of gold" and assures him that YHWH has granted him a sovereignty that echoes that of Adam (2:37–38).[23] Daniel 7 uses the imagery of the sea to mark the origin, and hence the essence, of what makes Gentile sovereignty finally unacceptable. That the sea has negative mythic connotations here seems certain. The contrast terms *heaven* and *sea* seem to point generally to the background of the cosmic conflict. And yet, if the mythic pattern of God's battle with the sea is being invoked here, it is invoked in ways that subvert it. In this respect both Day and Collins underread the complexity of the author's blending of traditions. Ambiguity enters the picture with the symbol of the four winds of heaven and the nature of their activity in "stirring up" the Great Sea. Four winds (Jer 49:36) or a particular wind (Exod 14:21; 15:8) may be used as a weapon of YHWH (cf. Marduk's use of four winds as weapons against Tiamat), and so Collins under-

---

22. The Persian roots of this schema and its later development were first examined by Joseph Ward Swain, "The Theory of the Four Monarchies: Opposition History under the Roman Empire," *CP* 35 (1940): 1–21. See also David Flusser, "The Four Empires in the Fourth Sibyl and in the Book of Daniel," *Israel Oriental Studies* 2 (1972): 148–75.

23. All biblical translations are by the author, unless otherwise specified.

stands the imagery to evoke the cosmic battle.[24] But the Aramaic participle *mĕgîḥān* complicates what might otherwise be a simple image. The sea is not represented as *itself* roiling or surging in an aggressive fashion, even though the Hebrew cognate of the Aramaic verb can be used of the activity of the sea, a river, or sea monsters (Ezek 32:2; Job 38:8; 40:23). Here, however, the sea is first *acted upon* by the winds. Agency does not belong to the sea. Other commentators, correctly in my view, recognize an allusion to Gen 1:2, in which a divine wind sweeps over the surface of the cosmic waters as the first activity of creation.[25] The full meaning of the imagery can only be grasped if one hears both elements in play at the same time. What will emerge from the sea is the political history of the four Gentile kingdoms. The echo of Gen 1:2 connotes that this process is part of God's creative control of historical as well as of cosmic processes. But the echo of the chaotic sea and of the combat myth indicates that there is something inherently unruly and dangerous in the Gentile kingdoms that will ultimately have to be dealt with through force. This imagery articulates the classic apocalyptic response to the mystery of evil, in contrast to the mythic model. In apocalyptic, evil forces are understood as never fully autonomous but as playing a designated role in a divine drama, a drama that leads to the ultimate destruction and elimination of those forces.

Similarly, Day underreads the complexity of the beasts from the sea because of his overreliance on the combat myth. Though he notes that their form is not like that of Leviathan from the combat myth, he suggests that they "play the *role* ascribed to the dragon Leviathan in Canaanite mythology."[26] But it is more complicated than that. The

---

24. Collins, *Daniel*, 294. Theodotion's translation explicitly takes it in that fashion: "The four winds kept assaulting the great sea."

25. Louis F. Hartman and Alexander A. Di Lella, *The Book of Daniel* (AB 23; Garden City, NY: Doubleday, 1979), 211; John E. Goldingay, *Daniel* (WBC 30; Dallas: Word, 1989), 160; and Klaus Koch, "Die Winde des Himmels über dem Völkermeer (Dan 7, 1f): Schöpfung oder Chaos?" in *"Unter dem Fussboden ein Tropfen Wahrheit": Festschrift für Johann Michael Schmidt zum 65jährigen Geburtstag* (ed. H.-J. Barkenings and U. F. W. Bauer; Düsseldorf: Presseverband der Evangelischen Kirche im Rheinland e.V., 2000), 43–46.

26. Day, *God's Conflict*, 152; emphasis original.

first three beasts do not engage in autonomous hostile activity. Instead, they are acted upon and commissioned by a voice that is not explicitly identified but is certainly God's (Dan 7:4–6). Though Day rightly recognizes the source of the imagery for the first three beasts in Hos 13:7–8,[27] he overlooks the significance of the simile in that passage:

> So I am become like a lion to them,
> Like a leopard I lurk on the way;
> Like a bear robbed of her young I attack them
> and rip open the casing of their hearts. (NJPS)

These are all comparisons for God's hostile agency. Whatever the violence done by these three kingdoms, it is not activity opposed by God but activity commissioned by God. Only the last beast displays its own agency and violence. Yet even the fourth beast itself does not seem to play the role of Leviathan. Scholarly opinion is divided as to whether Dan 7 originally included the material concerning the little horn or whether an earlier version of the chapter predated the Antiochene crisis and was later updated to refer to Antiochus. I find the arguments for a two-stage development of the chapter quite persuasive.[28] If that is the case, then it is noteworthy that the beast, though violent, does not direct its hostility toward God or other heavenly beings, but rather will "devour the whole earth." That is to say, it must be punished because it exceeds the authorization for violence given to each of the beasts. It behaves in just the way that the fourth kingdom does in the imagery of the statue in Dan 2 whose iron "crushes and shatters all" (2:40). Only with the addition of the material concerning the little horn is the motif of blasphemy against the Most High and aggression against the "holy ones" introduced. Even then, this motif does not appear to have its origin in the cosmogonic combat myth but in the tradition of the arrogant human kings who do not understand their role as God's instruments but presume to think that they act autonomously. The

---

27. Ibid., 153–57.

28. For a review of the issues, see Klaus Koch, *Das Buch Daniel* (EdF 144; Darmstadt: Wissenschaftliche Buchgessellschaft, 1980), 68–71; and Collins, *Daniel*, 278–80.

closest parallels are the rebukes to the king of Assyria in Isa 10 and 37. In both passages the motifs of arrogance and blasphemy are present (10:8–13; 37:27). Specific aggression against Jerusalem and its cultic images is mentioned in 10:11, and the punishment of the arrogant king is by fire (10:16–17), as is the punishment of the fourth beast.

A COURT JUDGMENT TYPE SCENE

The second major component of the vision in Daniel is a forensic type scene in which the divine court executes judgment upon the beasts, removing the first three from dominion and consigning the fourth to the fire. While the motif of a divine council is widespread in the ancient Near East, the passage in Dan 7 has its closest similarities with a set of passages from roughly contemporary texts: *1 En.* 14.18–23; 90.20; and 4Q530 Giants. More precisely, 4Q530 and *1 En.* 90.20 share with Dan 7:9–10 an action sequence concerning judgment based on records preserved in books; *1 En.* 14.18–23 and Dan 7:9–10 provide details concerning the divine throne and the appearance of God; 4Q530, *1 En.* 14.18–23, and Dan 7:9–10 enumerate the angelic attendants. Much ink has been spilled in attempting to specify the nature of the relationship among these texts, but with little consensus.[29] The complexity of the relationships among the four texts, including the "mix and match" nature of the elements that appear in different combinations and with different degrees of elaboration, argue against a model of direct literary dependence. More likely, descriptions of the divine throne and its attendants and descriptions of divine court judgment scenes were traditional, formulaic set pieces within apocalyptic literature that could be adapted for a variety of purposes. In the Enochic tradition, those who are judged are errant stars, disobedient angels, and the "seventy shepherds," angelic figures who are similar to the angelic princes of the nations in Dan 10. In any

---

29. The most judicious review of the evidence is the unpublished essay by Jonathan Trotter, "Throne Visions in Daniel, *1 Enoch*, and the *Book of the Giants*." Also good is Ryan E. Stokes, "The Throne Visions of Daniel 7, *1 Enoch* 14, and the Qumran *Book of Giants* (4Q530): An Analysis of Their Literary Relationship," *DSD* 15 (2008): 340–58, though I disagree with him about the literary relationships.

event, even those who argue for the strong influence of the combat myth on Dan 7 acknowledge that here the text deviates sharply from the myth, since there is no battle in Dan 7, only a forensic judgment. Moreover, the figure whom it has been argued most closely corresponds with the Baal function, "the one like a human," is nowhere on the scene when the demise of the fourth beast takes place.

MYTHIC PATTERNS INFLUENCING ANCIENT AUTHORS OR MODERN READERS?

So far, the only clear point of comparison between combat myth and Dan 7 is the mention of the Great Sea; yet even it does not function in ways closely analogous to Yamm in the Baal myth. What particularly attracts the partisans of the Baal myth theory, however, is the relationship between the seated deity who is called the "ancient of days" and the "one like a human" who comes "with the clouds of heaven" and to whom dominion is given after the fourth beast is killed. The argument is that these two figures model the relationship between El, "father of years," and Baal, "rider on the clouds," who receives kingship over the gods after the death of Yamm. The similarities are, to be sure, striking. But is it a case of the influence of a mythic pattern, even one transmitted indirectly, or an accidental resemblance created through other means of constructing the final scene? Even the partisans of the Baal myth theory have difficulty in explaining how a recollection of two divine beings, one of whom grants kingship to the other, could have been preserved in Israelite thought in such a fashion that it was available to influence the imagination of the author of Dan 7 in this way.

One needs to begin by considering the imaginative problem that the author was attempting to address. The authors who envisioned YHWH's delegation of earthly sovereignty to Gentile kingdoms generally did not consider how that delegation might be revoked. That extension of the imagination occurs first in Dan 2, where the figure of the rock cut out without human hands, that is, having a divine and not a human origin, smashes the statue representing the Gentile imperium and becomes "a great mountain and fills the whole earth" (2:34–35). Ambiguity exists as to whether this figure represents direct divine rule or whether the rock represents Israel as God's delegated earthly sovereign. The latter seems more likely, and the figure may echo Isa 51:1 ("Look to the rock from which you were hewn, / and to the quarry from which you were dug").

In the revisioning of this schema in Dan 7, the apocalyptic imagery with its developed angelology leads to a distinctive means of envisioning God's putting an end to the delegation of sovereignty to Gentile kingdoms. God's sovereignty will still be exercised through delegation, though it is envisioned as a dual sovereignty in heaven and on earth. The "holy ones of the Most High receive the kingdom" in heaven (v. 18), and "the people of the holy ones of the Most High" receive "the kingdom and the dominion and the greatness of all the kingdoms under heaven" (v. 27).[30] This view of reality comports well with the angelology in Dan 10—12, where the "princes" of the various nations are angelic powers whose struggles in heaven mirror those on earth. Thus the argument made by Collins and others that the one "like a human" in Dan 7:13 is to be understood as the archangel Michael (cf. 12:1) seems well grounded.

The notion of an angelic kingdom is attested in only a small number of other documents, most notably the Qumran War Scroll, which envisions at the end of the eschatological battle that God will "exalt the authority of Michael among the gods and the dominion of Israel among all flesh" (1QM 17.7–8). Similarly, Melchizedek, who is probably to be equated with Michael, assumes divine roles to judge and rule the people as an anointed prince in 11QMelchizedek. Both of these texts, however, are later than Daniel and show influence from that book. So they may be developments of the distinctive Danielic idea of angelic kingship rather than independent evidence for the notion.

---

30. See the thorough review of the debate over these terms in Collins, *Daniel*, 313–17.

What, then, might be the proximate source for imagining an angelic king to whom God delegates sovereignty? The most likely appears to be the ideology of Davidic kingship, which is in this case deflected upward as a model for angelic kingship. Psalm 2 models much of the dynamics reflected in the vision of Dan 7. There "kings of the earth" attempt to act autonomously ("let us break the cords of their yoke," vv. 2–3) and are confronted by the enthroned Lord (v. 4) who announces the installation of "my king on Zion, my holy mountain" (vv. 5–7). Though the kings are threatened with possible destruction (v. 9), they are finally admonished to serve in fear (v. 11), which is similar to the role of "all dominions" in Dan 7:27 (cf. 7:12) who are to "serve and obey" the people of the holy ones to whom God has given sovereignty. This understanding of Dan 7 and its relation to Davidic kingship may well be instrumental in drawing the figure of Melchizedek into speculation about angelic kingship, since in Ps 110 the Davidic king is declared to be "a priest forever according to the order of Melchizedek" (v. 4).

Might it be that one could make a case for a distant connection between the scene in Dan 7 and Ugaritic mythic traditions via the Davidic royal ideology? In at least one of the Davidic psalms, Ps 89, the covenant with David is contextualized within a celebration of God's own cosmic victory over the Sea and Rahab (vv. 10–11). This cosmic authority is associated with the Davidic king through the divine promise that "I will set his hand upon the sea, and his right hand upon the rivers" (v. 26). Yet even Paul Mosca, who has argued strongly for the royal Davidic ideology as the means of transmission of Ugaritic mythic patterns to the author of Dan 7, notes the "breaking" of the Canaanite pattern in Ps 89 and Dan 7 in that the angelic figure and the Davidic king are both assigned a role that is passive, unlike that of Baal.[31] While no one would deny that Baal motifs are important for the conceptualization of YHWH's kingship, they do not appear to have been transferred to the Davidic king in any significant manner. That the investiture scene in Dan 7 owes much to the pattern of Davidic kingship as a vice-regency conferred by the heavenly king

---

31. Paul Mosca, "Ugarit and Daniel 7: A Missing Link," *Bib* 67 (1986): 514.

seems likely. But it is not a vehicle for the transmission of a Ugaritic mythic pattern.

Finally, one must address the significance of the phrases "ancient of days" and "coming with the clouds of heaven," which are seen by the proponents of the Baal myth hypothesis as echoing epithets of El ("father of years") and Baal ("rider of the clouds"), and associating these with God and the "one like a human," respectively. If there is no significant presence of mythic elements in the plot of Dan 7, as I have argued, then these phrases are unlikely to have any independent force. Despite Collins's assertion that "Daniel 7 is exceptional in the Hebrew Bible in depicting God [as an aged god]," there are several biblical parallels to the phrase "ancient of days," including "God of Ages" (*'ēl 'ōlām*, Gen 21:33; *'ĕlōhê 'ōlām*, Isa 40:28), "the ancient God" (*'ĕlōhê qedem*, Deut 33:2, 7), and in Aramaic, "Lord of Ages" (*mārē' 'ālmayyā*, Gen. Ap. 21.2). Even Colpe, who is ultimately fairly sympathetic to the arguments for a Canaanite background to Dan 7, considers "father of years" to be a dubious parallel to "ancient of days."[32] At most it simply reflects the acknowledged fact that the conceptualization of YHWH frequently includes typological aspects shared with Canaanite El.

Regarding the other figure, the words "with the clouds of heaven one like a human being was coming" are a narrative predicate, not an epithet. To be sure, moving with the clouds is a feature characteristic of divine beings and is associated both with YHWH (Isa 19:1; cf. Deut 33:26; Pss 68:34; 104:3) and with Baal (*KTU* 1.2 IV 8, 29' etc.). Within the context of the Book of Daniel, it is one aspect of what I would term the *elohization* of the angels, that is, the tendency to describe them in terms drawn from descriptions of God (cf. 10:5–6). This tendency is strongly present in certain Qumran literature as well, including 11QMelchizedek and the Songs of the Sabbath Sacrifice. The phrase in Daniel does not point back to a distinctively "Baal-shaped" role for the one like a human.

In conclusion, it has not been my purpose in this article to deny that there are points of similarity between the Baal myth and Dan 7.

---

32. Carsten Colpe, "*Ho huios tou anthrōpou*," TDNT 8:417–18.

My purpose has been to clarify whether they are best understood as the product of an *authorial* intertextuality, however unconscious and indirect, or are best understood as the product of a modern *readerly* intertextuality generated by scholars who read Dan 7 alongside of the Baal myth and the *Enuma Elish*. In my opinion, it is largely the latter. There are, to be sure, mythic elements present, largely through the mention of the Great Sea, which bears a negative valance. Certain aspects of both El and Baal imagery contribute generally to the Israelite representation of YHWH, and various details of the chapter reflect this background. But when one investigates the proximate sources of the characters, scenes, actions, and plot elements that construct Dan 7, they point in other directions than the mythic pattern of the Baal story. Indeed, reading Dan 7 too strongly through the lens of the Baal myth leads to a misapprehension of the function and significance of key elements of the vision, in particular, the sea and the beasts that come from it. What initially seems the most likely place to find the shaping influence of the Baal myth, the investiture scene, does seem to point back to Davidic royal ideology. But when this is examined, the narrative patterns from this material that are most relevant to the formation of Dan 7 do not appear to be strongly informed by Canaanite mythic patterns. If the intention is to recover historical information about the traditions that were consciously or unconsciously formative of Dan 7, then I would argue that the recent practice of reading Dan 7 in light of the Ugaritic Baal cycle largely produces an optical illusion. The similarities and dissimilarities between the Baal cycle and Dan 7 may still be of hermeneutical interest, but they should be reconceived as a form of readerly intertextuality.

7

Creation Traditions in the Book of *Jubilees*

John C. Endres, SJ
(JESUIT SCHOOL OF THEOLOGY OF SANTA CLARA UNIVERSITY)

Recent decades have witnessed a revival of interest in creation traditions and theology in the Old Testament, and Richard J. Clifford has
played no small part in this revival. He has devoted much of his scholarly and professional life to the theology and traditions of creation,
demonstrating their deep significance for both Jews and Christians.[1]
He has traced creation traditions in ancient Near Eastern texts and various parts of the Hebrew Bible, especially Gen 1—11, the Psalms,
Wisdom literature, and Isa 40—55. Other colleagues of his have studied the development of creation motifs in some Jewish works from the
second century BCE to the second century CE, namely the Wisdom
of Solomon, Philo of Alexandria, and *4 Ezra*. Speculation on creation
also occupied Ben Sira, a Jewish sage from Jerusalem in the early second century BCE, and the author of the book of *Jubilees*, written in
Palestine in the same century. One goal of this study is to honor

---

1. E.g., Richard J. Clifford and John J. Collins, eds., *Creation in the Biblical
Traditions* (CBQMS 24; Washington: Catholic Biblical Association of America,
1992), especially the introduction, 1–15, and "Creation in the Psalms," 57–69; and
Richard J. Clifford, *Creation Accounts in the Ancient Near East and in the Bible*
(CBQMS 26; Washingon: Catholic Biblical Association of America, 1994).

Clifford's abiding passion for creation thought and theology by demonstrating its continuing influence for the author of *Jubilees*.

Jubilees, written in Hebrew in Palestine in the mid-second century BCE, offers a new version of the events that Jewish people knew from Genesis and the first half of Exodus. It contains traditions of primeval history, patriarchs, and matriarchs in the line of Abraham, and concludes with the exodus events. The ideology and theology of this text have provided fertile ground for recent scholarly discussion, but I wish to highlight a critical methodological guide for my own study of *Jubilees*, found in an essay by Daniel J. Harrington.[2] When I heard this paper at an annual meeting of the Society of Biblical Literature, it helped me to develop the methodology for my own dissertation, which led to the monograph *Biblical Interpretation in the Book of Jubilees*.[3] I was already schooled in this approach by a course on the Gospel of Luke with Dan, where redaction-critical study focused less on literary developments than on the theological perspectives that it could reveal. My essay, then, utilizes an approach I learned from Dan Harrington's teaching and uses it to explore a theological motif central to the work of his colleague, Dick Clifford. I intend to honor both of them and their collaboration over many years by indicating the contribution of *Jubilees* to the theological reflection on creation during the Second Temple era. I will argue that the author of *Jubilees* has reworked biblical traditions in order to demonstrate the inner connections between Sabbath, creation, and the sanctification of Israel.

Comparing materials in Genesis and *Jubilees*, especially those aspects where *Jubilees* differs from Genesis, offers an important perspective on *Jubilees*'s view of creation. Primary attention goes to *Jubilees*'s rewriting of the creation traditions in Gen 1 (in *Jub.* 2); there I observe considerable redaction as the author gives a concise synthesis of

---

2. Daniel J. Harrington, "Palestinian Adaptations of Biblical Narratives and Prophecies: I. The Bible Rewritten (Narratives)," in *Early Judaism and Its Modern Interpreters* (ed. R. A. Kraft and G. W. E. Nickelsburg; Philadelphia: Fortress, 1986), 239–47.

3. John C. Endres, *Biblical Interpretation in the Book of Jubilees* (CBQMS 18; Washington: Catholic Biblical Association of America, 1987).

Gen 1. Attention then passes to five prayers in *Jubilees*, all of them composed by this author. I attend to the way that God is addressed in them, and how this evidence might point to creation faith in the community for which the book was intended. Finally, I survey additional appearances of creation language in *Jubilees*, clustered around significant characters. Concluding reflections will complete the study.

JUBILEES 2 AND GENESIS 1

The Book of Genesis begins by recounting seven days, six of creation and the following Sabbath, narrated by a writer who knows the tradition well. This tradition focuses attention on the accounts of the creation of the cosmos and human beings in it. It is possible to read this beautifully patterned priestly "account" of creation as a liturgically oriented piece, designed to praise God the Creator who brought about an aesthetically beautiful and orderly world ("It was good"), which culminates in the Sabbath observance by God the Creator. The audience learns about the origins, in God's creative activity, of the entire human race; the election of a special people, Israel, only occurs later.

The book of *Jubilees*, however, begins very differently,[4] at Mount Sinai, a location pictured in the Book of Exodus. After the exodus from Egypt, Moses meets God and receives a revelation from the angel of the presence that contains all the events and contents of the tradition found in Genesis and Exodus. Then this angel of the presence tells Moses to write down all the "words about the creation—how in six days the Lord God completed all his works," and then established the Sabbath, which God set as a "sign for all his works"[5] (*Jub.* 2.1). *Jubilees* identifies the first topic of the revelation as "the creation," surely alluding to the first verbal form in Gen 1:1: "When God *created* the heavens and the earth."

Jubilees's readers should imagine that everything that follows was written down by Moses, as ordered and dictated by the angel of the

---

4. James C. VanderKam, "Genesis 1 in *Jubilees* 2," *DSD* 1 (1994): 300–21.

5. Translations of *Jubilees* are taken from James C. VanderKam, *The Book of Jubilees* (CSCO 511; ScrAeth 88; Leuven: Peeters, 1989). Emphasis throughout is mine.

presence (*Jub.*1.27). When we hear of later traditions about Moses as the author of the Torah/Pentateuch, we might recall this picture of Moses writing down all the traditions that comprise the book of *Jubilees*; the tradition of Mosaic authorship surely gained strength from this description. Remember also that this revelation occurs at Sinai, evoking memories of the events of the exodus and the experiences at Sinai, by which Israel enters into a covenant with God. This then is the sense of Jacques van Ruiten's comment that *Jubilees* offers a retrospective account of the events,[6] in which creation and Sinai covenant traditions have become inextricably bound together. Genesis 1, by contrast, portrays for its audience the very beginning of all these traditions and events.

JUBILEES 2 AND SABBATH

Jubilees 2 contains two distinct sections: (1) narration of the six days of creation (*Jub.* 2.2–14 // Gen 1:1–31); and (2) description of the Sabbath, its institution, and its significance for the people (*Jub.* 2.17–33, paralleling and developing Gen 2:1–3). Although Gen 2:3 recounts a Sabbath rest of God on the seventh day, the implications of this Sabbath for Israel are not spelled out. *Jubilees* claims that Sabbath was observed not only or primarily by God, as in Genesis, but also by the people Israel (*Jub.* 2.19–20) and by the most important groups of angels (*Jub.* 2.17–18). The angels and the people Israel should observe Sabbath together (*Jub.* 2.21) by eating, drinking, and blessing "the Creator of all" as God had blessed and sanctified them. So *Jubilees* has developed the Decalogue's view of the Sabbath related to God's rest on the seventh day to encompass the activity of God and the angels of the presence, who were given the Sabbath as a great sign and told to keep Sabbath with God "in heaven and on earth" (*Jub.* 2.18).

It may not be quite correct to claim that Sinai traditions precede the notion of creation in *Jubilees*, but the literary structure implies that

---

6. J. T. A. G. M. van Ruiten, *Primaeval History Interpreted: The Rewriting of Genesis 1–11 in the Book of* Jubilees (JSJSup 66; Leiden: Brill, 2000), 13.

we should connect Sabbath and creation notionally even as we consider them singly. The author draws a strong connection between Sabbath observance and God's creative activity by addressing God as "Creator of all" in this section on Sabbath, using the term "the Creator of all" twice (*Jub.* 2.31, 32). *Jubilees* reorients the "creation account" of Gen 1 into the life of the people Israel, as they are camped beneath Mt. Sinai and receive the sacred revealed words from God. This religious setting already reverences the Sabbath and observes it together with the angels in the heavens. Worship with the angels addresses God as "Creator of all" and surrounds (literarily) the creation account with the Sabbath, as it was prescribed from the time of Israel at Sinai.

GENESIS 1 AND *JUBILEES* 2 ON CREATION

Jubilees honors the literary structure of Gen 1:1 — 2:4a by dividing the acts of creation into six "days," but it alters the tradition significantly. While *Jubilees* narrates creative actions of God occurring during six days (*Jub.* 2.2–14), which resemble aspects of Gen 1, the Sabbath account and interpretation that follows is much longer than the account of creation (*Jub.* 2.15–33). In Genesis and in *Jubilees*, the first six days are numbered, but the literary structure shows considerable difference. In Genesis each day has a pattern: introductory formula ("God said"), divine command ("Let there be…"), execution of the command ("And there was…" or "God made" or "God created"), formula of divine approval ("God saw that it was good"), and conclusion formula ("There was evening and there was morning, the xth day").[7] *Jubilees*, however, omits the divine command, the execution of the command, and the formula of divine approval, but similar to the "execution formula," *Jubilees* describes an act of making/creating. In the Genesis pattern, the day's number comes only at the conclusion of each set of events, after the mention of evening and morning (e.g., "the first day," Gen 1:5). *Jubilees*, conversely, announces the number of the day both at the beginning and

---

7. Ruiten, *Primaeval History*, 9–10.

the conclusion of each day (e.g., "For on the first day he created the heavens...," *Jub.* 2.2; and "He had made seven great works on the first day," *Jub.* 2.3). To put it more pointedly, *Jubilees* avoids most of the dramatic elements of the Genesis account: God speaking ("Let there be..."), the execution of God's word, and the look of approval by God. One could say that *Jubilees* removes most anthropomorphic language about God's actions. Thus, much of the dramatic quality of the account has been lost by recasting all the actions into third person past action verbs; theologically, what has also been lost is the strong notion of creation by the word of God in Gen 1.

Jubilees uses the verb "created" four times (2.1, 2, 7, and 11); Genesis also employs it four times (1:1, 21, and 27 [2x]). *Jubilees* uses the verb *made* nine times (2.4 [2x], 7, 8, 10, 12, 13, and 14 [2x]); Genesis employs it only four times (1:7, 25, 26, and 31). On two occasions Genesis introduces the notion of God "blessing" (1:22, 28), with connotations of growth, fertility, and procreation. That precise vocabulary is not found in this section of *Jubilees*. When the word *bless* occurs, it applies not to all humanity, but rather to the chosen "descendants of Jacob": "[God] had blessed them and sanctified them for himself as a noteworthy people out of all the nations" (*Jub.* 2.20–21). This language of blessing in *Jubilees* connotes chosenness and election. From the earliest accounts of creation, *Jubilees* emphasizes the particularity of Jacob: Israel as chosen by God. Genesis, on the contrary, allows the audience to witness a gradual development of human beings, through a process of sin and error followed by an experience of God's love and grace, until the chosenness of Abraham's grandson Jacob is established. *Jubilees* cannot replicate that perspective because its narrative begins at Sinai, and the audience knows that Israel had already been chosen and entered into a covenant with God.

SIX DAYS OF CREATION

On the first day (*Jub.* 2.2–3 // Gen 1:1–5), God "created the heavens that are above, the earth, the waters, and all the spirits who serve before him…the depths, darkness and light" (*Jub.* 2.2). On this day God made seven great works, rather than (only) light and darkness as in Gen 1:4. The number of works is significant; all the works together will add up to twenty-two. But *Jubilees* offers three significant additions to the traditions of Genesis. First, the "spirits" constitute one work, the angels, which are described by categories; thus *Jubilees* can produce the beginnings of an angelology, which is not found in the Genesis account. Second, although *Jubilees* does not focus on God's speaking, it does indicate that these seven acts were "prepared through the *knowledge of his mind*" (*Jub.* 2.2). The closest biblical parallel to this notion might come from Ps 104:24 ("Your works…*in wisdom* you have made them all").[8] God's knowledge has become an instrument of his creating in *Jubilees*, a notion that became more common in late Second Temple documents. A closer parallel comes from the Qumran Hymn to the Creator: "Blessed be he who made the earth with his strength, establishing the world with his *wisdom*. With his *knowledge* he spread out the heavens" (11QPs^a XXVI, 14).[9] Third, the "spirits" (angels) play an active role in the events: "We saw his works and blessed him. We offered praise before him regarding all his works" (*Jub.* 2.3). In *Jubilees* the proper response to the created works of the first day is blessing and praise offered by the angels; this notion flows naturally from the perspective of *Jubilees* that an angel narrates these acts to Moses, and also that humans have not yet been created. This detail also contributes to a developing notion that angelic worship and praise parallels the worship of humans.

Jubilees introduces only a slight change when narrating the second day (*Jub.* 2.4 // Gen 1:6–7). In Genesis God created a dome/firmament that separated waters above from waters below, and God called it "sky." In *Jubilees* the firmament is the "only work that he made on the second day" (*Jub.* 2.4), but God does not name it as in Genesis (sky/heavens).

---

8. Translations of biblical texts are from the NRSV.

9. Florentino García Martínez, *The Dead Sea Scrolls Translated: The Qumran Texts in English* (trans. W. G. E. Watson; 2nd ed.; Leiden: Brill; Grand Rapids: Eerdmans, 1996), 309, emphasis added.

A reason for this omission could be that "the heavens" were already included in *Jubilees*'s list of beings created on the first day (*Jub.* 2.2).[10]

The third day of creation (*Jub.* 2.5–7 // Gen 1:9–13) seems to have two distinct parts in each text. In *Jubilees* dry land appears in the first part (*Jub.* 2.5–6), but in the second part God "created for them" reservoirs of water of various kinds and also everything that sprouts, as well as the Garden of Eden (*Jub.* 2.7). Thus *Jubilees* counts four "great types" on day three: dry land, water reservoirs, things sprouting from seed, and the Garden of Eden. For this day *Jubilees* alludes to God's speaking ("He did as he said to the waters"), which is recorded in Gen 1:9; moreover, it notes that "the waters did...as he told them" (*Jub.* 2.6). Only here does *Jubilees* give any hint of the normal pattern in Genesis of a divine command and an execution of the command by the waters.[11] In this text, in spite of fears of the mythic power of the waters, the waters seem to play some positive role, and their action does not threaten the notion of a powerful creator God.

The narration of creation on the fourth day (*Jub.* 2.8–10 // Gen 1:14–19) in both texts focuses on the three great lights in the cosmos. In *Jubilees* "the Lord made the sun, the moon, and the stars," the three works placed in the firmament to shine over the earth and rule over day and night (*Jub.* 2.8). *Jubilees*, however, elaborates only on the importance of the sun; it is the sign "for days, Sabbaths, months, festivals, years, Sabbaths of years, jubilees, and all times of the years" (*Jub.* 2.9). These details make sense in an ancient priestly calendar that depends on the movements of the sun. Everything growing on the earth needs that separation between light and darkness in order to prosper, "so that everything that sprouts and grows on the earth may prosper" (*Jub.* 2.10). Time notations referring to the moon and the

---

10. VanderKam, "Genesis 1 in *Jubilees* 2," 310.

11. In the Hebrew text of Gen 1:9, the "execution formula" is missing in this one case. But *Jub.* 2.6 contains a "memory" of such a formula: "The waters did so, as he told them; they withdrew from the surface of the earth to one place apart from this firmament, and dry land appeared." This formula may have formed part of the text of Genesis at an early stage; this is suggested by its presence in LXX Gen 1:9: "The water under the sky was gathered into its basin, and the dry land appeared" (Gen 1:9; NABRE includes it).

stars have disappeared in *Jub.* 2.9, indicating *Jubilees's* disdain for the lunar aspects of the rabbinic solilunar calendar. For *Jubilees* this formulation of the creation of lights that gives prominence to the sun provided its audience strong encouragement to follow the solar calendar, especially in their religious and worship life.[12]

The narration of the fifth day (*Jub.* 2.11–12 // Gen 1:20–23) introduces three more works. In *Jubilees* God "created" three works on this day: great sea monsters, beings that move about in the waters ("marine creatures"), and flying birds in "all their kinds." These three types parallel the creation in Genesis of great sea monsters, every living creature...in the waters, and every winged bird (Gen 1:21). *Jubilees*, however, again highlights (as in *Jub.* 2.10) the great beneficence of the sun: "The sun shone over them for (their) wellbeing and over everything that was on the earth—all that sprouts from the ground" (*Jub.* 2.12). This author continues to emphasize the great light, the sun, but here points not only to the solar calendar, but also to the great benefits of the light of the sun for marine animals and birds, as well as for "all fruit trees and all animate beings" (*Jub.* 2.12).

In the next part, *Jubilees* has replaced a more complex account of the events recounted in Gen 1:20–22. The Genesis account begins with a divine command that might be considered to compromise God's creative power: "Let the waters bring forth swarms of living creatures, and let birds fly above the earth" (1:20).[13] The retelling in *Jubilees* reflects some fear that this text might be viewed as an invitation from God to "the waters" to participate in this act of "creation." The Genesis account contains another unusual element, a blessing for these beings of sea and air: "Be fruitful and multiply and fill the waters in the seas, and let birds multiply on the earth." Both of these sentences are altered by the author of *Jubilees* so that the waters do not "bring forth swarms of living creatures" (*Jub.* 2.11 // Gen 1:20), and

---

12. James L. Kugel, *Traditions of the Bible: A Guide to the Bible as It Was at the Start of the Common Era* (Cambridge, MA: Harvard University Press, 1998), 79.

13. Here again *Jubilees's* author may have tried to avoid the role to be played by the waters in the LXX version of Genesis, which shows a more active role for the waters: "Which the waters brought forth according to their kinds."

God does not utter a blessing to these three (sea monsters, birds, every living being). In *Jubilees* there is no hint that any created being might be producing or causing any created entities to reproduce. God's creative power stands out all the more as singular.

The narration of the sixth day (*Jub.* 2.13–14 // Gen 1:24–31) gives further proof of *Jubilees*'s desire for a more succinct account by mentioning two distinct actions. God made land animals, cattle, and all creeping things; and God also made "mankind"—one man and a woman (*Jub.* 2.14). Thus, there are four works of God on the sixth day, and humankind is to rule over all things on earth, in the seas, and flying in the air. It appears that ruling over everything is the sole task given to humans in *Jub.* 2.14. One needs to consider the theological implications of the story in Genesis, however, to realize what the simple, direct account in *Jubilees* emphasizes and does not emphasize. In Genesis God first spoke of the earth "bring[ing] forth," then God "made" the three types, and after that God "saw that it was good" (Gen 1:24–25). *Jubilees* focuses more pointedly than Genesis on the creative activity of God as center of attention.

Concerning "humankind," in Genesis God spoke ("Let us make"), "created," "blessed," and assigned all to the humans, and then assessed ("saw everything that he had made, and indeed, it was very good" (Gen 1:31). Here, as on the fifth day, the priestly writer reflects on God's actions and assesses what God made or created. In each case, God's creative actions invite partnership ("let the earth" and "let us") and lead to more speaking by God, particularly in the case of the human beings. God blesses humans with words of promise: be fruitful, multiply, fill the earth, and "have dominion" over all the plants, fish, and every living thing on the earth. God has given all plants to humans for food; and all green plants were to be given to "everything that has the breath of life" (Gen 1:30). Instead of this artfully elaborated view, *Jubilees* simply states that God "made [humans] rule everything," wherever it was (*Jub.* 2.14).

As one continues reading in *Jubilees*, there is no doubt that the author values offspring, descendants, and procreation. But the theological impetus for humans to procreate does not stem from the creation materials as found in Gen 1; in *Jub.* 2 the blessing formula and the command to "be fruitful and multiply" are absent. These notions only emerge in *Jub.* 6.5 (the aftermath of the flood, drawing on Gen 9:1). In an extensive study of attitudes toward sexuality in this literature, William Loader interprets this omission of language about procreation in *Jub.* 2 not as a negative comment on procreation, but as possibly reflecting an "emphasis on companionship in the accounts of the creation of woman both in Genesis and in *Jubilees*, which make no mention of procreation."[14]

PRAYERS IN THE BOOK OF *JUBILEES*

Prayers are more commonly found in texts from the Hellenistic Jewish milieu of the Second Temple era than in the Hebrew Bible. For our purposes, they provide intriguing information because of the ways in which they address and imagine God. The appellations in the literary prayer forms give strong indications of the images and beliefs about God that can be derived from them.[15] Another consideration when examining prayer texts for notions of creation belief is that they almost never have a precise biblical counterpart, so the forms of address, with their attributions of divine actions and motifs, can be considered as intentional expressions and compositions of the author.[16] Unlike the various creation references in *Jub.* 2, where we must observe subtle differences between the text of *Jubilees* and its biblical counterpart in

---

14. William Loader, *Enoch, Levi, and Jubilees on Sexuality: Attitudes towards Sexuality in the Early Enoch Literature, the Aramaic Levi Document, and the Book of Jubilees* (Grand Rapids: Eerdmans, 2007), 236. He comments on the absence of Gen 1:26–27 in this part of *Jubilees*, but also notes that the "image or likeness of God" motif does appear in *Jub.* 6.8, where it derives from Gen 9:6.

15. For a study of various ways of addressing God in *Jubilees*, see Christfried Böttrich, "Gottesprädikationen im Jubiläenbuch," in *Studies in the Book of Jubilees* (ed. M. Albani, J. Frey, and A. Lange; TSAJ 65; Tübingen: Mohr Siebeck, 1977), 221–41.

16. The basic outline of this section is heavily indebted to an article I prepared for a Festschrift for Betsy Halpern-Amaru. See John C. Endres, "Prayers in Jubilees," in *Heavenly Tablets: Interpretation, Identity and Tradition in Ancient Judaism* (ed. L. LiDonnici and A. Lieber; JSJSup 119; Leiden: Brill, 2007), 31–47.

Genesis, these prayer texts stand out as coherent literary phenomena and can be examined by a more direct exegetical approach than the redaction-critical investigative tools needed for *Jub.* 2.

In an earlier study of prayers in *Jubilees*, I surveyed several definitions of prayer from the last centuries BCE and then focused on one offered by Judith Newman: it is speech by which humans address God, that is not conversational in nature, and that is in the second person, although it may include description of God in the third person.[17] This particular description of prayer guided the selection of five prayers for that essay.

(1) Prayer of Moses (*Jub.* 1.19–21). This first prayer in *Jubilees* is uttered by Moses on behalf of his people, Israel, after he learns from God how they will turn away from God, but then turn again to God. Moses prays for "mercy" for God's people and begs God to "*create* for them a just spirit" and to "*create* for them a pure mind and holy spirit" (1.20–21). He also prays that the spirit of Belial (a leader of evil spirits) not rule over them (1.20). Although Moses does not address God as Creator, he does employ the imperative, "create," when petitioning God to fashion the mind and spirit of this people, and to protect them from the spirit of evil (1.20–21).

(2) Prayer of Noah (*Jub.* 10.3–6). Noah has brought his family through the flood, which was precipitated by sins of the people (injustice and violence [*Jub.* 5.2; 7.23]) and of the Watchers (miscegenation with human women). In an important prayer text, Noah petitions God to preserve him and his descendants from the power of the evil spirits that are offspring from the Watchers. For his descendants he prays: "Now bless me and my sons so we might *increase and grow numerous and fill the earth*" (10.4). This language requesting a blessing would remind readers of the God of creation in Gen 1:22, 28. This prayer also binds together

17. Judith H. Newman, *Praying by the Book: The Scripturalization of Prayer in Second Temple Judaism* (SBLEJL 14; Atlanta: Scholars Press, 1999), 6–7.

notions of creation with the need to protect the chosen people from evil spirits.

(3) First Prayer of Abraham (*Jub.* 11.17). *Jubilees* views the generation of Abraham's father as given over to idolatry, so in his youth he begins to pray to God, "to the *Creator of all* so that he might save him from the straying of the sons of men" (11.7). This straying results from the pernicious activity of another prince of evil spirits, Mastemah, so the notion of protection for the people again appears, along with the notion of God as "Creator of all."

(4) Second Prayer of Abraham (*Jub.* 12.19–21). Abraham has been staying in Haran with his father Terah, and he has been awake at night, gazing at the stars, trying to learn what he can about weather patterns. During his vigil he perceives a voice assuring him that everything stands under the control of the Lord, so he wonders what use there is for his investigations of the skies. In that night he prays and says, "My God, my God, God most high, You alone are my God. You have *created* everything; everything that was and has been is the product of your hands" (12.19). Clearly he addresses the Creator God, and in the next line he begs to be saved from the influence of the evil spirits: "Save me from the power of evil spirits who rule the thoughts of people's minds" (12.20). "God most high" is here a term connected with God the Creator, once again addressed as defender of the people against the evil spirits.

(5) Prayer of Abraham at the Festival of Shavuot (*Jub.* 22.7–9). At the end of his life, Abraham celebrates the Shavuot festival, and Rebecca bakes bread and gives it to her son Jacob to take to Abraham to "eat (it) and bless the Creator of everything" before he dies (22.4b). At the same time, Isaac brings offerings for his father who blesses "the most high God who *created* the heavens and the earth, who made all the fat things of the earth, and gave them to mankind to eat, drink, and bless their *Creator*" (22.6). Later in his prayer Abraham asks God to allow his descendants to "become your chosen people" (22.9). Here language of a Creator God joins with the notion of Abraham's people,

Israel, the elect of God. This binding together of election and creation reminds us of the opening scene in *Jubilees*, where the people chosen by God hear the creation story anew and observe the Sabbath.

ADDITIONAL REFERENCES TO CREATION

Two other definitions of prayer allow for "celebration of a deity"[18] or "words...spoken in praise of God."[19] When we include blessing prayers in our category of creation-oriented prayers, the number of texts that mention creation increases significantly. I will note some significant examples, grouping them together according to the characters who utter them.

Noah makes an offering of first fruits: "It will be offered as first-fruits that are acceptable before the most high Lord, the *Creator* of heaven, the earth, and everything, so that they may offer in abundance the first of the wine and oil as first fruits" (*Jub.* 7.36). Bringing first fruits of the crops (in the fourth year in this case) naturally connects with the God of creation.

Abraham's references to the Creator God are numerous. He exhorts his father Terah to worship only the one God: "Worship the God of heaven who *makes* the rain and dew *fall* on the earth and *makes* everything on earth. He *created* everything by his word; and all life (comes) from his presence" (*Jub.* 12.4). Two notions come together here: God created everything, and he created "by his word" (a notion not featured in *Jubilees*'s rewriting of Gen 1).

Abraham also prays at the first festival of Tabernacles, a seven-day celebration. A high point comes when he blesses "his Creator who had created him in his generation because he had created him for his

---

18. Mark Kiley, ed., *Prayer from Alexander to Constantine: A Critical Anthology* (London: Routledge, 1997), 2.

19. Eileen Schuller, "Petitionary Prayer and the Religion of Qumran," in *Religion in the Dead Sea Scrolls* (ed. J. J. Collins and R. A. Kugler; Grand Rapids: Eerdmans, 2000), 30–31.

pleasure" (*Jub.* 16.26). The continuation of this prayer even claims that from Abraham there would be "holy descendants so that they should be like *the one who had made everything*" (*Jub.* 16.26). One wonders whether "being like" the Creator is a challenge or a privilege. Later, at a banquet celebrating the weaning of his son Isaac, Abraham prays "with his full voice…[and] blessed the *Creator* of everything" (*Jub.* 17.3). Many years later, Abraham delivers testaments to his off-spring before he dies. In one of them, addressed to his son Isaac, he proclaims: "I have personally hated idols in order to keep myself for doing the will of the *one who created* me" (*Jub.* 21.3). Finally, as he is dying, Abraham and Jacob lie down, and he blesses his grandson, praying: "The most high God is the God of all and *Creator* of every-thing who brought me from Ur of the Chaldaeans to give me this land…and raise up holy descendants" (*Jub.* 22.27). The Creator God directly connects with the elect people, Israel, the children of Jacob.

In the Jacob section of *Jubilees*, several references to God the Creator emerge. Rebecca offers an unusual and beautiful blessing prayer for Jacob (*Jub.* 25.11–23). *Jubilees* introduces her invocation to the Creator God: "Then she lifted her face to heaven, extended her fin-gers, and opened her mouth. She blessed the most high God who had *created* the heavens and the earth and gave him thanks and praise" (*Jub.* 25.11). Later, Jacob invites Isaac to travel with him to fulfill a vow with a sacrifice, but Isaac declines because of his age and infirmity. Still, he urges Jacob to carry out his vow, proclaiming, "May *the one who has made everything*, to whom you made the vow, be pleased (with it)" (*Jub.* 31.29). When Jacob spends a night at Bethel, God appears to him dur-ing the night and blesses him, saying, "I am the Lord who *created* heaven and earth. I will increase your numbers and multiply you very much" (*Jub.* 32.17–18). This self-identification by God as Creator gives motivation for his people to address him in this way.

When Isaac gives a farewell speech to Esau and Jacob, he exhorts them to live harmoniously, and then orders them to swear an oath by the "great *name which made the heavens and the earth and everything together*—that you will continue to fear and worship him" (*Jub.* 36.7). Lastly, when Jacob is reunited with his son Joseph in Egypt, and all the sons eat food and drink wine before their father, Jacob blesses "the Creator of all who had preserved him and preserved his twelve sons for him" (*Jub.* 45.5). Even in a foreign court, he blesses God as Creator.

CONCLUDING REFLECTIONS

Creation traditions play a very important role in the revelatory scheme of *Jubilees*. At Sinai God says "to an angel of the presence: '*Dictate* to Moses (starting) from the beginning of the creation until the time when my temple is built'" (*Jub.* 1.27). A few verses later, the "angel of the presence" tells Moses to write down "all the words about the creation," including its seven-day schema comprised of six days of creation and the Sabbath, "sanctified...for all ages" (*Jub.* 2.1). Creation and Sabbath are inseparable from the very beginning, and for this reason *Jubilees* reiterates the notion that "the Creator of all" established the Sabbath, first for the angels, and then for Israel alone (*Jub.* 2.31). Sabbath, creation, and the sanctification of Israel form a triad for the religious scheme of *Jubilees*, which exists on two planes, angelic and human.

Jubilees emphasizes that the angels kept Sabbath "before it was made known to all humanity" to keep Sabbath on earth (*Jub.* 1.30). *Jubilees's* audience should pay careful attention to Sabbath observance since the revealed account of this book begins with Sabbath and also ends with it (*Jub.* 1.29; 2.1, 15–33; 50.6–13). Even though God made this known to all humanity, he pointedly intended and directed it for Israel (*Jub.* 2.31).

Although *Jubilees* moves the audience away from the more poetic language and structure of the priestly creation account, this strategy heightens the role of God as Creator of everything. The description of the fifth day works against a notion that the waters might have taken any part in the creation processes of sea monsters, marine animals, and flying birds: God alone created. And even though God created three great lights, only one should be significant for Israel: the sun would buttress a solar calendar for this worshiping community, and would also prove beneficial for all kinds of living, growing beings. For all practical purposes, the moon played no role in the community's life.

The notion of God as Creator of all, Creator of heaven and earth, stands uppermost in the view of *Jubilees* because it ties together the most important aspects of Israel's life, especially covenant and creation. Moses, Noah, and Abraham call on God as Creator in their prayers, and Jacob and Rebecca address their concerns to the God of creation. Continual references to God as Creator shape a theological texture where humans and angels worship together, especially on Sabbath, and Israel shares the privileges and responsibilities of an elect people, living in covenant with their God.

8

Blessing the Lord with the Angels

Allusion to Jubilees 2.2 in the Song of the Three Jews

Christopher G. Frechette
(BOSTON COLLEGE SCHOOL OF
THEOLOGY AND MINISTRY)

The third chapter of the Book of Daniel tells of the astonishing rescue of three faithful Jews from the flames of a furnace. Although serving at the Babylonian royal court, they refused to worship a golden image as ordered by the king and so were bound and cast into the fire. Daniel was written in the second century BCE, but this story, like the others in Dan 1—6, is set in the Babylonian court during the exile of the Jews in Babylon in the sixth century BCE.

The tales of Dan 1—6 offered a model for Jews living in the Diaspora, encouraging them to participate in the life of foreign nations while insisting on fidelity to Jewish religion, which prohibited worshiping any foreign deity.[1] In connection with the book's concern to address persecution of the Jews, these tales encouraged faithfulness even when it might precipitate dire consequences. To this end, Dan 3 offered potent, persuasive images through narrating the deadly threats facing the Jewish protagonists, their heroic fidelity in the face of those

---

1. John J. Collins, *Daniel: A Commentary on the Book of Daniel* (Hermeneia; Minneapolis: Fortress, 1993), 51.

118

threats, and the intervention of God on their behalf. The superiority of Yʜwʜ, the God of Israel, over foreign gods and rulers is demonstrated in the astonished reaction of Nebuchadnezzar to the miraculous deliverance of the three Jews. Indeed, this image of astonishment captures the central aim of the story to draw the Jewish audience into an experience of astonishment and so to foster enthusiastic worship and loyal service of their God.[2]

Within this dramatic narrative, some ancient versions place a lengthy song in the mouths of the heroes. Scholars agree that the song was part of an insertion made after the ancient Aramaic version of the narrative was complete. This raises the question, how might this song function in the redactor's rhetorical purpose?

After describing the three men falling bound into the furnace (v. 23), the ancient Aramaic version of the narrative preserved in the Masoretic Text (MT) differs greatly in its account of what happens next from other ancient manuscripts. Scholars group these in five main traditions, one each in Aramaic, Syriac, and Latin, and two in Greek, known as Old Greek and Theodotian.[3] The insertion (Dan 3:24–90, NABRE, NETS) begins with the three men walking in the flames while singing and blessing God, and one of them, Azariah, offers a prayer of twenty verses that is largely penitential and petitionary in tone. Six verses of narrative follow, including a description of how the angel of the LORD comes into the furnace and drives the flames out of it, making it as pleasant as if a dew-laden breeze were blowing. The three men then glorify and bless God together by singing, and the words of their song, roughly thirty-nine verses, conclude the insertion. Thereafter, the other traditions generally agree with the MT, which reports the king's astonishment when he sees the three men walking unbound in the fire accompanied by a fourth who looks like a god.

---

2. Ibid., 192.

3. One can readily observe this difference by comparing Dan 3 in translations corresponding to the canons of Jews and Protestants, which accept the Hebrew version (NJPS, NRSV), and Catholic and Eastern Orthodox canons, which accept the Greek version (NABRE, NETS). The inserted text is found in the NRSV Apocrypha as a separate text. All citations and translations of Dan 3 correspond to the NETS. All other biblical translations are from the NRSV.

The Song of the Three Jews, also called the Song of the Three Young Men (henceforth, "the Song"), has been regarded as a liturgical composition that originated independently of Dan 3 and was inserted there sometime after the narrative preserved in the MT was complete.[4] In support of this view, scholars have noted that mention of the three men (v. 88) serves as the only explicit reference in the Song to the Daniel narrative and the only obvious adaptation of it for insertion into Dan 3. John Collins suggests that the purpose of the insertion was essentially pious embellishment prompted by the emphasis on praise in the Song and the correspondence between the fire in the narrative and the mention of fire in the Song.[5]

Yet, there is evidence that those responsible for inserting the Song intended it to cultivate faithfulness in their ancient Jewish audience in *specific* ways and that the thematic links between the Song and the narrative are richer and more complex than first meets the eye. Consideration of a central activity of the Song, blessing God, affords an avenue into this evidence. The Song commands angels, all humanity, and specifically all Israel and the heroes of the narrative to bless God in solidarity with the Jewish audience. The present essay demonstrates that rather than supplying mere pious embellishment, the Song supplements the narrative by giving the audience a concrete way to imagine how their activity of blessing God in response to the narrative in Dan 3 is vital for their participation in God's saving activity.

The present analysis diverges methodologically from much prior scholarship concerning differences among ancient textual traditions of the Song. Prior studies have prioritized reconstructing a putative original Song and so have disregarded certain variants in favor of others.[6] Echoing the trend in textual criticism discussed elsewhere in the present volume by Eldon Epp, this study assumes that certain textual tra-

---

4. See the table below for a schematic comparison of the Song's two Greek traditions.

5. Collins, *Daniel*, 198.

6. For a detailed presentation and analysis of all the ancient witnesses of the Song that takes this approach, see Klaus Koch, *Deuterokanonische Zusätze zum Danielbuch: Entstehung und Textgeschichte* (2 vols.; AOAT 38; Neukirchen-Vluyn: Neukirchener, 1987), 1:97–127; 2:85–141. For an overview of the textual evidence for Daniel, see Collins, *Daniel*, 2–12.

ditions can represent purposeful adaptation of the Song's elements according to distinctive poetic purposes. Incorporating observations from all five traditions of the Song, the present argument pertains to the two main Greek traditions, and by implication, the Latin, which was based upon them.

The essay proceeds in four sections. First, it explains that blessing God, as distinct from praising God, expresses not only recognition of and reverence for God, but commitment to serve God obediently. Next, it explores the purpose of having angels and other nonhuman subjects—from sun and snow, to mountains and animals—among those commanded to bless God. Then, it argues that, by allusion to a tradition of the first day of creation preserved in another ancient Jewish text, the book of *Jubilees*, the commands to all nonhuman subjects be understood as addressed to angels. It concludes by explaining how the blessing of God by angels and humans in the Song supplements the function of Dan 3.

Early in my studies, Dick Clifford, SJ, and Dan Harrington, SJ, taught me and directed my STL thesis on Dan 7 and Rev 4—5. Since joining them on the faculty at Weston Jesuit School of Theology and then Boston College, I have benefited greatly from their gracious and wise mentorship. It is with pleasure that I return to the Book of Daniel to honor them.

BLESSING GOD

To understand "blessing God" in its biblical context, it is essential to recognize that in describing human practices directed toward YHWH, the Bible in many places employs ancient Near Eastern customs regulating interactions between rulers and their subjects.[7] Multiple biblical traditions depict YHWH as a king and the Israelites as his subjects. Many postexilic biblical traditions present YHWH's reign

---

7. I am currently preparing a technical essay on blessing God. For a less technical treatment, see my "Why Bless God?" in *Reading the Old Testament: Pastoral Essays in Honor of Lawrence Boadt, CSP* (ed. C. Carvalho; New York: Paulist, 2013), 111–19.

as universal, as does the Song's portrayal of God enthroned in the heavens (vv. 54–56). The stipulations of the Sinai covenant, foundational for Israel, are stated in terms similar to those of Near Eastern treaties between more powerful kings and subordinate kings. Even though such relationships are inherently asymmetrical, they were stylized as fundamentally personal, favorable, and reciprocal. These qualities also apply to the covenant relationship between Israel and YHWH.

As distinct from praising God, the concept of blessing God fundamentally entails recognition of the existence of a relationship that is asymmetrical yet personal, favorable, and reciprocal. Although what humans do when they bless God is clearly not identical to what God does in blessing them, the same verb is used in both cases. In biblical Hebrew and other Semitic languages, the verbs commonly translated "to bless" can also mean "to greet," and it is this meaning that provides a key to the aspect of meaning shared when it is predicated both of humans and of God toward each other. In the formalized setting of an audience, in which a subordinate enters the presence of a ruler or deity in the biblical world, "to bless" can express a salutation of each party by the other that affirms recognition of and commitment to the relationship between them. The formal conventions of greeting by the subordinate typically included formalized speech and hand gestures; the superior, typically seated, could also gesture with a hand. By observing these conventions, superior and subordinate communicated to each other both recognition and acceptance of their roles and status in relationship to each other. In this respect, the exchange is analogous to a modern military salute.

For a faithful Israelite at prayer, to bless YHWH would communicate both reverence and commitment to loyal, obedient service. At the same time, it would anticipate being recognized favorably by YHWH. Without compromising God's freedom, such anticipation could cultivate hope that God would respond in commitment to the covenant relationship that Jewish traditions affirmed. God would act in ways identified as blessings: by giving life, fertility, and protection. Such concrete blessings are properly understood as emanating from God's ongoing recognition of the Jewish people and commitment to covenant relationship with them.

Thus the Song's emphasis on blessing brings particular emphasis to the concern of Daniel that its Jewish readers not assimilate to the religious practices of the other peoples among whom they lived, but faithfully observe their own traditions, including the worship and service of YHWH alone. Yet how is it that not only humans but also angels, fire, animals, and meteorological phenomena are commanded to bless God?

ANGELS IN LATE SECOND TEMPLE JUDAISM

For ancient Jewish literature, *angel* serves as a useful term to classify all spiritual agents that inhabit the heavens but also appear in visions and cause events on earth, in some cases taking physical form. This category includes Hebrew terms translated "angel" (*mal'āk*), "spirit" (*rûaḥ*), and many other particular designations. Speculation about angels increases in postexilic biblical writings and becomes most fully developed in those of the late Second Temple period (c. 200 BCE–70 CE).[8] Angels have central significance not only in Daniel, but also in Tobit and in noncanonical works such as *1–2 Enoch, Jubilees,* and various Qumran documents. This increase in discourse about angels "indicates that those authors found the speculation on the heavenly world a useful way to explore serious religious and theological issues."[9] I suggest that reference to angels in the Song served such a function in Dan 3.

Although the precise manner of portraying angels and the significance of doing so is not uniform among the various Jewish sources of this period, there are commonalities.[10] Angels assume increasing capacities as agents of God's will, although a dualistic view developed in which some angels were understood to oppose it. The angels who serve God are conceived in a hierarchical manner, where the head

---

8. Carol A. Newsom, "Angels: Old Testament," *ABD* 1:249.

9. Ibid.

10. This paragraph is heavily indebted to Newsom, "Angels," 251–53.

may be either a single angel or a small group of archangels or "angels of the presence." The head angel is sometimes identified as Michael, who has particular responsibility for Israel in Dan 12:1 and may also be identified with the figure known as the Angel of Truth or the Prince of Light in Qumran literature. God's dwelling in heaven, which is depicted in imagery from both the temple and royal court, is populated with myriads of angels (e.g., Dan 7:9–10), whose role is to worship and serve God. Their tasks of service are portrayed variously in different sources and could include teaching, executing punishment, mediating revelation, assisting humans, having authority over nations, and controlling all the physical processes of the cosmos. The conflict between the Jewish people and the nations who oppose them has a counterpart in a heavenly conflict between armies of angels who serve God and those who oppose God, as depicted in apocalypses (e.g., Dan 10:13, 20; 12:1) and developed more fully in the Qumran War Scroll. Imagining such conflicts offered a way to attribute the righteous suffering of Jews not to God's will but to angels who opposed it.

Although God is increasingly portrayed as acting indirectly via angels, at the same time angels are portrayed in various attitudes of worship before God and so providing the Jewish audience with a means of gaining proximity to God by joining the angels' transcendent worship. Cecelia Wassen situates this phenomenon, as attested in Qumran literature, within the wider imaginative climate of this period: "The close encounter between humans and angels, often expressed in joint worship, reflects an apocalyptic climate in which the heavenly and terrestrial worlds were close together."[11] The importance placed on the joining of humans and angels in worship accounts for the inclusion of both in the Song. However, the question remains as to why the Song names phenomena other than angels and humans in the act of blessing God.

It is plausible that the Song could be countering ancient beliefs that these various natural elements were either deified or served some deity other than YHWH. Most of the natural elements named in the Song

---

11. Cecilia Wassen, "Angels in the Dead Sea Scrolls," in *Angels: The Concept of Celestial Beings. Origins, Development and Reception* (ed. F. Reiterer, T. Nicklas, and K. Schöpflin; Deuterocanonical and Cognate Literature Yearbook, 2007; Berlin: de Gruyter, 2007), 519–20.

are attested in the ancient Near East as deified. These include: calf (cattle), day, dew, dove (birds), *dynamis* (power), eagle (birds), earth, fire, heaven, Helios (sun), lightning, moon, mountains and valleys, night, oak (what grows in the ground), river, sea, Shemesh (sun), source (spring), stars, Tannin (sea monster), and wind-gods.[12] It is also possible that the Song was contesting the view, well attested in Mesopotamian sources, that all manner of natural phenomena could serve as conduits for communicating inauspicious fates on behalf of the deity sending them and so function as angels of deities other than YHWH.[13] In Mesopotamia, the chief deity responsible for sending fates was the sun god (Shamash). Against beliefs that natural phenomena were either deified or served as angels of deities other than YHWH, the Song asserts that all such phenomena are creations of YHWH and must therefore serve and worship only YHWH.

Allowing this general context, evidence in the Song, in particular the Greek versions of it, indicates that its editors intended a specific understanding of the natural phenomena addressed and their relationship to angels as understood in Judaism. This evidence suggests that grasping this intended meaning required readers to recognize the Song's allusion to a particular tradition concerning angels and the first day of creation.

ALLUSION TO THE FIRST DAY OF CREATION AS RECOUNTED IN *JUBILEES* 2.2

Among beliefs about angels current in late Second Temple Judaism was the notion that God assigned angels to the various natural phenomena of creation in order to carry out God's will through

---

12. For each of these terms, see the corresponding lemma in *DDD*[2]. The terms in parenthesis give the corresponding term from the Song.

13. See Stefan M. Maul, "How the Babylonians Protected Themselves against Calamities Announced by Omens," in *Mesopotamian Magic: Textual, Historical, and Interpretative Perspectives* (ed. I. T. Abusch and K. van der Toorn; Ancient Magic and Divination 1; Groningen: Styx, 1999), 123–29.

them. This belief is attested in *1 Enoch* (60.16–22; 82.9–20) and *Jubilees* (2.2).[14] The Song in all its ancient versions may well have assumed this belief about angels and, consequently, the following rationale for addressing natural phenomena: by addressing them, the Song actually addresses the angels controlling them. Moreover, the Greek versions of the Song show evidence that their editors alluded to a particular tradition that preserves such a conception, namely, the retelling of the first day of creation from Gen 1 as it is preserved in *Jub.* 2.2.

Jubilees is a retelling of much of Genesis and the first half of Exodus and is believed to have been written originally in Hebrew, though the only complete extant manuscript of it is in Ethiopic. Although certainly translated into Greek, only fragments of the Greek version are known.[15] With marked differences from Gen 1, *Jub.* 2.2 recounts that on the first day God created seven works: heavens, earth, waters, spirits, depths, darkness (*skotos*), and light. For spirits, the text employs both "angels" (*aggeloi*) and "spirits" (*pneumata*) and names the particular spirits created on that day as follows:[16]

> [He created]...(2b) all the spirits who serve before him, namely: (2c) the angels of the presence; the angels of holiness; the angels of the spirits of fire; the angels of the spirits of the winds [*pneumatōn pneontōn*, lit., "blowing spirits"]; the angels of the spirits of the clouds, of darkness [*gnophōn*], snow, hail, and frost; the angels of the sounds, the thunders, and the lightnings; and the angels of the spirits of cold and heat, of winter, spring, autumn, and summer, (2d) and of

---

14. On these passages from *1 Enoch*, see George W. E. Nickelsburg and James C. VanderKam, *1 Enoch 2: A Commentary on the Book of 1 Enoch, Chapters 37–82* (Hermeneia; Minneapolis: Fortress, 2012).

15. See the standard edition by James C. VanderKam, *The Book of Jubilees: A Critical Text* (2 vols.; CSCO 510–511; ScrAeth 87–88; Leuven: Peeters, 1989), 2:i–xviii.

16. See the detailed discussion of *Jub.* 2.2–3 by Jacques van Ruiten, *Primaeval History Interpreted: The Rewriting of Genesis 1–11 in the Book of Jubilees* (JSJSup 66; Leiden: Brill, 2000), 20–27. The Greek terms are provided for purposes of comparison to the Song. They are from the edition of Greek fragments of *Jubilees* by Albert-Marie Denis, "Liber Jubilaeorum," in *Fragmenta pseudepigraphorum, quae supersunt graeca: Una cum historicorum et auctorum judaeorum hellenistarum fragmentis* (PVTG 3; ed. A. M. Denis and M. de Jonge; Leiden: Brill, 1970), 70–102.

all the spirits of his creatures which are in the heavens, on earth, and in every (place).[17]

The importance of angels is apparent both in the amount of detail dedicated to describing them and in that among the seven works listed, they occupy the fourth and central position.[18] The account concludes with the angels blessing and praising God: "Then we saw his works and blessed him. We offered praise before him regarding all his works because he had made seven great works on the first day" (*Jub.* 2.3). Here as elsewhere in the book, *Jubilees* emphasizes angelic worship.[19]

The relative dating of *Jubilees* (mid-second century BCE) and of the Greek translations of Daniel (late second century BCE) allows that *Jubilees* could have been known to those who inserted the Song into the various textual traditions of Dan 3. Moreover, one should not discount the possibility that the tradition appearing in *Jub.* 2.2 could have circulated independently of the complete work and been known in that way. It is thus plausible that either *Jubilees* or the tradition of creation on the first day that it preserves could have been known to the editors of the Song in the Old Greek (OG) and Theodotian (TH) traditions.

Two aspects of the Song suggest that those editors intended to allude to that tradition.[20] Both aspects would have been in some way puzzling to the ancient readers until recognition of the allusion resolved the puzzle. The first aspect involves the unexpected image of God looking upon the depths from the heavenly throne (v. 54 [OG] = 55 [TH]).[21] The mention of "depths" in the Song is unique when compared with multiple texts from the Psalter that portray God looking out from the heavenly throne. Seeing no rationale for this image among

---

17. *Jub.* 2.2b–d, trans. VanderKam, *Jubilees*, 2:7–8.

18. Ruiten, *Primaeval History*, 24.

19. Jacques van Ruiten, "Angels and Demons in the Book of *Jubilees*," in Reiterer, Nicklas, and Schöpflin, *Angels*, 585–609.

20. On the issue of allusion in biblical texts, see G. Brooke Lester, "Inner-Biblical Allusion," *Theological Librarianship: An Online Journal of the American Theological Library Association* 2 (2009): 89–93.

21. The Greek *abyssous*, "depths," often translates Hebrew *těhômôt*.

biblical conventions, some scholars suggest replacing it with some-thing else.[22] Klaus Koch suggests "correcting" it to the Aramaic ver-sion, "You who have lowered the depths and seated yourself upon the cherubim."[23]

The second aspect involves a rationale for the structure of the Song, specifically the section in verses 57–73. Scholars agree that these verses constitute a major subsection of the whole, and most see it as divided into two parts (vv. 57–63 and vv. 64–73), but they do not agree on the rationale for its structure.[24] Some have suggested that the two parts have seven units each, the first focusing on heavenly phenomena, the second on natural phenomena or what comes down from heaven.[25] However, to arrive at seven units in each, they must argue for deleting several verses from what they consider to have been the original.

The following discussion demonstrates that the key to both the Song's puzzling reference to the depths and its structuring rationale lies in its allusion to the seven works that God created on the first day according to the tradition preserved in *Jub.* 2.2. Thus, this allusion refers the reader to the portrayal of angels in that tradition, according to which they were created by God to serve God (2.2b) and to control natural phenomena (2.2d); they respond to God's action by blessing God (2.3), affirming their status as God's obedient servants.

---

22. Citing Pss 11:4; 14:2; 33:14; 53:3; and 102:20, Curt Kuhl (*Die drei Männer im Feuer [Daniel, Kapitel 3 und seine Zusätze]: Ein Beitrag zur israelitisch-jüdischen Literaturgeschichte* [BZAW 55; Giessen: Töpelmann, 1930], 157) observes that the psalms describe God looking down from heaven upon either the earth or its inhabi-tants, but never upon the depths.

23. Koch, *Deuterokanonische Zusätze*, 2:91.

24. See Koch's summary comparison of how Elmer Christie, Mathias Delcor, Otto Eissfeldt, Curt Kuhl, and Carey Moore structure the Song (ibid., 1:126). An impor-tant manuscript in the OG tradition (Papyrus 967) locates vv. 62–63 after v. 77. Accepting this ordering, Alexander Di Lella divides the Song into seven sections of five verses, plus vv. 88–90, considered additions ("A Textual and Literary Analysis of the Song of the Three Jews in Greek Daniel 3:52–90," in *Studies in the Greek Bible: Essays in Honor of Francis T. Gignac, SJ* [ed. J. Corley and V. Skemp; Washington: Catholic Biblical Association of America, 2008], 49–64).

25. Carey Moore, *Daniel, Esther, and Jeremiah: The Additions* (AB 44; Garden City, NY: Doubleday, 1977), 72. Here, Moore concurs with Elmer Christie, "The Strophic Arrangement of the Benedicte," *JBL* 47 (1928): 188–93.

Echoing the angels in *Jub.* 2.3, the entire Song involves blessing God as a response to divine action. The narrative introduces the Song by describing the three men singing hymns, glorifying, and blessing God from the furnace in which they have just been rescued. After the opening verses of the Song address God in formulaic language of blessing, more than thirty verses follow, each naming one or two addressees with the formula, "Bless the Lord, X, sing hymns and highly exalt him forever." The Greek *kyrios* ("Lord") here is likely intended to represent Yhwh, the Hebrew name of Israel's God. The concluding verse of the Song (v. 90) adapts Ps 136:2 by inviting all who worship the Lord to "bless" the God of gods.

SEE TABLE NEXT PAGE

> *Heavens/earth, spirits*: The Song employs two pairs of terms to organize all the works of God addressed in it. In both OG and TH, the introductory verse 56 classifies as works created by God all the addressees that follow. The next two verses introduce overarching subcategories that, along with their counterparts, categorize the contents of the entire Song: angels (v. 58) correspond to humans (v. 82); and heavens (v. 59) correspond to earth (v. 74). The underlying logic is that both pairs constitute merisms, conventional sets of terms that indicate the parts of a whole. Heavens/earth is an obvious merism. Angels/humans also constitutes a merism, if in addressing all nonhuman phenomena, the Song was understood to address angels, and if humans were understood as distinct from angels. The two traditions differ, in that the OG names angels before heavens, and TH reverses this order. Placing angels before heavens may have been a way to emphasize that angels exist in heavens and earth; reversing the order might reflect the notion that such emphasis was unnecessary.
>
> *Waters/spirits*: Besides being paired with humans, spirits are paired with waters as a significant structural feature of verses 58–65 of the Song, slightly differently in OG and TH (see table).

Schema of the Song of the Three Jews

The Two Main Greek Traditions Structured by Addressee
Highlighting the Seven Works of Creation on the First Day (*Jub.* 2.2)

Columns labeled *Works* list works created on the first day according to *Jubilees*: heavens, earth, waters, spirits, depths, darkness, and light. Translation, with some adaptation, and verse numbers follow the NETS.

Works		
	52	Blessed are you, O Lord, God of our ancestors…and blessed is your glorious holy name
	53[26]	Blessed are you in the shrine of your holy glory
	54[27]	Blessed are you upon the throne of your kingdom
depths	55	Blessed are you who (OG: view) (TH: look upon) the depths sitting upon the cherubim
	56	Blessed are you in the firmament (TH: of heaven)
	57	Bless the Lord, all you works of the Lord sing hymns, and highly exalt him forever.

	Old Greek			Theodotian	
Works			Works		
spirits	58 (I) angels of the Lord		heavens	59 (I) heavens	
	set of seven			*set of seven*	
heavens	59	(A) a heavens	spirits	58	(A) a angels of the Lord
waters	60	a all waters above the heavens	waters	60	b all waters above the heavens
spirits	61	a all powers of the Lord (= a class of angels)		61	c every power
	62	b sun and moon		62	c sun and moon
	63	b stars of heaven		63	c stars of heaven
waters	64	a' all rain and dew [= waters below]	waters	64	b' all rain and dew [= waters below]
spirits	65	a' all spirits (or *winds*)	spirits	65	a' all spirits (or *winds*)
	set of seven			*set of seven*	
	66	a *fire* and *heat*		66	a *fire* and *heat*
	67	b chill and *winter cold*		67	b *winter cold* and *summer heat*
	68	b dews and falling snow		68	b dews and falling snow
	69	b *ice* and *cold*	light	71	c nights and days
			darkness	72	light and darkness (*skotos*)
	70	b *snows* and hoarfrosts		69	b' *ice* and *cold*
darkness	71	c nights and days		70	b' hoarfrosts and *snows*
light	72	darkness (*skotos*) and light			
	73	a' *lightnings* [= fire from heaven] and *clouds*		73	a' *lightnings* [= fire from heaven] and *clouds*
earth	74 (B) earth		earth	74 (II) earth	

	Old Greek & Theodotian
Works	
	set of seven
	75 mountains and hills
	76 all that grows in the ground
	77[28] rain storms and springs
	78 seas and rivers
	79 sea monsters and all that move in the waters
	80 all birds of the air
	81[29] four-footed and wild animals of the land
	82[30] (OG: II; TH: B) all humans on earth
	83 Israel
	84 priests (OG: servants of the Lord)
	85 (TH: servants)
	86 spirits and righteous souls
	87 you who are holy and humble in heart
Images parallel depths.	88 Hananiah, Azariah, Mishael for he has rescued us from Hades saved us from the hand of death delivered us from the midst of the burning flame (TH: of the furnace) (OG: released) (TH: delivered) us from (TH: the middle of) the fire
	89 Acknowledge the Lord, for he is kind, for his mercy is forever.
	90 All who worship the Lord **bless** the God of gods; sing hymns, and acknowledge him, for his mercy is forever.

According to *Jub.* 2.4, the firmament divided all waters so
that "half of them went up above and half of them went
down below [it]." Since the pair "rain and dew" (Song, v. 64)
is a general expression in *Jubilees* for waters that come down
from heaven (*Jub.* 12.4), it balances "waters above the heavens" (Song, v. 60). Mention of dew in verse 68 of the Song
has a different purpose, recalling the intervention of the
angel in the narrative, when the furnace became as if a moist

---

26. This line is in TH only.

27. Lines 54–55 reflect the order in OG; the lines are reversed in TH.

28. Lines 77–78 reflect the order in OG; the lines are reversed and read differently in TH: "seas and rivers / springs."

29. TH reads differently: "wild animals and cattle."

30. This line begins a set of seven commands to bless the Lord in the OG. Since TH splits OG 84 into two lines (84–85), the introductory line falls out of the set of seven.

breeze, literally a "wind of dew," was blowing through it. The occurrence of *pneumata* in verse 65 of the Song is usually translated "winds" in keeping with the perception that verses 64–73 focus on natural elements. Yet even if *pneumata* here could evoke the image of physical winds, it certainly evoked the notion of spirits as divine agents. Greek *pneuma* translates Hebrew *rûaḥ*, and both can mean wind, breath, or spirit. Yet even wind may be regarded as an obedient agent of God (cf. Ps 148:8). Allusion to *Jub.* 2.2, with the important role that the spirits play there, strongly favors seeing here a primary reference to the general notion of spirits. In TH verses 58 and 60, along with verses 64–65, form a chiastically arranged *inclusio* (angels–waters; waters–spirits) enclosing verses 61–63, the entire section consisting of seven addressees. In OG mention of angels (v. 58) is introductory and falls outside the grouping of seven that follows, but verse 61 "powers of the Lord" makes more explicit than the same verse in TH (simply "powers") that the addressee is a class of angels. Thus in OG verses 60–61 and verses 64–65 form a nonchiastic *inclusio* (waters–angels; waters–spirits). In both traditions, angels and spirits enclose and so symbolically contain the sun, moon, and stars, considered major deities in their own right in neighboring cultures.

Depths: In biblical understanding, the depths symbolize chaos that can be manifested in various types of suffering and death. Many biblical images for chaos preserve the dual notion that it represents an adversary to God but that God has confined it within boundaries in the past and always has the potential to master it; yet God may allow chaos to encroach on creation and so need to confine it once again.[31] However, *Jub.* 2.2e asserts that even the depths are a work of God and therefore under God's power. Allusion to this tradition explains God's looking into the depths, for it endows the

---

31. See Jon D. Levenson, *Creation and the Persistence of Evil: The Jewish Drama of Divine Omnipotence* (Princeton: Princeton University Press, 1994).

Song with an added means of affirming God's power over anything that threatens faithful Jews. This allusion unifies the opening and closing sections of the Song by anticipating the account of God's action of rescuing the heroes from Hades and death (v. 88), metaphors that overlap with depths. Psalm 71:20 recounts: "You who have made me see many troubles and calamities will revive me again; from the depths of the earth you will bring me up again." Blessing is the logic that unites the two actions: God delivered them because, upon seeing their suffering, God must have blessed them, that is, acknowledged God's convenant relationship with them.

Spirits, darkness/light: The Song's sequence in verses 66–73 is designed to address a number of elements for which angels/spirits are named in *Jub.* 2.2 and to embed within them the final pair of works created on the first day, darkness and light. Excluding verses 71–72, almost all the elements named in verses 66–73 of the Song are also associated in *Jub.* 2.2 with the angels/spirits created for them (see table). Dawn and evening were considered not a separate work, but a manifestation of darkness and light. It follows that even though both of these pairs are commanded to "bless the Lord" in verses 71–72, the double addressee could be considered a single poetic unit because each line refers to the same pair of works. With this understanding, in both OG and TH the total number of poetic units in verses 66–73 is seven, the unit of verses 71–72 surrounded by six invocations. The sequence of verses 66–73 begins and ends with fire, and this emphasis corresponds to the prominence of both fire and the angel in the narrative. Lightning (v. 73) was understood as fire, apparently from the observation that when striking the earth, it could cause fire. Like wind, fire is also regarded as an angel serving God (*Jub.* 2.2; Ps 104:4).

ANGELS, BLESSING, AND THE SONG'S FUNCTION IN DANIEL 3

The Song does not merely embellish the narrative, but like other songs that were probably inserted into existing biblical narratives, it shows signs of careful editing so that its characters become a means for drawing the audience into the narrative and into a broader theological stance.[32] Regardless of the degree to which the Song may have existed as a single composition prior to its insertion in Dan 3, its two Greek traditions contain particular means of advancing the goal of the narrative to foster proper worship and obedience to God. The joining of angels and humans in blessing God constitutes the core of the underlying poetic logic.

The Song supplements the narrative in two ways. First, as a liturgical composition to be sung, the Song has a particular capacity to draw the audience into solidarity with the angels in God's presence and to reassure them of God's help. By alluding to the tradition of the first day of creation preserved in *Jub.* 2.2, the Song affirms the angels' obedient worship and service of God and their control over natural phenomena. Thus it offers the audience a way to imagine how God's favorable will on their behalf is being enacted by the angels.

Second, by portraying as a unity what the narrative recounts as separate human, angelic, and divine actions, the Song makes the obedience of the angels and heroes an extension of God's saving activity. The narrative articulates separately the heroes' obedience, God's sending an angel, and the angel's obedient intervention. The Song, however, does not recall any of these actions but sees only the action of God. God looks into the depths and rescues the heroes, and these two actions frame the sequence of angels' and humans' blessing God. This frame conveys poetically the basis for the imperative that the audience join the angels in blessing God. Doing so—recognizing who God is to them and committing to serve God obediently—is the very thing that unites them to God's saving activity manifested in the astonishing rescue of the heroes from the fiery furnace.

---

32. Other such songs include Exod 15:1b–18 and 1 Sam 2:1–10. See James W. Watts, *Psalm and Story: Inset Hymns in Hebrew Narrative* (JSOTSup 139; Sheffield, UK: JSOT Press, 1992).

9

Prose Prayers in *Biblical Antiquities*[1]

Eileen M. Schuller
(MCMASTER UNIVERSITY)

Among the lesser-known works from Judaism in late antiquity is a chronicle of some sixty-five chapters retelling the history of Israel from the time of Adam until the death of Saul. Written by an unknown author, this book was transmitted in the same manuscript as Philo's *De Vita Contemplativa* and *Quaestiones et Solutiones in Genesim*, and thus the author came to be designated as Pseudo-Philo; the book itself is usually given the English title *Biblical Antiquities*.[2] Almost certainly written in Hebrew, it was translated into Greek and then into Latin, which is the only version that has survived in eighteen manuscripts. The work comes from the Palestinian Jewish world, and scholars continue to debate whether it was written before the destruction of the temple (70 CE) or slightly later.[3]

---

1. It is fitting to include an article on Pseudo-Philo in this Festschrift since Daniel Harrington played such an important role in bringing this oft-neglected work to the attention of both scholars and more general readers. He edited the Latin text in *Pseudo-Philon: Les antiquités bibliques* (trans. J. Cazeaux; SC 229; Paris: Cerf, 1976); and produced the translation and introduction for "Pseudo-Philo" in *OTP* 2:297–377. The latter is the most accessible English translation and the one used throughout this essay.

2. The medieval manuscripts preserve a number of titles; the *editio princeps* of Joannes Sichardus in 1527 gave it the title *Liber Antiquitatum Biblicarum*.

3. For a review of major proposals, see Howard Jacobson, *A Commentary on Pseudo-Philo's* Liber Antiquitatum Biblicarum *with Latin Text and English Translation* (2 vols.; AGJU 31; Leiden: Brill, 1996), 1:199–210; and Bruce N. Fisk, *Do You Not Remember?: Scripture, Story and Exegesis in the Rewritten Bible of Pseudo-Philo* (JSPSup 37; Sheffield, UK: Sheffield Academic Press, 2001), 34–41.

The book is puzzling on many levels. It is a narrative retelling that follows the general course of biblical history by summarizing and rephrasing many biblical narratives, omitting others, and adding whole new sections of popular stories and traditions, some known from Josephus and rabbinic tradition, and some unique to this work. Attempts to link the author to any specific social milieu or to identify an overarching purpose for the work in terms of polemics or ideological/theological ideas (e.g., Essene, anti-Samaritan, pro-rebellion, anti-Zealot) have proven frustrating and unconvincing. And so many scholars are content simply to say that it represents "fairly mainstream scribal Judaism in first-century Palestine."[4]

One feature of *Biblical Antiquities* that has frequently been noted by commentators is the significance given to prayer. There are two long and striking poetic-style passages that correspond to similar hymnic compositions in the biblical text: the Song of Deborah (32.1–17 // Judg 5) and the Song of Hannah (51.3–6 // 1 Sam 2:1–10). Other hymnic compositions are added where there is no biblical precedent: the lament of Seila, daughter of Jephthah, when she is condemned to death (40.5–7); a song of David after his anointing by Samuel (59.4); and the song that David played for Saul so that the evil spirit would depart from him (60.2–3). There are declarative comments about prayer: for instance, that the norm is to pray out loud, not silently (50.5); that the dead cannot pray for anyone (33.5); and that prayer is efficacious and moves God to act (e.g., God frees the people not because of Jephthah's leadership "but because of the prayer that Israel prayed" [39.11; also 12.10]). In a few places, there are references to prayer but no text; for example, in the choice of a new leader in 49.3, Nethez exhorts the people, "Let us pray again and let us cast lots by cities," but the wording of their prayer is not given.[5]

Above all, what plays a major role in creating the "prayer-rich" impression of this book are the frequent short prayers in prose (not

---

4. Frederick J. Murphy, *Pseudo-Philo: Rewriting the Bible* (New York: Oxford University Press, 1993), 7.

5. Indeed, unlike the casting of lots that is described in detail, it is not clear that the people actually prayed, though this might be implied by 49.6: "They prayed *again* to the Lord."

poetry), over twenty in all, scattered throughout from chapter 10 to chapter 56.[6] These vary from the single-sentence petition of Jael for God's assistance as she prepares to smite Sisera ("Strengthen in me today, Lord, my arm on account of you and your people and those who hope in you" [31.7]), to the much lengthier and more complex prayer of Moses in which he intercedes for the people when God threatens to forsake them after they have made the golden calf (12.8–9). These compositions, both short and long, are certainly modeled on the biblical text itself, where there are more than fifty prose prayers in which individuals, and less commonly the people as a whole, call upon God, particularly in times of need, with spontaneous words of petition, lament, and less frequently, praise.[7] In other biblical retellings of the Second Temple period, prayers are likewise added in places where they do not appear in the biblical text. For example, *Jubilees* records prayers of Moses (1.19–21), Noah (10.3–6), and Abraham (11.17; 12.19–21; 22.7–9);[8] and *Genesis Apocryphon* the prayer of Abraham (20.12–16).[9] But the large number of such additions in *Biblical Antiquities* is sui generis and suggests that these texts merit a closer examination. Since it is not possible to analyze each of the twenty-plus prayers in detail, this paper will undertake a more general overview, noting where and why prayers are omitted or added, and highlighting some distinctive features of style and content.

---

6. For a discussion of the exact number and the difficulty in determining the number, see the discussion below. The absence of prose prayers in chs. 2–9 (ch. 1 is virtually all genealogy) is striking, especially given the fact that there are prayers in the corresponding chapters of Genesis and Exodus.

7. It is equally difficult to give a precise number of biblical prose prayers since so much depends on definition. For a list of over fifty, see Patrick D. Miller, *They Cried to the Lord: The Form and Theology of Biblical Prayer* (Minneapolis: Fortress, 1994), appendix A. Moshe Greenberg lists ninety-two "nonpsalmic prayers" in his classic study *Biblical Prose Prayer: As a Window to the Popular Religion of Ancient Israel* (Taubman Lectures in Jewish Studies; Berkeley: University of California Press, 1983), 59–60n3.

8. John C. Endres, "Prayers in Jubilees," in *Heavenly Tablets: Interpretation, Identity and Tradition in Ancient Judaism* (ed. L. LiDonnici and A. Lieber; Leiden: Brill, 2007), 31–47.

9. For a comprehensive survey, see Michael D. Matlock, *Discovering the Traditions of Prose Prayers in Early Jewish Literature* (Library of Second Temple Studies 81; New York: T & T Clark, 2012).

WHAT IS CONSIDERED A PRAYER?

The delineation of a corpus of materials demands establishing some criteria for deciding what constitutes a prayer.[10] A very simple definition, "an address to God in petition and/or praise," will have to suffice for our purposes here and does serve to highlight the basic features of style (second-person language for God) and content. There are "grey areas," particularly in narrative passages where a character enters into an extended conversation with God (e.g., Gen 3:9–13; 18:1–33).[11] Furthermore, prayers are customarily distinguished and treated separately from blessings, and so I will not be discussing the latter, though they are also frequent in *Biblical Antiquities* (e.g., blessing of the people: "And Joshua blessed them and said: The Lord grant that your heart may abide in him" [21.10]; and blessings of God: "Blessed be the Lord who has revealed all the schemes of these men" [25.5]; also 26.6; 27.13; 31.9).

In drawing up a list of prose prayers in *Biblical Antiquities*, I began with those places where the text itself uses the language of prayer, that is, where there is an introductory formula, "He prayed saying" (*oravit dicens*), or some close variation thereof, "Praying, they said" (*orantes dixerunt*) or "He prayed and said" (*oravit et dixit*), followed by the actual words uttered. There are thirteen such passages:

12.8–9: the prayer of Moses interceding for the people after they have made the golden calf;

19.8–9: the final intercessory prayer of Moses before his death;

22.7: the prayer of the tribes of Rueben, Gad, and Manasseh after they built an altar at Gilgal;

25.6 and 27.7: two prayers of Kenaz[12] (the first in conjunction

---

10. I share totally the sentiments of Samuel Balentine in his work on biblical prayer, *Prayer in the Hebrew Bible: The Drama of Divine-Human Dialogue* (OBT; Minneapolis: Fortress, 1993), 30: "The question of definition is especially difficult, and despite several years' investment in this study, I remain somewhat frustrated that precision in this matter seems so elusive."

11. See n. 15.

12. Although in the Bible Kenaz, father of Othniel the first judge, is mentioned only

with all the assembly), for revelation about the identity of the sinners, and before going into battle;

39.7: the prayer of the people, at the instruction of Jephthah, for divine help;

42.2 and 42.5: the prayers of Elumah and of Manoah, parents of Samson, concerning the birth of their child;

43.7: the prayer of Samson bound between the pillars;

46.4: the prayer of Phinehas demanding answers from God about Israel's defeat;

49.6: the prayer of the people when choosing Elkanah as judge;

50.4: the prayer of Hannah for a son;

55.1: the prayer of Samuel when the ark is taken by the Philistines.

These thirteen passages contain the expected features of biblical prose prayers: an explicit address to God (which I will discuss later) and an imperative or jussive verb(s) articulating a petition, most often for deliverance from distress or for revelation; additional elements include statements of lament about the situation/suffering and the motivation for God to act. Yet even these basic components are not mandatory in order for something to be introduced as a prayer. For example, the words of Manoah in 42.5 ("Behold I am not worthy to hear the signs and wonders that God has done among us or to see the face of his messenger") have no direct address to God and no petition (even though the corresponding passage in Judg 13:8 is petitionary), and yet they are introduced with "He went to the upper chamber and prayed and said (*oravit et dixit*)."[13]

In the Hebrew Bible some of the most clear and formally structured prayers (e.g., Gen 24:12–14; 32:10–12; and 2 Chr 20:6; to give both early and late examples) are introduced simply with "And he said"

---

in passing (Josh 15:17; Judg 1:13; 1 Chr 4:13), Pseudo-Philo makes him the first judge after Joshua, and a leader almost equivalent to Moses and Joshua.

13. Other examples are 46.4, where Phinehas asks God a series of questions introduced by *oravit*, and the words of Samuel in 55.1 introduced with *oravit* but with no second person address to God or petition.

(*wayyo'mar*). In *Biblical Antiquities* there are nine instances of *dixit*, "He said," followed by direct address to God in the second person along with the standard elements of petition, lament, and/or motivation:

10.4: prayer of Moses before crossing the Red Sea;
15.7: prayer of Moses after sending out the spies to the land;
18.4: prayer of Balaam for enlightenment;
19.14: prayer of Moses for revelation about the time of the end;
21.2–6: intercessory prayer of Joshua for the people;
31.5 and 31.7: two prayers of Jael, while preparing and then directly before striking Sisera;
47.1–2: prayer of Phinehas that God will reveal the cause of wickedness;[14]
56.5: prayer of Samuel at the choice of Saul.

Given what we have just observed in the previous listing, that the language of *oravit* can occasionally be used even when there is no direct address or petition, there are a couple of other passages that might well be considered prayers: the lament of Kenaz and the people in 28.5; the question of the people about God's intent in 46.4a; and the second question of Samuel to God in 55.2.[15] Thus we end up with a list of between twenty-two and twenty-five prose prayers.

WHO PRAYS AND WHEN?

Since *Biblical Antiquities* is not a "free" composition but a creative reworking of an already existing narrative, the question of where and why prayers are inserted cannot be separated from larger ques-

---

14. The words of Phinehas are immediately followed by the statement, "And the Lord saw that Phinehas had *prayed* earnestly before him" (47.3).

15. There are other texts that I do not count as prayers, especially places where God is addressed in the second person with specific questions for concrete information to which he gives an immediate answer (e.g., the question of Kenaz in 26.2, "Should we burn these precious stones in the fire or consecrate them to you?"; the question of the people in 49.8 about which of Elkanah's sons will rule or prophesy; and the question of Samuel in 59.1 about the kingdom of Saul).

tions concerning Pseudo-Philo's unique techniques and style of bibli-cal rewriting.[16] While it is never possible to know for certain if we have managed to uncover why Pseudo-Philo added a prayer in one place and not in another, a few suggestions can be made about how he seems to have proceeded.

For four of the prayers (possibly five, if 39.7 is considered a refashioning of Judg 10:10), there is a prayer in the corresponding bib-lical text (prayer of Moses after the golden calf episode in 12.8–9 = Exod 32:11–13; prayer of Moses after the sending of the spies in 15.7 = Num 14:13–19; prayer of Manoah at the birth announcement in 42.5 = Judg 13:8; prayer of Samson when bound between the pillars in 43.7 = Judg 16:28). In these cases, prayers are treated in much the same way as Pseudo-Philo handles all his material; he does not repeat the biblical text nor paraphrase it, but writes a new composition. Occasionally, the basic idea is carried over from the biblical passage though it is expressed quite independently (the plea of Samson in 43.7), but often the content and purpose are quite different.

For seventeen prayers there is no corresponding biblical prayer. In a few cases these involve incidents that have no biblical parallel (the prayers of Kenaz in 25.6 and 27.7; the prayer of the people at the choosing of Elkanah in 49.6). Occasionally, Pseudo-Philo seems to be supplying what could be considered as missing in the biblical text. For example, 1 Sam 1:10–11 relates that Hannah "was deeply distressed and prayed to the LORD, and wept bitterly. And she vowed a vow." Her vow is explicitly stated but there is no prayer. Pseudo-Philo resolves this gap by supplying the actual prayer that Hannah said (50.4). A more subtle reworking, almost a hypercorrection of the biblical text, might be behind the insertion of the prayer of Moses in 10.4. In Exod 14:15 the Lord said to Moses, "Why do you cry out to me?" But there is no referent for the question, since Moses has not been talking to

---

16. See the recent and comprehensive discussion by Howard Jacobson, "Biblical Interpretation in Pseudo-Philo's *Liber Antiquitatum Biblicarum*," in A *Companion to Biblical Interpretation in Early Judaism* (ed. M. Henze; Grand Rapids: Eerdmans, 2012), 180–202.

God. *Biblical Antiquities* gives the actual words of Moses in 10.4 so that God's question in 10.5 makes perfect sense.[17]

Certainly, one of the effects of adding so many prayers is to give a more religious tone to the book as a whole and to highlight specific incidents and people. An obvious example is the story of Sisera's death at the hand of Jael. The addition of two prayers very close together—in 31.5, while Jael is milking, and in 31.7, the short plea for divine help just before she delivers the deadly blow—leaves no doubt that Jael is justified in her conviction that "you act with me, Lord" (31.5). Indeed, it is probably not by chance that almost half of the prayers (nine) come during the violent and unsettled era of the Judges.[18] Many commentators have pointed out the particular attention that Pseudo-Philo devotes to the issue of proper leadership in the community and to women.[19] It is not by chance that one-third of the prayers are allotted to the leadership triumvirate (Moses, Joshua, and Kenaz), and that Jael, Eluma (the wife of Manoah), and Hannah are allotted prose prayers (in addition to the hymn of Deborah and the lament of Seila).

FORM AND CONTENT OF THE PROSE PRAYERS

In any study of prayer, the way that God is addressed deserves special attention. The most common address (ten times) is the one word "Lord," *Domine*, with no further elaboration or titles.[20] Second

---

17. This may explain why the prayer in 10.4 is the only one introduced by the verb *exclamare*, "Moses cried out to the Lord and said"; that is, Pseudo-Philo is picking up the verb *ts'q* of Exod 14:15 (in 10.5 Pseudo-Philo renders *ts'q* with *exclamavit*).

18. Contrast the very different way of handling this problematic period in Ben Sira's retelling, where it is passed over quickly, almost in embarrassment, in just two verses in 46:11–12.

19. See George W. E. Nickelsburg, "Good and Bad Leaders in Pseudo-Philo's *Liber Antiquitatum Biblicarum*," in *Ideal Figures in Ancient Judaism: Profiles and Paradigms* (ed. G. W. E. Nickelsburg and J. J. Collins; SBLSCS 12; Chico, CA: Scholars Press, 1980), 49–65; and Pieter van der Horst, "Portraits of Biblical Women in Pseudo-Philo's *Liber Antiquitatum Biblicarum*," *JSP* 5 (1989): 29–46.

20. See 18.4; 19.8; 19.14; 21.2; 31.5; 31.7; 39.7; 46.4; 50.4; and 56.5.

in terms of frequency is the phrase "Lord God of our fathers," *Domine Deus patrum nostrorum* (25.6; 27.7), along with the slight variations "Lord God of my fathers" (43.7) and "God of our fathers" (22.7; 47.1). Other formulas of address are used only once each: "Lord God of Israel" (49.6); "Lord God of all flesh" (42.2); and "O God" (12.8). The simple address "Lord" is taken from many biblical prose prayers (e.g., Exod 32:11; Num 14:13; Judg 13:8; 2 Sam 24:10; 2 Kgs 20:3). In the Hebrew Bible, the only occurrence of "Lord God of our fathers" as an address in prayer is in the words of Jehoshaphat (2 Chr 20:6), but it appears in other Second Temple texts—for example, "Lord Almighty God of our fathers" (Prayer of Manasseh 1:1) and "God of our fathers" (Tob 8:5; LXX Dan 3:29)—though it is difficult to know if Pseudo-Philo was familiar with either of these. Given that the phraseology of "God of our fathers" became common in synagogue prayer ("Our God and God of our fathers") and in private rabbinic prayers ("May it be your will, O Lord, my God and God of my fathers"),[21] it may be that Pseudo-Philo's predilection for this phrase was not just because of the single Chronicles passage but also due to some influence from early liturgical practice in synagogue or in *bet midrash* circles.

A development that Claus Westermann pointed out in his classic study regarding certain later prose prayers of the Deuteronomist and the Chronicler is the inclusion of expressions of praise and blessing before the petition (e.g., 1 Kgs 8:56; 1 Chr 29:10; 2 Chr 20:6; Neh 9:5–6), and this innovation is well attested in many Second Temple prayers (e.g., 2 Macc 1:24–29; Judg 9:12; Add Esth 13:9; 3 Macc 2:2; 6:2).[22] More specifically, petitionary prayers are sometimes introduced with a blessing (*baruk* or *baruk 'atta*) formula (e.g., Tob 8:5; 1 Macc 4:30; GenAp 20:12–13; also LXX Dan 3:26). This latter style is almost certainly influenced by "a trend toward the systematic use of opening and closing blessings in liturgical prayers already in the middle of the

---

21. Joseph Heinemann, *Prayer in the Talmud: Forms and Patterns* (SJ 9; Berlin: de Gruyter, 1977), 31, 182.

22. Claus Westermann, *Praise and Lament in the Psalms* (trans. K. R. Crim and R. N. Soulen; Atlanta: Knox, 1981); and Judith H. Newman, *Praying by the Book: The Scripturalization of Prayer in Second Temple Judaism* (SBLEJL 14; Atlanta: Society of Biblical Literature, 1999), 19–54.

Second Temple period."[23] In light of these developments, it is note-worthy that in *Biblical Antiquities* there are no examples of the *baruk* formula to introduce a prayer of petition. There are occasional general affirmations of divine qualities (e.g., 12.9: "You are he who is all light"; 21.4: "You who are before all ages and after all ages still live"), but these are woven into the narrative of the prayer, rather than being part of the address. Five prayers (12.8; 19.8; 31.5; 42.2; 55.1) begin with *ecce*, "behold" (three of these with *ecce nunc*), presumably going back to *idou* in Greek and *hinneh* in Hebrew. This formula of introduction seems distinctive to Pseudo-Philo.[24]

If we adopt Westermann's formulation that there are "two basic modes of speaking to God: praise and petition,"[25] all the prose prayers in *Biblical Antiquities* belong to the second category. There are no prayers of praise or thanksgiving in prose. Let me comment briefly on a few features of different sorts of petitionary prayers (very short pleas, laments, intercessory prayers, and petitions for a revelation) in order to highlight how Pseudo-Philo continues with very standard biblical forms and patterns, while at the same time introducing distinctive elements of content (including didactic and apocalyptic motifs, and the narration of previously unmentioned events).

The prayers of Samson bound between the pillars (43.7), of Samuel for guidance for the people in the choice of a king (56.5), and of Jael before she smites Sisera (31.7) stand out because they are all only a single sentence: an address and a plea. There are antecedents for such concise, almost blunt, petitions in Moses' appeal for Miriam, "O God, please heal her" (Num 12:13; also 2 Kgs 6:20), and in Judith's cry of appeal to God before she cuts off the head of Holofernes, "Give me strength this day, O Lord God of Israel" (Jdt 13:7). Indeed, Jael's

---

23. Esther Chazon, "Looking Back: What the Dead Sea Scrolls Teach Us about Biblical Blessings," in *The Hebrew Bible in Light of the Dead Sea Scrolls* (ed. N. Dávid et al.; FRLANT 239; Göttingen: Vandenhoeck & Ruprecht, 2012), 160.

24. In biblical prose, *hēn/hinnēh* frequently begins conversations between God and Moses (e.g., Exod 6:12; 6:30), but does not open formally structured prayers.

25. Claus Westermann, *The Praise of God in the Psalms* (trans. K. R. Crim; Richmond, VA: Knox, 1965), 35.

prayer is sometimes taken as a direct quotation from Judith,[26] and, if so, would be perhaps the clearest example of intertextual influence that extends beyond what later came to be canonical boundaries. This type of prayer is never followed by an explicit statement that God has heard or accepted the prayer (as is sometimes the case after longer prayers); its efficacy is apparently sufficiently clear from the resolution of the crisis.

We have already made note of instances (42.5; 46.4; 55.1) where the specific language of praying (*oravit*) is introduced even when there is no explicit request, but only statements about the situation of crisis or a series of questions directed to God. Passages such as these fall into that category recognized phenomenologically by Gerardus Van der Leeuw as prayers that are "simply the expression of a pious or reverential, an anxious or some other type of mood."[27] The rhetorical function of the questions in this context is not informative as much as emotive. Comparison can be made not only with certain biblical prose prayers (the lament of Joshua after the defeat of Ai in Josh 7:7–9, or the lament of the Benjaminites in Judg 21:3), but also, most significantly, with psalms where lament is articulated through the direct interrogation of God (e.g., Pss 4:2; 10:1; 74:1; 80:4).[28] In the longer example, 49.6, the people go on to narrate at length to God (as if he didn't know!) all the concrete facts of the situation — they found they had discovered a leader in Elkanah but he refused them. In this way, these prayers combine the more universal and emotive aspects of psalmic language with the specificity that inserts them into, and indeed limits them to, the specific narrative context.

Five prayers by Moses and Joshua can be grouped together as intercessory prayers (10.4; 12.8–9; 15.7; 19.8–9; 21.2–6) of a leader

---

26. For instance, it is italicized and identified as a quotation by Harrington in *OTP*.

27. G. Van der Leeuw, *Religion in Essence and Manifestation* (2 vols.; Harper Torchbooks 100–101; New York: Harper & Row, 1963), 2:426.

28. The dependence of biblical prose prayers on psalmic patterns was developed at length by Greenberg, *Biblical Prose Prayer*, expanding on earlier comments by Sigmund Mowinckel, *The Psalms in Israel's Worship* (Nashville: Abingdon, 1962), 1:41 "Experience shows that so-called 'free prayer' is to a large extent dependent on the pattern set by the prayers and psalms of public worship."

pleading for his people; they share similar petitions for preservation, the restraint of divine anger, and the granting of mercy.[29] As Roger Le Déaut observed some years ago in a general study of intercessory prayers in the Second Temple period, the value of intercession is often linked to the merits and moral rectitude of the intercessors;[30] however, this is not the case in *Biblical Antiquities*, where the personal merits of Moses and Joshua are not part of the prayer or its introduction.

The prayer of Moses (12.8–9) after he has destroyed the golden calf, although comparable to similar intercessions of Moses (see Exod 32:11–13, 31–32; Num 14:13–19; Deut 9:26–29), is developed quite differently. In contrast to the bold and passionate pleading in the biblical prayers through a lengthy recalling of the previous acts of deliverance in the exodus and the promise to the ancestors, 12.8–9 is surprisingly reserved, offering an abstract and literary meditation on Israel as God's vine. There is no articulation of the immediate situation involving the golden calf, only a vague allusion that "the vine has lost its fruit and has not recognized its cultivator" (12.8). Although the biblical image of Israel as a vine recurs in multiple places throughout the book (18.10–11; 23.11–12; 28.4; 30.4; 39.7), it is within this prayer that Pseudo-Philo chooses to expand and introduce new cosmological dimensions, from the abyss to the heavenly throne, with descriptions of God as "you who are all light," and of his "house" (the temple? the universe?) as adorned with exotic spices and perfumes, precious stones and gold, and rich food and drink. Many commentators have suggested that Pseudo-Philo may have looked intertextually to *1 En.* 24 or some similar apocalyptic speculation for his imagery, though in the end, he concludes the prayer with a rather standard plea, "Now let your anger be restrained from your vine." This passage, perhaps more

---

29. The reuse of the divine attribute formula of Exod 34:6–7 and the emphasis on divine mercy in the prayer of Moses in 19.8–9 has been studied by Judith H. Newman, "The Staff of Moses and the Mercy of God: Moses' Final Intercession in Pseudo-Philo 19," in *Israel in the Wilderness: Interpretations of the Biblical Narratives in Jewish and Christian Traditions* (ed. K. E. Pomykala; Themes in Biblical Narrative 10; Leiden: Brill, 2008), 137–56.

30. R. Le Déaut, "Aspects de l'intercession dans le Judaïsme Ancien," *JSJ* 1 (1970): 35–57.

than any other, illustrates how the basic framework of petitionary prayer could be expanded to include wisdom speculation, didactic teaching, and apocalyptic motifs.[31]

The prayer of Moses (19.8–9), coming after his impending death has been twice announced (vv. 2 and 6), is another illustration of originality. While the preservation of memorable last words or blessings from a great man (Isaac in Gen 27, Jacob in Gen 49, Moses in Deut 32 — 33, David in 2 Sam 23:1–7) is thoroughly biblical, none of these figures actually prays a deathbed prayer. Here Pseudo-Philo may be following the lead of *Jubilees*, which first introduces a prayer of Abraham on his deathbed (*Jub.* 22.6–7). In Moses' deathbed prayer, in addition to the usual elements of address, petition, and rhetorical questions, there is the long section of biblical material quoting directly from the call of Moses in Exod 3:1–6. This "forward-background" movement (from the end of Moses' life to the beginning) is Pseudo-Philo's most distinctive compositional technique: an incident is omitted completely in its proper sequential place in the narrative and subsequently introduced by being recalled in a totally different context.[32] Here a procedure that is pervasive and works so well in speeches throughout the book (9.9; 12.2; 17.2; 19.10–12; 20.5) is carried over into prayer (also in the prayers of Joshua in 21.3 and Phinehas in 47.1), where it is logically less appropriate—after all, in prayer one does not need to tell God past history! But again, the standard structure of petitionary prayer proves flexible enough to absorb elements quite unprecedented in biblical examples.

What is missing from *Biblical Antiquities* are prayers of penitence and confession. Recent scholarship has placed a great deal of emphasis on penitential prayer as a significant and changing genre,

---

31. Petitions for a revelation that are typical of apocalypses (e.g., 2 Bar 54:6, 20; 4 Ezra 4:48; 5:56; 12:8) may have also influenced the frequency of prayers containing requests for some revelation associated with the future (18.4; 19.14; 25.6; 42.2; 47.1–2). In biblical narrative, such prayers are not unknown (cf. 1 Sam 23:10), but are infrequent since the divine will is usually sought through a direct oracular inquiry via a priest.

32. This technique was recognized already by Otto Eissfeldt, "Zur Kompositionstechnik des Pseudo-Philonischen Liber Antiquitatum Biblicarum," *NTT* 56 (1955): 53–71, and is discussed at length with many examples by Fisk, *Do You Not Remember?*

ranging from simple confessions of guilt (Judg 10:10, "We have sinned against you because we have abandoned our God"), to confession plus petition (Judg 10:15; 1 Sam 12:10; 2 Sam 24:10), to extended confession prefaced by a lengthy historical prologue (Neh 9:6–38; Ezra 9:6–15; Dan 9:4–9; Baruch 1:15 — 3:8; the Words of the Luminaries 4Q504).[33] Why not in *Biblical Antiquities*? It is not that opportune moments are lacking. In 39.7, Pseudo-Philo reworks the explicit confession, "We have sinned," of Judg 10:10–15 into a petition, "May you not destroy the vine that your right hand has planted"; in another place where it is expected that Reuben, Gad, and Manasseh would confess their sin, we find instead a "lament of innocence" ("You know that our ways were not undertaken out of wickedness…we have not strayed from your way" [22.7]). It is not what is said in prayer, but what is *not* said that serves a theological purpose; that is, the omission of confession of sin reinforces Pseudo-Philo's consistent downplaying of the repentance element in the Deuteronomistic sin-punishment-repentance-deliverance cycle, and enhances his emphasis on the gratuity of divine mercy and divine faithfulness, not human agency, as the guarantee of Israel's ultimate salvation.[34]

CONCLUSION

Biblical Antiquities has been often neglected in the study of Second Temple literature, and the numerous prose prayers in this work have been neglected in the study of both prayer formulation and the function of prayers within biblical retellings. This brief essay has only been able to touch on a few selected features. In addition to

33. The development of penitential prayers has been the subject of much study in recent scholarship; see the three volumes edited by Mark Boda, Daniel K. Falk, and Rodney A. Werline, *Seeking the Favor of God* (SBLEJL 21–23; Atlanta: Society of Biblical Literature, 2006–8).

34. This foundational aspect of Pseudo-Philo's theology, that "he [God] will never entirely abandon them [his people]," was articulated already by Leopold Cohn in his early study "An Apocryphal Work Ascribed to Philo of Alexandria," *JQR* 10 (1898): 322, and has been reiterated by virtually every modern commentator; see Frederick J. Murphy, "The Eternal Covenant in Pseudo-Philo," *JSP* 3 (1988): 45–57.

attempting to draw up a list of what should be categorized as a prose prayer (itself not an easy or uncontroversial task), I have drawn attention not only to many similarities with biblical prose prayers, but also to many ways in which Pseudo-Philo introduces new elements and subtly transforms traditional usage. What seems like a very simple rewriting of biblical prayers and adding a few new ones turns out, on closer examination, to be much more intricate and innovative. If the book as a whole is a "difficult, complex and problematic text,"[35] the same can be said for the prayers per se, and these fascinating texts warrant much further study.

---

35. The conclusion of Howard Jacobson after years of work on this text; from his review of Murphy, *Pseudo-Philo: Rewriting the Bible* in *JJS* 45 (1994): 309.

III

NEW TESTAMENT DEPLOYMENTS OF SCRIPTURE AND TRADITION

10

Paul's Use of Scripture in the Collection Discourse (2 Corinthians 8—9)[1]

Thomas D. Stegman, SJ
(BOSTON COLLEGE SCHOOL OF THEOLOGY AND MINISTRY)

Paul employs several persuasive strategies in his exhortation to the church in Corinth to give generously to his collection project for the *hagioi* ("holy ones") in Jerusalem (2 Cor 8:1—9:15).[2] Prominent among these strategies are two Scripture citations introduced with the formulaic "as it is written" (*kathōs gegraptai*; 8:15 and 9:9). Beyond

---

1. This essay is offered as a token of *pietas* and gratitude to two great Jesuit biblical scholars, Daniel Harrington and Richard Clifford. They were my teachers at Weston Jesuit School of Theology and directors of my STL thesis. They were the ones who encouraged me to pursue doctoral studies in New Testament and then recruited me to join them on the faculty at Weston Jesuit (now Boston College School of Theology and Ministry). I have since had the pleasure of coteaching with each, which has afforded me the opportunity to continue to learn from them. They are esteemed colleagues, valued mentors, and—best of all—generous and trustworthy brother Jesuits and friends.

2. For studies on the collection, see, e.g., Keith F. Nickle, *The Collection: A Study in Paul's Strategy* (SBT 48; Naperville, IL: Allenson, 1966); Dieter Georgi, *Remembering the Poor: The History of Paul's Collection for Jerusalem* (Nashville: Abingdon, 1992); Stephan Joubert, *Paul as Benefactor: Reciprocity Strategy and Theological Reflection in*

direct citation, he also alludes more subtly to Scripture throughout 9:6–10, near the climax of his discourse.[3]

This essay explores Paul's use of the biblical passages that he cites and alludes to in 2 Cor 8—9. I limit myself to two lines of inquiry. First, what significance might there be to Paul's changing any words or the syntax of the texts he cites or refers to (insofar as such things can be determined from the best LXX texts)? Second, how does the original context of the various passages he cites or echoes illuminate his meaning? The latter question is indebted to the seminal work of Richard B. Hays,[4] who has argued that Paul's use of Scripture is more than perfunctory (e.g., for proof texting). Instead, the apostle often evokes the broader literary context of the texts he cites or alludes to in order to engage them theologically. Hays's proposal, which has been widely accepted in scholarly circles, has the virtue of making more "audible the range of theological harmonics sounding within Paul's letters."[5] I analyze the relevant texts in sequential order.

Paul's Collection (WUNT 2/124; Tübingen: Mohr Siebeck, 2000); and David J. Downs, *The Offering of the Gentiles: Paul's Collection for Jerusalem in Its Chronological, Cultural, and Cultic Contexts* (WUNT 2/248; Tübingen: Mohr Siebeck, 2008). For studies on 2 Cor 8—9, see, e.g., Hans Dieter Betz, *2 Corinthians 8 and 9: A Commentary on Two Administrative Letters of the Apostle Paul* (Hermeneia; Philadelphia: Fortress, 1985); and Kieran J. O'Mahony, *Pauline Persuasion: A Sounding in 2 Corinthians 8—9* (JSNTSup 199; Sheffield: Sheffield Academic Press, 2000).

3. In line with several recent commentaries, this essay operates from the premise of the literary integrity of 2 Corinthians as a whole, and thus of chs. 8—9. For a discussion of the latter, see Stanley K. Stowers, "*Peri men gar* and the Integrity of 2 Cor. 8 and 9," *NovT* 32 (1990): 340–48.

4. Richard B. Hays, *Echoes of Scripture in the Letters of Paul* (New Haven: Yale University Press, 1989).

5. John M. G. Barclay, "Manna and the Circulation of Grace: A Study of 2 Corinthians 8:1–15," in *The Word Leaps the Gap: Essays on Scripture and Theology in Honor of Richard B. Hays* (ed. J. R. Wagner, C. K. Rowe, and A. K. Grieb; Grand Rapids: Eerdmans, 2008), 409.

CITATION OF LXX EXODUS 16:18 IN 2 CORINTHIANS 8:15

Paul begins his collection appeal by referring to "the grace of God" that has been manifested through the generosity of the churches in Macedonia, a phenomenon all the more remarkable given the Macedonians' "extreme poverty" (2 Cor 8:1–5). Their response to his appeal has inspired Paul to send his coworker Titus to Corinth to resume the facilitation of the collection there (8:6).[6] Between exhortations to the Corinthians to excel in their own generosity and love (8:7–8) and to complete what they had previously started (8:10–12), Paul sets before them "the grace of our Lord Jesus Christ" who, "though he was rich, became poor for your sake, in order that you might become rich by his poverty" (8:9).[7] Paul then clarifies that he is not asking the Corinthians to impoverish themselves in the process; rather, he envisions a type of mutuality. In the present time, the Corinthians are positioned to help the needs in Jerusalem. But in the future, the tables might be reversed, and the Jerusalemites will then assist the church in Corinth. Paul refers to this reciprocal response to need as *isotēs* ("mutuality" or "equality"; 8:13–14). It is this idea of *isotēs* that he grounds in Scripture by quoting Exod 16:18: "As it is written, 'The one who [gathered] much did not have surfeit, and the one who [gathered] little did not lack'" (8:15).

The cited text occurs in the narrative about God's provision of manna for the Israelites in the wilderness of Sin, shortly after the exodus and before their arrival at Sinai (Exod 16:1–36). In response to the people's complaints about not having food, God bestowed bread every morning (as well as quail every evening). The gift of manna was to be collected each day, an *omer* for every person (16:16). It was to be consumed daily, with nothing left over to the next day (16:19). When the

---

6. Paul had previously given the Corinthians instructions concerning the collection (1 Cor 16:1–4). A breakdown in the relationship between him and the community, however, led to a stoppage in their participation. See, e.g., Thomas D. Stegman, *Second Corinthians* (CCSS; Grand Rapids: Baker Academic, 2009), 20–23.

7. Translations of biblical texts are my own, unless otherwise indicated.

Israelites gathered the manna and then measured it out, "those who gathered much had nothing over, and those who gathered little had no shortage; they gathered as much as each of them needed" (16:18, NRSV).[8] What the Exodus text does not make explicit is the reason why the gift of manna was equally distributed. Was it because of the people's cooperation and compliance with God's instructions (as possibly suggested by 16:17)? Or was it due to some miraculous intervention by God to bring about equal measurement regardless of the amounts gathered?

Interpretation of the manna story and the lessons to be gleaned from it has a long history, beginning with the Jewish Scriptures (see, for instance, Deut 8:3; Ps 78). For our limited purposes, it is instructive to look briefly at the allegorical use of the story by Paul's contemporary Philo in his treatment of *isotēs* in "Who Is the Heir of Divine Things?" (*Her.* 141–206). According to Philo, *isotēs* refers first and foremost to God and to God's activity—in particular, to God's wise governance of creation, including the proportional bestowal of gifts (e.g., wisdom) to people according to their individual capacities. It is in this connection that Philo cites Exod 16:18 (*Her.* 191).

That Paul intends something different by referring to the Exodus text is suggested, in the first place, by the way he changes the syntax:[9]

LXX Exod 16:18—*ouk epleonasen ho to polu, kai ho to elatton ouk ēlattonēsen*

2 Cor 8:15—*ho to polu ouk epleonasen, kai ho to oligan ouk ēlattonēsen*

Notice that Paul reverses the order of the first clause, placing the subject *ho to polu* ("the one who [gathered] much") before the predicate *ouk epleonasen* ("did not have surfeit").[10] As L. L. Welborn suggests,

---

8. LXX Exodus 16 is very close to the MT on which English translations are based.

9. See Christopher D. Stanley, *Paul and the Language of Scripture* (SNTSMS 74; Cambridge, UK: Cambridge University Press, 1992), 231–33; and L. L. Welborn, "'That There May Be Equality': The Contexts and Consequences of a Pauline Ideal," *NTS* 59 (2013): 87–88.

10. The change of *to elatton* to *to oligan* is not so significant; the terms are synonymous.

the effect of this change "is to destroy the chiastic structure of the Septuagint text, a structure which linguistically mirrors the miracle of divine equalization."[11] The notion of "divine equalization" is what Philo drew from the manna story. But Paul's word order draws attention to the contrast between the one who gathered much and the one who gathered little. I will return to the significance of this point momentarily.

Before doing so, it will be helpful to take up Hays's project of looking at the broader context of Exod 16:18 for clues to Paul's meaning. In fact, Hays himself analyzes 2 Cor 8:15 in his groundbreaking study. He points to two features of the manna story that Paul draws on in his exhortation to the Corinthians. First, the story is an "economic parable" that teaches that God provides in abundance for those who trust in him, a theme Paul later makes explicit with reference to material resources (2 Cor 9:8–12). Second, the vignette about those Israelites who attempted to save some manna for the following day—an act of disobedience against the divine command—only to find that it had rotted (Exod 16:19–20) functions as an admonition to the Corinthians not to hoard their possessions.[12] In short, Paul employs the manna story (1) to convince them to trust in God to provide, and (2) to share, not hoard, their material abundance with the Jerusalem church. Hays concludes that Paul's "application of the story taps and draws out hermeneutical potential that is fairly oozing out of the Exodus narrative—or more precisely, Paul taps Exodus 16 and then walks away, leaving the reader to draw out the sap."[13]

John M. G. Barclay, while expressing admiration for Hays's interpretation, argues that Paul's use of the manna story is even more complex. The apostle now reads and understands that story in the light of the Christ event. Recall that, a few verses prior to the Exodus citation,

---

11. Welborn, "That There May be Equality," 88. The chiastic structure here is predicate-subject-subject-predicate.

12. Cf. 1 Cor 10:1–6 for other examples of warnings to the Corinthians via the wilderness generation.

13. Hays, *Echoes of Scripture*, 90. See also Frank J. Matera, *II Corinthians: A Commentary* (NTL; Louisville: Westminster John Knox, 2003), 193.

Paul reminds the Corinthians of the self-giving love of Jesus (2 Cor 8:9). For Paul, the Christ event not only exemplifies self-giving love but also empowers participation in his self-gift. The *isotēs* Paul desires here entails the sharing of material resources befitting a community of believers whose source of life is "grace," the self-gift of God revealed in Christ. The manna story, read through the lens of the Christ event, does more than encourage trust in God and warn against hoarding; it also reveals a new "economy" rooted in God's self-giving love. Barclay therefore argues that "there is more than one tree being tapped here, and it is precisely the *blend* of juices that makes this reading of Exodus so unusual and so theologically creative."[14]

This reading complements the observation above about Paul's syntax. The linear rather than chiastic structure, which highlights the contrast between "the one who [gathered] much" and "the one who [gathered] little," functions, as Welborn notes, "to advocate equality between persons of different resources through redistributive action."[15] That is, the divine self-giving revealed in the Christ event creates the possibility of a "christological economy"[16] played out in practical terms in the arena of human agency. Paul thereby complements the theme of God's grace with the necessity of human activity. This activity is an ongoing participation in and expression of divine grace (a point to which the apostle will return in 2 Cor 9:9).

Another feature of the manna story merits comment. The gift of manna is preceded by a manifestation of "the glory of the LORD" (Exod 16:10). The glory of the Lord is a prominent theme for Paul in 2 Corinthians. He offers a midrash of the story of Moses' face reflecting the Lord's glory (2 Cor 3:12–18; cf. Exod 34:29–35). For Paul, the Lord's glory now refers to "the glory of Christ, who is the image of God" (2 Cor 4:4). The manner by which Christ manifests the divine glory, however, is paradoxical—through his self-giving love revealed in his dying for all (5:14–15), which has brought about "new creation"

---

14. Barclay, "Manna and the Circulation of Grace," 413 (emphasis original); see also 419–26.

15. Welborn, "That There May be Equality," 88.

16. The phrase is Barclay's ("Manna and the Circulation of Grace," 426).

(5:17). Through the gift and empowerment of the Spirit, "we all" (i.e., those in Christ) are transformed into "the same image from glory to glory" (3:18). In other words, the Spirit enables recipients to enter into the dynamic of self-giving love; and in so doing, they show forth God's glory. Blending the juices, or, to change the metaphor, mixing the notes of Paul's prior treatment of "glory" with the echo of "the glory of the LORD" from the manna story adds to the resonance of the apostle's theological harmonics. The Corinthians' generous participation in the collection redounds to—and manifests—God's glory (as made explicit in 2 Cor 9:13–15).

ALLUSIONS TO LXX PROVERBS IN 2 CORINTHIANS 9:6–7

Following the citation of Exod 16:18, Paul announces that he is sending Titus and two "brothers" ahead of him to Corinth to facilitate and administer the community's contribution. He vouches for these emissaries and exhorts the Corinthians to welcome them and to cooperate with them (2 Cor 8:16–24). Paul also appeals to the Corinthians' sense of honor (not to mention, their shame) by informing them that, in the past, he has boasted to the Macedonian churches about their generosity (9:1–4). He therefore exhorts the community in Corinth to have their previously promised contribution ready for his arrival, a contribution that should be given "as a blessing" (*hōs eulogian*; 9:5).

Paul then launches into a rhetorically powerful encouragement to generosity, one that is saturated with scriptural allusions.[17] Picking up on the theme of blessing (*eulogia*), he offers a proverbial saying from the sphere of agriculture: "The point is this: the one who sows sparingly will reap sparingly, and the one who sows bountifully (*ho speirōn ep' eulogiais*) will reap bountifully (*ep' eulogiais kai therisei*)" (2 Cor 9:6). Maxims involving the sowing and reaping metaphor—with the

---

17. For a helpful summary of the argumentative force of 2 Cor 9:6–10, see Bart B. Bruehler, "Proverbs, Persuasion and People: A Three-Dimensional Investigation of 2 Cor 9.6–15," *NTS* 48 (2002): 209–24, esp. 218–19.

sense that one reaps what one sows—were a commonplace in both Greco-Roman and Jewish literature.[18] Variants of the maxim are found in a number of sapiential texts in the LXX: Prov 11:21, 24, 26; 22:8; Job 4:8; and Sir 7:3. Does Paul have a particular text in mind here? Given that he alludes to LXX Prov 22:8a (the first line of a couplet not found in the MT) in the very next verse (2 Cor 9:7), it is possible that he has Prov 22:8 in mind. However, the preponderance of passages from Prov 11 is also suggestive.

The latter proposal, particularly Prov 11:24 and the verses immediately following, leads to some intriguing interpretive possibilities.[19] To be sure, the sowing/reaping metaphor in LXX Prov 11:24 is not a direct parallel to 2 Cor 9:6. The former reads: "There are some who scatter their own, and make it more; and there are some also who gather, yet have less."[20] But then LXX Prov 11:25a continues: *Psychē eulogoumenē pasa haplē* ("Blessed is every sincere soul"). The participle *eulogoumenē* echoes the "blessing" terminology in 2 Cor 9:5–6. Even more striking is the occurrence of the adjective *haplē*. The related substantive *haplotēs* is an important term in 2 Corinthians, especially in the collection discourse (see 1:12; 8:2; 9:11, 13; 11:3).[21] The opposite of *dipsychia* ("double-mindedness"), *haplotēs* connotes singleness of mind and purpose. Its meaning can also shade into "sincerity" as well as "open-heartedness" and thus "generosity." As we will see, Paul desires that the Corinthians keep their eyes and hearts fixed on God's loving provision for them so that they can emulate the divine generosity with confidence. Lastly, LXX Prov 11:26 comments: "May he that hoards corn leave it to the nation: but blessing (*eulogia*) be on the head of him that gives it."[22] Notice how the context of the allusion to Prov 11:24 bolsters the warn-

---

18. See, e.g., Margaret E. Thrall, *The Second Epistle to the Corinthians* (2 vols.; ICC; Edinburgh: T &T Clark, 1994–2000), 2:575.

19. Alfred Ralphs's edition of the LXX (*Septuaginta* [Stuttgart: Deutsche Bibelgesellschaft, 1979]) suggests that the allusion is to Prov 11:24.

20. Lancelot C. L. Brenton, *The Septuagint Version: Greek and English* (Grand Rapids: Zondervan, 1970).

21. These represent five of the eight occurrences of the term in the New Testament (see also Rom 12:8; Eph 6:5; and Col 3:22).

22. Brenton's translation.

ing against hoarding and amplifies the theme of blessing, which Paul takes up again in 2 Cor 9:8 (see further).

Paul follows up the sowing/reaping maxim by advising the Corinthians, "Each one should give as [he has determined] in his heart, not from regret or from compulsion" (2 Cor 9:7a).[23] He then reinforces his advice not to give reluctantly with an allusion to LXX Prov 22:8a: "For 'God loves a cheerful giver'" (2 Cor 9:7b). Paul slightly modifies the scriptural text:

LXX Prov 22:8a—*andra hilaron kai dotēn eulogei ho theos*
2 Cor 9:7b—*hilaron gar dotēn agapai ho theos*

The most significant alteration involves the change of the verb from *eulogeō* ("bless") to *agapaō* ("love"). At first glance, the alteration is surprising, given the blessing terminology in 2 Cor 9:5–6; that is, the LXX's formulation would seem to offer the perfect reinforcement for his advice.

While it is possible that Paul follows a Greek version of Prov 22:8a no longer available to us, most commentators think that he deliberately changed the verb. But why? Indeed, there are potential problems with emphasizing God's love for cheerful givers. Doesn't God love everyone, including sinners (cf. Rom 5:8)? And doesn't Paul undermine his exhortation to the Corinthians to give generously out of pure motivation by suggesting the winning of God's love? Dieter Georgi, in my opinion, offers the most cogent explanation of the apostle's use of *agapaō*. He argues that Paul refers here to divine love as the source of human love: "When Paul speaks of God's love elsewhere, he refers primarily to the kind of love that brings about salvation and was made apparent in the crucifixion. Hence, God's love would have to be, not the consequence, but rather the origin—indeed, the very ground—from which human charity evolves."[24] Georgi's interpretation has been

---

23. LXX Deut 15:10 may very well be in the background here: "You shall surely give to him, and you shall lend him as much as he wants, according as he is in need; *and you shall not grudge in your heart* as you give to him" (Brenton's translation, slightly modified, emphasis added).

24. Georgi, *Remembering the Poor*, 96.

criticized for being "too elaborate" and for importing theological and christological meaning into the text.[25] However, I contend that his reading appropriately "blends the juices" of the sap from Prov 22 with the sap from what Paul himself has previously set forth. In 2 Cor 8:8–9, he juxtaposed the notions of the genuineness (*gnēsios*) of the Corinthians' love with "the grace of our Lord Jesus Christ," thereby suggesting a linkage between their love and the love revealed in the Christ event. It is little wonder he will juxtapose, in the final benediction, "the grace of the Lord Jesus Christ and the love of God" (13:14).[26]

The broader context of LXX Prov 22:8a also reverberates with themes that echo Paul's line of thought. The preceding couplet is another instance of the sowing/reaping maxim: "The one who sows bad things will reap evil" (LXX 22:8). What follows immediately is encouragement to be merciful and generous: "He that has pity on the poor shall himself be maintained; for he has given of his own bread to the poor. He that gives liberally secures victory and honor" (LXX 22:9–9a).[27] A few lines later, we read, "The Lord loves (*agapai*) holy hearts" (LXX 22:11), which may explain the connection with *agapē* that Paul makes with Prov 22. Once again, the theological harmonics sound forth more richly when one takes into account the broader context of the alluded to passage.

CITATION OF LXX PSALM 111:9 IN 2 CORINTHIANS 9:9

After encouraging the Corinthians to contribute liberally, freely, and cheerfully (2 Cor 9:6–7), Paul reminds them of God's capacity to supply for their generosity: "God is able to provide you abundantly with every blessing in order that, always having enough in all things, you may share abundantly in every good work" (9:8). He then cites

---

25. E.g., Thrall, *Second Epistle to the Corinthians*, 2:577.

26. Cf. 2 Cor 5:14: "The love of Christ impels us...."

27. Brenton's translation (spelling modifed).

LXX Ps 111:9:[28] "As it is written, 'He dispersed, he gave to the poor; his righteousness remains forever'" (2 Cor 9:9). Paul cites the text almost verbatim: *eskorpisen, edōken tois penēsin, hē dikaiosynē autou menei eis ton aiōna.*[29]

What is the apostle's reason for citing LXX Ps 111:9? The answer to this question depends on determining who is intended as the grammatical antecedent of the pronouns "he" and "his." On the one hand, many factors point to God as the antecedent. God is the explicit subject of the allusion to LXX Prov 22:8a in 2 Cor 9:7 and of the main clause in 9:8. God is also the implicit subject of the following verse (9:10). Since Paul offers no indication of a change in subject, God would seem to be the implied subject in 9:9. The actions described in LXX Ps 111:9 ("He dispersed, he gave to the poor") are similar to the actions attributed to God in 2 Cor 9:10 ("He who supplies seed to the sower…will supply and multiply"). Furthermore, the statement concerning a righteousness that remains forever seems most appropriate as a description of divine righteousness (cf. LXX Ps 110:3). Thus some commentators interpret Paul's citation of LXX Ps 111:9 as providing scriptural support for the divine provision described in 2 Cor 9:8.[30]

On the other hand, the "he" in LXX Ps 111 is a "man" (*anēr*; 111:1). More precisely, the subject of this psalm is the righteous person who fears and trusts in the Lord, and who is generous in giving alms to those in need. While God is the subject of the main clause in 2 Cor 9:8, the subordinate clause—which immediately precedes Paul's citation of LXX Ps 111:9—has as its subject the plural "you," referring to the Corinthians. Moreover, at the end of 2 Cor 9:10, Paul refers explicitly to the Corinthians' righteousness. Thus other commentators, indeed the majority of them, interpret Paul's use of the psalm "to substantiate from Scripture his assurance in verse 8 that his readers will always be sufficiently supplied with the wherewithal for their own almsgiving: Scripture itself speaks of the man whose benef-

---

28. LXX Ps 111:9 = Ps 112:9 in the MT and English translations.

29. Paul omits the final phrase *tou aiōnos* from LXX Ps 111:9.

30. E.g., Betz, *2 Corinthians 8 and 9*, 111–14.

icence to the poor is perpetual."[31] The "he" in 9:9, on this reading, seems to refer to the ideal Corinthian giver.

Before adjudicating the issue, it is important to appreciate that LXX Pss 110–111 function together as, in effect, a literary diptych.[32] One "panel" sings the praise of God (LXX Ps 110), while the other blesses the ideal righteous person (LXX Ps 111). The "hinge" between these panels is the statement in 110:10 that "the fear of the Lord is the beginning of wisdom," which is followed immediately by the macarism "blessed is the man who fears the Lord" (111:1). There are a number of parallels in these psalms. Both God and the God-fearing man are characterized by mercy and compassion (110:4; 111:4). Both are generous in providing for those in need (110:5; 111:5, 9). And the righteousness of both remains forever (110:3; 111:3, 9). Noting "the peculiar bond" between these psalms and "the deliberate vagueness" with which Paul employs the citation of LXX Ps 111:9, Georgi interprets the apostle's meaning thus: "God is the true origin of human compassion and…his righteousness is the true source of our righteousness."[33]

Georgi's suggestion of a linkage between divine and human characteristics puts us on the right track. Such interplay, suggested by the diptych of LXX Pss 110–111, also finds an echo in Paul's collection discourse. As David I. Starling points out, 2 Cor 8–9 has a similar "interplay between the different senses and referents of *charis*, a word that is thematic for the whole section."[34] Indeed, the term *charis* appears ten times in the collection discourse, but with different nuances of meaning: God's grace (i.e., the outpouring of God's love—2 Cor 8:1; 9:14); the "gracious act" of Christ, through which God's grace is preeminently expressed (8:9); the "favor" of participating in the collection (8:4); the collection itself (8:6, 7, 19); the material blessings God provides for the Corinthians' generosity (9:8); and thanksgiving rendered to God (8:16; 9:15). In light of the Christ event, Paul

---

31. Thrall, *Second Epistle to the Corinthians*, 2:582.

32. LXX Pss 110–111 = Pss 111–112 in the MT and English translations.

33. Georgi, *Remembering the Poor*, 99.

34. David I. Starling, "Meditations on a Slippery Citation: Paul's Use of Psalm 112:9 in 2 Corinthians 9:9," *JTI* 6 (2012): 248.

suggests a vigorous synergism between God's *charis* and human *charis*. In doing so, he invites the Corinthians "not just to imitate God's dynamic of grace toward the world but to embody it, to continue and extend it in their own giving to meet the needs of others."[35]

Blending the juices of the sap of LXX Pss 110—111 with that of Paul's treatment of *charis* in the collection discourse gives flavor to his understanding of the relationship between God's righteousness and human righteousness. Recall that the clause "His righteousness remains forever" pertains both to God (110:3) and to the God-fearing generous person (111:3, 9). The ambiguity of reference in 2 Cor 9:9, I submit, suggests that both are in the background for Paul. Human beings can participate in and imitate God's righteousness and generosity—that is, God's self-giving love as revealed by Jesus—because they are empowered by God to participate in these characteristics. In fact, earlier in the letter, Paul states that, in Christ, it is now possible that "we might become the righteousness of God" (5:21).[36] By trusting in God's loving provision of material blessings and by imitating the divine generosity, the Corinthians' righteousness—expressed in their generosity in the collection—will be increased (9:10). This is what the apostle's citation of LXX Ps 111:9 reinforces.

The references to *dikaiosynē* ("righteousness") in 2 Cor 9:9–10 also connect with what Paul says earlier in the letter about his role as a minister of the new covenant (3:6). He describes the new covenant ministry as "the ministry of the Spirit" (*hē diakonia tou pneumatos*; 3:8) and as "the ministry of righteousness" (*hē diakonia tēs dikaiosynēs*; 3:9). The Spirit-empowered ministry is one through which God's righteousness continues to be embodied and enacted. This ministry is particularly manifested as "the ministry of reconciliation" (*hē diakonia tēs katallagēs*; 5:18), which is a sign of the "new creation" (5:17). The fact that Paul now refers to the collection as a *diakonia*—more precisely, as "the ministry for the holy ones" (*hē diakonia hē eis tous*

---

35. Ibid., 249.

36. Starling (ibid., 249–53) correctly makes this connection. See also Thomas D. Stegman, "Paul's Use of *Dikaio*-Terminology: Moving Beyond N. T. Wright's Forensic Interpretation," *TS* 72 (2011): 500–4.

hagious; 8:4 and 9:1)—is suggestive. The collection taken from the (mostly) Gentile churches for the members of the Jerusalem church is, to be sure, a response to real socioeconomic need. But is it also, and more fundamentally, a concrete expression of the ministry of reconciliation that seeks to bring about unity and solidarity in God's people? The final scriptural allusion to be analyzed will intimate such is the case.

ALLUSION TO LXX ISAIAH 55:10 IN 2 CORINTHIANS 9:10

Paul brings the line of thought begun in 2 Cor 9:6 to a conclusion in 9:10. In this verse he repeats and expands on the point made in 9:8 about God's generous provision, and resumes from 9:6 the use of the sowing/reaping metaphor: "He who supplies 'seed to the sower and bread for eating' will supply and multiply your seed and increase the harvest of your righteousness." That is, Paul reinforces to the Corinthians his conviction that God, now portrayed as the sower, can and will continue to provide them with abundant "seed"—a reference to material blessings—so that they are equipped to be generous in their contribution to the collection. Their generosity will represent a "harvest of righteousness" enabled by God's generous "sowing."

Second Corinthians 9:10 contains two scriptural allusions. The phrase "the harvest of your righteousness" (*ta genēmata tēs dikaiosynēs hymōn*) echoes a formulation found in LXX Hos 10:12.[37] It is particularly apt for Paul because of the harvest metaphor and the reference to "righteousness," which bolsters the point made in 2 Cor 9:9. For our purposes, I limit my focus here to the expression "seed to the sower and bread for eating" (*sporon tōi speironti kai arton eis brōsin*), an allusion to LXX Isa 55:10.[38] The words to which Paul alludes occur in a

---

37. LXX Hos 10:12 reads: "Sow to yourselves for righteousness, gather in for the fruit of life: light for yourselves the light of knowledge; seek the Lord till the fruits of righteousness (*genēmata dikaiosynēs hymin*) come upon you" (Brenton's translation, slightly modified).

38. Paul's change of *sperma* ("seed"; LXX Isa 55:10) to *sporon* is not significant; the terms are synonymous.

passage in which Isaiah compares the power and efficacy of God's word to the life-giving effects of rain and snow. Just as the latter fall from the heavens and do not return there until they have watered the earth and, in doing so, enable it to bring forth vegetation and grain—"giving seed to the sower and bread for food"—so God's word does not return to him without accomplishing its purpose (55:10–11). Paul employs the allusion as scriptural warrant for three important claims: (1) God has provided and will continue to provide material blessing upon the Corinthians; (2) such blessing has a divine purpose: it should be shared generously with those in need; and (3) the collection is ultimately God's work.

Does Paul also intend to allude to the broader context of Isa 55:10? Although some commentators look to the entirety of Isa 55 (esp. vv. 1–7) in their interpretation,[39] I submit that it is more fruitful exegetically to look at what follows the line to which he alludes. It is striking to observe that, four verses later, the prophet exhorts on behalf of God, "Do [in the sense of enact] righteousness" (*poiēsate dikaiosynēn*; LXX 56:1), an exhortation that fits perfectly within Paul's discourse. More relevant is the content that follows, where the prophet speaks of "foreigners" (*allogenes*) who become part of God's people (56:3, 6), who join themselves to God and minister to him as servants (56:6). Moreover, God will bring these foreigners to his holy mountain and gladden them in his house of prayer. Their offerings will be acceptable to God, whose house is to be called "a house of prayer for all the nations" (56:7).

Thus, what the passage following the allusion to LXX Isa 55:10 describes is the coming together of Jews and Gentiles—two traditional rivals—into God's people. This description of the joining of Gentiles with Jews as one people resonates in the background at the climax of the collection discourse. While not employing the language of reconciliation per se, David J. Downs's assessment of the collection is on target: "'The offering of the Gentiles' (Rom 15:16) served an important ecumenical purpose. This gift, according to Paul, symbolized the unity of Jews and Gentiles under the one gospel of

---

39. Georgi, *Remembering the Poor*, 99–102.

Jesus Christ."[40] Given Paul's concern for reconciliation and unity throughout 2 Corinthians (e.g., 2:5–11; 5:18—6:2; 6:11–13; 7:2–4)— a major ramification of God's having reconciled the world to himself through Christ (5:18–19)—it should come as no surprise that these themes would reemerge in the collection discourse. And it is surely no coincidence that the letter to the Romans, which Paul dictates from Corinth shortly after writing 2 Corinthians, emphasizes the unity and solidarity of Jews and Gentiles, now reconciled together into the body of Christ (see, e.g., Rom 3:28–30; 10:8–13; 12:1—15:13, esp. 15:7–13; cf. Eph 2:11–22).

That Paul intends the allusion to LXX Isa 55:10 to echo the portrayal of "foreigners" joining God and God's people (56:1–8) is strengthened by one final observation. The Isaian passage climaxes with references to prayer and to sacrifices in God's temple, which is to be a house of prayer for all. Similarly, Paul concludes the collection discourse (2 Cor 9:11–15) with images of worship and prayer. The Corinthians' generosity to the Jerusalem church will glorify God (9:13), as well as lead to the Jerusalemites' giving thanks to God (9:11–12, 15) and praying for the Corinthians (9:14). Paul views the collection—with the subsequent praise of God and the mutuality of support (including prayer) between Jews and Gentiles who are in Christ—as the embodiment of Isaiah's vision, now seen through the prism of reconciliation and unity. Here is another case where the blending of intertextual juices leads to fuller theological understanding.

CONCLUSION

Paul's use of Scripture in the collection discourse is subtle and complex. On the surface level, his citations of Exod 16:18 and Isa 55:10 and allusions to texts from Proverbs and Psalms function to convince the Corinthians of God's abundant provision for them, and to exhort them to be generous in giving to the collection. But when one digs deeper, several themes and images emerge that add texture to

---

40. Downs, *Offering of the Gentiles*, 161.

Paul's exhortative strategy. Careful attention to the ways he alters texts and appeals to their broader contexts reveals that he taps into theological themes that are prominent not only in 2 Cor 8—9 but also throughout the whole letter: the manifestation of God's glory, single-hearted commitment to God's ways, participation in and embodiment of God's righteousness, and the enactment of reconciliation and unity. Paul draws both from the sap of the texts he echoes and from the sap of the Christ event to create a rich theological mixture. In doing so, the apostle "achieves the effect of drawing an attentive reading community into a transformative intertextual meditation on themes that are at the heart of the letter."[41]

---

41. Starling, "Meditations on a Slippery Citation," 254, referring to 2 Cor 9:9. This description is apt for Paul's use of Scripture throughout the collection discourse.

11

Reading with Double Vision

Isaiah and the Gospel of Mark

John R. Donahue, SJ

(EMERITUS, ST. MARY'S SEMINARY
AND UNIVERSITY)

Charting the influence of the Old Testament in the New has been a major focus in biblical studies in recent decades, and has enriched our knowledge of the Jewish Scriptures and their importance for sounding the depth of first-century Judaism and the literature of emerging Christianity. A major area within the larger field of New Testament studies is the relation and influence of the Jewish Scriptures on the New Testament, which has moved beyond the traditional emphases on explicit and implicit citations to a study of the ongoing influence of traditions and themes. Throughout his multiple and diverse publications, Daniel Harrington has been a leader in the study of the "rewritten Bible"[1] and in the study of the Gospels. This essay will attempt to highlight ways in which the Gospel of Mark has taken up themes and texts from the Book of Isaiah, including an overview of the massive exegetical puzzle of Mark 4:10–12, with special emphasis on

---

1. For example, Daniel J. Harrington, "Abraham Traditions in the Testament of Abraham and in the 'Rewritten Bible' of the Intertestamental Period," in *Studies on the Testament of Abraham* (ed. G. W. E. Nickelsburg; Missoula, MT: Scholars Press, 1976), 165–71; and idem, "Palestinian Adaptations of Biblical Narratives and Prophecies: The Bible Rewritten (Narratives)," in *Early Judaism and Its Modern Interpreters* (ed. R. A. Kraft and G. W. E. Nickelsburg; Philadelphia: Fortress, 1986), 239–47.

its use of Isa 6:9–10.[2] My purpose is to provide resources for continued reflection rather than to enter into detailed discussion or to attempt any new solutions.

Craig Evans, a recognized leader in the area of the presence of Old Testament references in the New Testament, has noted more than four hundred instances "where the New Testament either quotes, paraphrases, alludes to, or echoes passages from the Book of Isaiah."[3] In his thorough and comprehensive study of the influence of the Old Testament upon the New Testament, Rikki Watts finds sixty-nine Old Testament references in Mark and notes that among the prophets "Isaiah is particularly influential," with nineteen references (which equal the number of references to the Torah).[4]

Of particular importance are the first words of Mark's Gospel:

The beginning of the good news of Jesus Christ, the Son of God.

As it is written in the prophet Isaiah,
"See, I am sending my messenger ahead of you [Exod 23:20],
    who will prepare your way [Mal 3:1];
the voice of one crying out in the wilderness:
    'Prepare the way of the Lord,
    make his paths straight'" [Isa 40:3]. (Mark 1:1–3)

---

2. The choice of the topic is also to acknowledge the significant studies of Richard Clifford on the Book of Isaiah. For example, Richard J. Clifford, *Fair Spoken and Persuading: An Interpretation of Second Isaiah* (New York: Paulist, 1984); and idem, "The Unity of the Book of Isaiah and Its Cosmogonic Language," *CBQ* 55 (1993): 1–17.

3. Craig A. Evans, "From Gospel to Gospel: The Function of Isaiah in the New Testament," in *Writing and Reading the Scroll of Isaiah: Studies of an Interpretive Tradition* (ed. C. C. Broyles and C. A. Evans; 2 vols.; VTSup 70; Leiden: Brill, 1997), 2:651.

4. Rikki Watts, "Mark," in *Commentary on the New Testament Use of the Old Testament* (ed. G. K. Beale and D. A. Carson; Grand Rapids: Baker Academic, 2007), 111. See also Morna Hooker, "Isaiah in Mark's Gospel," in *Isaiah in the New Testament* (ed. S. Moyise and M. J. J. Menken; New Testament and the Scriptures of Israel; London: T & T Clark, 2005), 35–49. Hooker notes that in "the overall pattern of citations in Mark's gospel, it would seem significant that more are drawn from Isaiah than from any other book" (49).

This concise introduction foreshadows many of the most important themes of Mark. Morna Hooker has noted that these verses are "the equivalent of all the 'fulfillment quotations' in Matthew put together."[5] Mark's is the only Gospel that explicitly calls itself "good news" (*euangelion*). The initial description of the work as the *archē* is both significant and ambiguous. If a period is placed after "Son of God," 1:1 is a kind of title or *incipit* to the whole work. But if a comma is placed after "Son of God," the beginning refers to the fulfillment of the prophecy quoted in 1:2–3 so that the origin of the Gospel is rooted in Isaiah ("The beginning…as it is written…").[6]

The attribution of the good news to Isaiah characterizes not only the beginning of Mark, for echoes of Isaiah permeate the Gospel.[7] One finds numerous citations and allusions to Isa 40–66 in Mark's prologue (1:1–15): the voice in the wilderness at 1:3 (see Isa 40:3), the herald proclaiming the joyful news of God's coming in strength at 1:7 and 14 (see Isa 40:9–10), the opening of the heavens at 1:10 (see Isa 64:1), the use of *katabainein* to describe the descent of the Spirit at 1:10 (see Isa 63:10), and the Servant in whom God delights at 1:11 (see Isa 42:1). Equally important are the thematic similarities between Isa 40–66 and the Gospel of Mark. Both begin with the voice in the wilderness, both promise a new manifestation of divine rule, and both look to the inclusion of Gentiles (or the nations) in God's saving plan (see Isa 42:1, 6; 43:9; 49:6; 52:10; 55:5; 56:7 [= Mark 11:17]; 66:18). Moreover, both portray a prophetic figure who suffers and is rejected by his own people (Isa 52:13–53:12; Mark 8:31; 9:31; 10:33–34). There are also structural similarities. Second Isaiah (chs. 40–55) begins with the voice of promise in the wilderness and ends with "nations that you do not know" running to join God's people (55:4–5),

---

5. Hooker, "Isaiah in Mark's Gospel," 35.

6. See John R. Donahue and Daniel J. Harrington, *The Gospel of Mark* (SP 2; Collegeville, MN: Liturgical Press, 2002), 59–61.

7. As Hooker notes ("Isaiah in Mark's Gospel," 49), "Readers of Mark may well discover that the story he tells is one that is as 'written in Isaiah the prophet' in more ways than Mark himself ever imagined."

while Mark begins with the voice in the wilderness (1:3) and ends with the confession of the Gentile centurion (15:39).[8]

Along with a multitude of allusions, Mark has eight explicit quotations from Isaiah: 1:2–3 (Isa 40:3); 4:12 (Isa 6:9–10); 7:6–7 (Isa 29:13); 9:48 (Isa 66:24); 11:17 (Isa 56:7); 12:32 (Isa 45:21); 13:24 (Isa 13:10); and 13:25 (Isa 34:4).[9] Paramount among these is the inaugural quotation in Mark 1:2–3. Though attributed to Isaiah, the quotation is really a conflation of Exod 23:20; Mal 3:1; and Isa 40:3. Some have suggested that this situation is evidence of the use of a pre-Markan *testimonia* or collection of Old Testament texts assembled with reference to the Christ event. But as Joel Marcus notes, this theory "would be more convincing if the citation from Isaiah *preceded* the conflation," though he still admits that the texts may have been combined prior to Mark.[10] In Mark, however, they sound the themes of the rest of the prologue, which progresses "from God's promise to Jesus to send a messenger before him (1:2b), to a description of the messenger as a voice crying in the wilderness (1:3a), to a summary of his message which consists of two parallel imperative clauses (1:3b)"[11]—"prepare the way" and "make his paths straight." Whatever the origin of the conflation, the texts are united by reference to the "way."

The most important aspect of Mark 1:2–3 is the attribution of the whole conflation to Isaiah. Mark in effect says that the whole good news to be proclaimed and enacted by Jesus is ultimately rooted in the prophet Isaiah. In Isaiah as a whole, and in Mark, the different connotations of the term "way" (*hodos*) are of special importance. It can mean "a way for traveling or moving from one place to another" or "the action of traveling," but also "a course of behavior, a way of life."[12] This double sense appears especially throughout Isaiah as a descrip-

---

8. Donahue and Harrington, *Gospel of Mark*, 449.

9. See Hooker, "Isaiah in Mark's Gospel," 35; and Sharyn Dowd, "Reading Mark Reading Isaiah," *LTQ* 30 (1995): 133.

10. Joel Marcus, *Mark 1—8: A New Translation with Introduction and Commentary* (AB 27: New York: Doubleday, 2000), 145, emphasis original.

11. Ibid.

12. BDAG, 691.

tion of behavior (2:6; 8:11; 26:7; 30:11, 21; 40:14; 48:17; 49:9; 59:8), and in Second Isaiah more frequently for the path by which God will bring the people back from exile (40:3; 42:16; 43:16, 19; 49:11; 51:10).[13] It is also central to Mark, who captures the double meaning of "way" as a "path" or "journey" (2:23; 4:4, 15; 6:8; 8:3; 10:17; 10:46), as well as the way of true discipleship (8:27; 9:33–34; 10:32; 10:52; 11:8; 12:14).[14]

Language associated with "preparing the way" and "making paths straight" (with the nuance of walking according to the way) in Isaiah has overtones of exhortations to faithful observance of God's word and to conversion or return to the proper way when the people have strayed. Both overtones of exhortation foreshadow the demands, challenges, and failures of discipleship in Mark. Walter Brueggemann compares the Book of Isaiah to "a mighty oratorio whereby Israel sings its story of faith."[15] In contrapuntal fashion, Isaiah alternates harsh oracles indicting the sinful ways of the people and threats of judgment with oracles of mercy and hope often couched in the language of following or walking in God's ways. For example,

> O house of Jacob,
>   come, *let us walk*
>   in the light of the LORD!
> For you have forsaken *the ways* of your people. (2:5–6)

In addition, after speaking of fear and disobedience as precipitating the oncoming assault of Assyria, the Lord speaks to the prophet "while his hand was strong upon me, and warned me not to walk in *the way* of this people" (8:11). The language of "way" and "walk" appears again, now in an oracle of hope:

---

13. Joseph Blenkinsopp, *Opening the Sealed Book: Interpretations of the Book of Isaiah in Late Antiquity* (Grand Rapids: Eerdmans, 2006), 179–82.

14. Dennis Duling, "Interpreting the Markan Hodology," *Nexus* 17 (1974): 2–11.

15. Walter Brueggemann, *Isaiah* (2 vols.; Westminster Bible Companion; Louisville: Westminster John Knox, 1998), 1:1.

In the latter time he will make glorious *the way* of the sea,
the land beyond the Jordan, Galilee of the nations.
The people *who walked* in darkness
   have seen a great light;
those who lived in a land of deep darkness—
   on them light has shined. (9:1–2)

The theology of "the way" is summed up in the oracle of 26:7–8:

The way of the righteous is level;
   O Just One, you make smooth the path of the righteous.
In the path of your judgments,
   O LORD, we wait for you;
your name and your renown
   are the soul's desire.

After the people have returned from exile, the call of the Holy One of Israel continues:

I am the LORD your God,
   who teaches you for your own good,
   who leads you in the way you should go. (48:17)

Yet the negative nuance of "the way" reappears:

The way of peace they do not know,
   and there is no justice in their paths.
Their roads they have made crooked;
   no one who walks in them knows peace.

Therefore justice is far from us,
   and righteousness does not reach us;
we wait for light, and lo! there is darkness;
   and for brightness, but we walk in gloom. (59:8–9)

The initial call of the "voice in the wilderness" in Mark 1:2–3 is rooted deeply in Isaiah's dialectical use of "way"; indeed, this usage provides the framework for the use of Isaiah in Mark. Hooker notes that when John appears in 1:4, "he prepares the way of the Lord by proclaiming a baptism of repentance for the forgiveness of sins" so that:

> God offers the forgiveness of sins to those who repent…. Nevertheless, the promised forgiveness requires repentance. The fact that Mark's account of the ministry of Jesus begins, in 1:14, with the words "After John had been handed over," indicates straight away that not everyone has welcomed his proclamation, and that the coming of the Lord will inevitably mean judgment, as well as salvation.[16]

I would add that the initial proclamation of Jesus, "The time is fulfilled, and the kingdom of God has come near; repent, and believe in the good news" (Mark 1:15), contains the familiar dialectic of promise and demand, and anticipates the alternation of rejection of Jesus and his continued reaching out to people.

All of Mark's explicit citations of Isaiah appear in settings of threat or criticism. The most dramatic use of Isaiah as a warning or threat occurs in Mark 4:10–12, after the parable of the sower. Apart from the crowd, Jesus addresses "those who were around him along with the twelve":

> To you has been given the secret (*mystērion*) of the kingdom of God, but for those outside, everything comes in parables; in order that (*hina*)
> "they may indeed look, but not perceive,
>   and may indeed listen, but not understand;
> so that they may not (*mēpote*) turn again and be forgiven."
> (4:11–12, citing Isa 6:9–10)

Winston Churchill's description of the Soviet Union in 1939 as "a riddle, wrapped in a mystery, inside an enigma" might well describe this text! More reflection and research has perhaps been devoted to this saying and its background in Isaiah than to any other saying of Jesus in the

---

16. Hooker, "Isaiah in Mark's Gospel," 38.

New Testament.[17] As a prelude to further engagement, some observations on the original context and use of Isa 6:9–10 may be helpful.

ISAIAH 6:9–10 IN CONTEXT

Unlike other prophetic books, Isaiah does not begin with the call or commission of the prophet, but presents a series of bitter indictments of Israel and Judah (1:1 – 5:30), with the call of Isaiah appearing only in 6:1–13. The people as a whole are described at the outset as

Ah, sinful nation,
>   people laden with iniquity,
offspring who do evil,
>   children who deal corruptly,
who have forsaken the LORD,
>   who have despised the Holy One of Israel,
>   who are utterly estranged! (1:4)

Their worship is but a sham (1:10–15). But in a dialectical pattern that characterizes the whole work, accusation and judgment are followed by a call for conversion leading to forgiveness:

Wash yourselves; make yourselves clean;
>   remove the evil of your doings
>   from before my eyes;
cease to do evil,
>   learn to do good;

---

17. A selection, with emphasis on recent works, includes: Mary Ann Beavis, *Mark's Audience: The Literary and Social Setting of Mark 4.11–12* (JSNTSup 33; Sheffield: JSOT Press, 1989); eadem, "Mark's Parables of the Kingdom (Mark 4:1–34)," in *The Challenge of Jesus' Parables* (ed. R. N. Longenecker; MacMaster New Testament Studies; Grand Rapids: Eerdmans, 2000), 79–101; Donald E. Hartley, *The Wisdom Background and Parabolic Implications of Isaiah 6:9–10 in the Synoptics* (Studies in Biblical Literature 100; New York: Lang, 2006); Rikki Watts, "Mark," 150–54 (with massive bibliography); and Hiroaki Yoshimura, *Did Jesus Cite Isa 6:9–10? Jesus' Saying in Mark 4:11–12, and the Isaianic Idea of Hardening and Remnant* (Åbo: Åbo Akademi University Press, 2010). The standard commentaries also discuss these difficult verses; see below on those of Marcus, Beavis, Adela Yarbro Collins, and Clifton Black.

seek justice,
   rescue the oppressed,
defend the orphan,
   plead for the widow. (1:16–17)

After these exhortations comes the following message:

Though your sins are like scarlet,
   they shall be like snow;
though they are red like crimson,
   they shall become like wool.
If you are willing and obedient,
   you shall eat the good of the land. (1:18–19a)

The charges, however, escalate in the following chapters:

Their land is filled with idols (2:8);

For Jerusalem has stumbled
   and Judah has fallen,
because their speech and their deeds are against the LORD,
   defying his glorious presence (3:8);

and

The vineyard of the LORD of hosts
   is the house of Israel,
and the people of Judah
   are his pleasant planting;
he expected justice,
   but saw bloodshed;
righteousness,
   but heard a cry! (5:7)

Yet amid such denunciations and threats occur words of hope (2:1–5, 20–22; 4:2–6).

Though other prophetic writings begin with the call/commission of a prophet, the encounter between "the voice of the Lord" and Isaiah occurs only in 6:1–13. Following the massive oracles of judgment in Isa 1–5, "the main function of chap. 6 is to set the prophet apart from the people in clear fashion (6:7) and reveal to the reader the content of his commission, in all its historical breadth and theological force (6:11–13)."[18] Upon receiving the vision of the heavenly court—which underscores one of the major themes of Isaiah, the holiness and transcendence of God— the prophet exclaims: "Woe is me! I am lost, for I am a man of unclean lips, and I live among a people of unclean lips" (6:5). Only after under- going a symbolic purification so that "your guilt has departed and your sin is blotted out" (6:7) does Isaiah accept the Lord's commission:

> Go and say to this people:
> "Keep listening, but do not comprehend;
> keep looking, but do not understand."
>> Make the mind of this people dull,
>> and stop their ears,
>> and shut their eyes,
> so that they may not look with their eyes,
>> and listen with their ears,
> and comprehend with their minds,
>> and turn and be healed. (6:9–10)

These verses are the fountainhead of traditions of interpreta- tions, ancient and modern, and the source of the challenge of Mark 4:10–12. Evans argues that, in Isaiah, "the prophet's word was a harsh word of judgment intended to promote obduracy and to make the people ripe for judgment."[19] The judgment will bring about desola- tion and loss, but "even if a tenth part remains in it" like the stump of a fallen tree, it will become "the holy seed" (6:13). Evans notes that the linkage of these two ideas, destruction and remnant, "mirrors the theology of Isaiah in its canonical whole"; in fact, "whereas First Isaiah speaks mainly of judgment....Second and Third Isaiah offer consolation and hope, reminding Israel of God's love and faithful-

---

18. Christopher Seitz, "Isaiah, Book of (First Isaiah)," *ABD* 3:479.

19. Craig A. Evans, *To See and Not Perceive: Isaiah 6.9–10 in Early Jewish and Christian Interpretation* (JSOTSup 64; Sheffield, UK: JSOT Press, 1989), 163.

ness."[20] Torsten Uhlig also addresses the question of the hardening of Israel and notes that it permeates the rest of Isa 1—39, and lasts until "the audience of Isa 40—55 and Isa 56—66 is addressed in their specific situations....But now their hardness can be overcome when they listen to the voice of the servant (Isa 50:10) and to the proclamation of the prophet (Isa 57:14; 58:1—59:18)."[21] Through the theme of hardening and reversal, "the prophetic book serves to form the new people of Judah and Jerusalem."[22] Too often, however, discussions of Isa 6:9–10 in Mark have not attended enough to the context of the quotation in Isaiah or to the larger context of the dialectic between judgment and forgiveness, blindness and enlightenment, that characterizes the Book of Isaiah as a whole.

INTERPRETATION OF MARK 4:10–12 IN RECENT COMMENTARIES

The main focus of the discussion on Mark 4:10–12 has been on the meaning of "in order that" and "so that they may not," since ostensibly the purpose of Jesus' speaking in parables is to create blindness and deafness, which would rule out conversion and forgiveness. A phalanx of solutions confront the reader, ranging from suggestions about the Aramaic substratum to Jesus' words to multiple interpretations of *hina* (e.g., interpreting it as "because" [see Matt 13:13]; or as a result rather than the purpose of parabolic teaching; or as a code word for the fulfillment of Scripture).[23] Nevertheless, the notion of purposeful use, where the function of Jesus' parabolic teaching is

---

20. Ibid.

21. Torsten Uhlig, "Too Hard to Understand? The Motif of Hardening in Isaiah," in *Interpreting Isaiah: Issues and Approaches* (ed. D. G. Firth and H. G. M. Williamson; Downers Grove, IL: IVP Academic, 2009), 82.

22. Ibid.

23. Joachim Jeremias, *The Parables of Jesus* (rev. ed.; New York: Scribner, 1955), 13–18. See also John R. Donahue, *The Gospel in Parable: Metaphor, Narrative and Theology in the Synoptic Gospels* (Philadelphia: Fortress, 1988), 40–42.

understood to cause blindness with all the attending problems, has emerged as the dominant interpretation.[24] This interpretation has been strengthened by Evans's thorough study of Isa 6:9–10,[25] and is accepted, albeit with modifications, in most recent commentaries.[26]

Joel Marcus, who has grappled with this pericope since publishing his dissertation in 1985,[27] addresses it most comprehensively in his commentary. While continuing to accept that the purpose of the parables is to cause blindness and deafness, he expands on this interpretation in the commentary. Initially, he stresses the divine sovereignty and inscrutability of God rooted in the Old Testament, especially in the tradition of the hardening of Pharoah's heart in Exod 7:3, 13.[28] But Isa 6:9–10 remains the foundation of Mark's view that outsiders will be prevented from receiving the mystery of the kingdom of God. This harsh view of Isaiah, however, is tempered by other sections that contain the alternation of harsh judgment and reversal; for example:

> Then the eyes of those who have sight will not be closed,
> and the ears of those who have hearing will listen.
> (Isa 32:3–4)[29]

The use of Isa 6:9–10 in the New Testament is rooted in the "perplexing rejection of the gospel by the Jewish people as a whole."[30] But the rejection theme has renewed valence during the persecution

---

24. These meanings have been covered extensively in Hartley, *Wisdom Background*, 268–81.

25. Evans, *To See and Not Perceive*.

26. Amid the number of recent commentaries, I limit my coverage to two oriented mainly to scholars, and two that mediate technical scholarship for a wider audience.

27. Joel Marcus, *The Mystery of the Kingdom of God* (SBLDS 90; Atlanta: Scholars Press, 1986). He argues that "according to 4:11b–12 the effect of parables so defined upon the outsiders is blindness, lack of understanding, and hardness of heart" (103).

28. Marcus, *Mark 1—8*, 306, 428.

29. Walter Brueggemann (*Isaiah*, 1:253) notes that Isaiah 32 follows "a series of chapters all of which begin with a woe (28:1; 29:1; 30:1; 33:1)," but "this one begins with 'See,' a dramatic summons to attention for an important announcement which is a harbinger of radical newness from God."

30. Marcus, *Mark 1—8*, 307.

of the Markan community during the violence of the Jewish War (66–70 CE).[31] During this chaotic period, Mark 4:10–12 was interpreted through an "apocalyptic determinism," to "assure the hard-pressed faithful that their suffering does not signal a loss of divine control." Markus concludes that "the hiding of truth described in our passage [Mark 4:10–12], then, in the end must serve the revelation of truth; for Mark as for Isaiah, human blindness, deafness, and condemnation will not have the last word."[32]

In the second major commentary on Mark from the last decade, Adela Yarbro Collins calls attention to a text from Qumran that may shed light on Mark's theology: "[Gaze upon the mystery] that is to come, and comprehend the birth-times of salvation, and know who is to inherit glory (= glorious immortality?) and toil."[33] She observes that the notion of "the mystery to come" in the Dead Sea Scrolls is analogous to the idea of "the mystery of the kingdom of God" in Mark 4:11, and that "the mystery of the kingdom is the divinely willed way in which the rule of God will manifest itself and come to fulfillment through the agency of Jesus."[34] Collins goes on to suggest that the passage in Isaiah, as well as that in Mark, may reflect circumstances in which many people had rejected the word proclaimed to them, and "this discouraging situation is made bearable by interpreting it in terms of an authoritative text and by accepting it as part of the divine plan."[35] She notes that the Markan "community has its own language

---

31. Ibid., 33–37. Marcus rejects the common view that the persecutions faced by the community (see Mark 10:29; 13:9–13) reflect a Roman setting, but rather places them in the inner Jewish struggles prior to the destruction of the temple. For a summary of the arguments for a Roman setting, see John R. Donahue, "Mirrors and Windows: The Setting of Mark's Gospel," *CBQ* 57 (1995): 1–26.

32. Marcus, *Mark 1–8*, 307.

33. Adela Yarbro Collins, *Mark: A Commentary* (Hermeneia; Minneapolis: Fortress, 2007), 248, citing 4Q417 2 I, 10–11, a text first published by John Strugnell and Daniel J. Harrington in *Qumran Cave 4, XXIV: 4QInstruction (Sapiential Texts), Part 2* (ed. J. Strugnell et al.; DJD 34; Oxford: Clarendon, 1999), 173, 176.

34. Collins, *Mark*, 249.

35. Ibid.

and only a member of it can speak and understand that language," and then only after a reflection on the passion and death of Jesus.[36]

Mary Ann Beavis offers a more literary proposal on the enigma of Mark 4:10–12 by noting that, ironically, those who should recognize Jesus do not do so, while marginal figures do so. Thus faith, not fear, is the key to recognition of Jesus, and "the vision imparted by faith constitutes a sort of 'apocalyptic epistemology'—a special way of knowing about the true meaning of events through divine revelation—that Markan characters display to varying degrees."[37] Beavis agrees with previous interpreters that Mark 4:10–12 speaks of a deliberate divine intention that some people should misunderstand and be impenitent, but also of "an assurance that the divine purpose will be done, despite (or even by means of) human obduracy and error" so that, although "'the word' (missionary preaching, 4:15) will not always be efficacious, it will be spectacularly successful with some hearers, and the reign of God will prevail."[38]

Clifton Black, by a combination of traditional methods and original literary criticism, finds that Mark's genius lies not in telling a story about Jesus, "but in creating conditions under which the reader may *experience* the peculiar quality of God's good news" (1:14).[39] He locates the quandary of Mark 4:10–12 in the apocalyptic horizon of Mark where mysteries are revealed only to a select few, and attributes to Mark "an epistemological predestination: those who do not understand Jesus and his ministry *cannot* understand, by God's design….As baffling as that seems, such a claim has a conceptual affinity with Exodus (9:12; 10:20; 11:10), in which the Lord hardens Pharaoh's heart against Moses' demands."[40] Similarly, in 1 Corinthians, "God's gospel of the crucified Messiah withholds understanding from those

---

36. Ibid.

37. Mary Ann Beavis, *Mark* (PCNT; Grand Rapids: Baker Academic, 2011), 23, under "Themes of Mark."

38. Ibid., 81.

39. C. Clifton Black, *Mark* (ANTC; Nashville: Abingdon, 2011), 38, emphasis original.

40. Ibid., 121, emphasis original.

who have not received God's spirit."[41] In the larger context, "while the parables in Mark 4 have a deceptive charm, there is nothing cute about them. Their accessibility lulls readers into dropping their guard just long enough to realize that the gospel of God (1:14) has invaded their world to convict them of their own blindness, deafness and spiritual sclerosis."[42]

As this somewhat cursory survey indicates, the scandal of Mark 4:10–12—where the parables of Jesus cause blindness and deafness to outsiders—is not circumvented by suggesting an Aramaic original or by claiming that *hina* has a causal significance, but rather must be faced squarely. Extensive examinations of the quotation from Isa 6:9–10 reveal a pattern of divinely willed rejection that is followed by oracles of acceptance and forgiveness by God, which bequeaths to the New Testament a way of dealing with both the rejection of the gospel message and its continuing invitation to respond through conversion or change of heart (*metanoia*).

MARK 7:6–8

The next explicit use of Isaiah in Mark occurs in the bitter conflict between Jesus and some Pharisees and scribes "who had come from Jerusalem" (7:1), precipitated by the charge that Jesus' disciples do "not live according to the tradition of the elders, but eat with defiled hands" (7:5). In his reply, Jesus immediately quotes Isa 29:13:

This people honors me with their lips,
     but their hearts are far from me;
     in vain do they worship me,
     teaching human precepts as doctrines. (Mark 7:6–7)[43]

---

41. Ibid.

42. Ibid., 131.

43. The Markan text is almost identical to the LXX (Marcus, *Mark 1–8*, 444), though 29:13b, when translated from the Hebrew, reads: "Their worship of me is a human commandment learned by rote."

Jesus applies this quotation to his questioners: "You abandon the commandment of God and hold to human tradition" (Mark 7:8). The narrative then unfolds with further attacks by Jesus on a legalism that allows for the violation of the command in the Decalogue to honor parents (Deut 5:16), and concludes with instruction that true purity entails interiority rather than ritual observance.

The explicit citation of Isaiah here continues the polemical use of Isaiah found in Mark 4:10–12. Rikki Watts notes that Isa 29:13 "belongs to that series of woe oracles (Isa 28—31) that, in building on the earlier polemics against idolatrous wisdom, constitute Isaiah's most sustained attack on the nation's rulers."[44] Isaiah 29 follows a harsh judgment on the "scoffers who rule this people in Jerusalem," who have made a "covenant with death" (28:14–15), which most likely refers to the alliance with Egypt against Sennacherib. The following chapters echo the familiar pattern in Isaiah, that judgment is followed by deliverance, and the "recurring theme" throughout "that Jerusalem's obduracy is at the behest of Yahweh, even as is Jerusalem's belated capacity for positive response to Yahweh."[45]

The polemic in Isa 29:13 follows somewhat obscure statements that, though Jerusalem "will be visited by the LORD of hosts / with thunder and earthquake and great noise, / with whirlwind and tempest, and the flame of a devouring fire," in some unknown way the city will be preserved (29:6–8). God himself will cause blindness and deep sleep to fall upon the people (29:9–12), which results in following rules and rituals of piety without a conversion of the heart.[46] Again, the paradox emerges that God causes blindness (cf. Isa 6:9–10), and yet this is a prelude to deliverance:

---

44. Watts, "Mark," 163, citing David L. Petersen, "Isaiah 28, a Redaction Critical Study," in *Society of Biblical Literature 1979 Seminar Papers* (ed. P. J. Achtemeier; 2 vols.; Missoula, MT: Scholars Press, 1979), 2:101–22. See also Marvin A. Sweeney, *Isaiah 1–4 and the Post-Exilic Understanding of the Isaianic Tradition* (BZAW 171; Berlin: de Gruyter, 1988), 56–58; and T. C. Vriezen, "Essentials of the Theology of Isaiah," in *Israel's Prophetic Heritage: Essays in Honor of James Muilenburg* (ed. B. W. Anderson and W. J. Harrelson; New York: Harper 1962), 134n9.

45. Brueggemann, *Isaiah*, 1:218, calling attention also to Isa 6:9–10.

46. Ibid., 1:234–35.

On that day the deaf shall hear
the words of a scroll,
and out of their gloom and darkness
the eyes of the blind shall see.
The meek shall obtain fresh joy in the LORD,
and the neediest people shall exult in the Holy One of
Israel. (29:18–19)

While adopting Isaiah's polemic against having hearts far from God that results in vain worship, Mark does not explicitly quote Isaiah's later statement that the deaf will hear and the blind see. But, the long instruction that concludes this pericope, that no external impurity can enter the heart in contrast to diverse evils that can proceed "from the heart" (Mark 7:17–23), echoes Isa 29:13 that the human heart can be far from God.

OTHER EXPLICIT CITATIONS OF ISAIAH

Space does not permit a close examination of the other explicit citations of Isaiah noted by both Hooker and Sharyn Dowd, but as a group they gather up negative judgments by the prophet. After Mark 7, the next citation of Isaiah occurs as part of Jesus' harsh judgment on those who scandalize the "little ones" (9:42–48), where the quotation in 9:48 of the final verse of Isaiah — "where their worm never dies, and the fire is never quenched" (66:24) — stands in stark contrast to the positive statements immediately preceding (9:38–40). When Jesus drives out buyers and sellers from the temple, and overturns the tables of money changers, he asks,

Is it not written,
"My house shall be called a house of prayer for all the
nations"?
But you have made it a den of robbers. (Mark 11:17, citing
Isa 56:7 and Jer 7:11)

186

Though Isa 56:7 is not a threat but a promise about the gathering of non-Jews in the temple, by adding Jer 7:11, Mark turns it into a threat, which elicits the plan of the Jerusalem leaders to kill Jesus (11:18).[47] In response to continued opposition, Jesus then tells a parable in which "a man planted a vineyard, put a fence around it, dug a pit for the wine press, and built a watchtower" (12:1). This is a virtual paraphrase of Isa 5, where "the vineyard of the LORD of hosts is the house of Israel," which yielded not justice and righteousness but bloodshed and a cry (see Isa 5:7). Though Mark does not follow the details of Isaiah's text, it becomes a virtual allegory of the rejection of Jesus. The vineyard workers murdered the "beloved son," and "threw him out of the vineyard" (12:6–8). Both texts begin with the care for the vineyard and end with violence, so again Isaiah is used in a context of warning or judgment. The final citations of Isaiah occur at the end of Mark's eschatological discourse, and may be part of stock references to the coming day of the Lord: "the sun will be darkened, and the moon will not give its light" (Mark 13:24, citing Isa 13:10)—again a threat of judgment.

DO MANY THREADS MAKE A TAPESTRY?

As is often noted, the term "text" comes ultimately from the Latin *texere* ("to weave"), so every text resembles an interwoven tapestry. My attempt has been to uncover various threads in Mark's Gospel that are spun out from its beginning with the words of Isaiah the prophet, a "voice…in the wilderness," summoning people to "prepare the way of the Lord, make his paths straight" (Mark 1:3, citing Isa 40:3). This proclamation is both gift and demand, and explicit citations from Isaiah capture the dialectic that runs through the whole of that work: the holiness of God is mocked by infidelity and injustice,

---

47. Hooker, "Isaiah in Mark's Gospel," 41–42. These chapters embody the familiar pattern of judgment and forgiveness. Isaiah 56 is followed by some of the most bitter judgments on Israel's infidelity (Isa 57), which itself evokes a call to conversion with a promise of forgiveness (Isa 58).

which bring about judgment and ruin (Isa 1:2–8). But this is a prelude to conversion and forgiveness:

> Cease to do evil,
>> learn to do good, seek justice....
> Though your sins are like scarlet,
>> they shall be like snow;
> though they are red like crimson,
>> they shall become like wool. (1:16–18)

Judgment upon the pattern of human deafness, blindness, and hardness of heart; upon the sham of false worship; upon oppression of the vulnerable; and upon rejection of God's continuing outreach dominates the early chapters of Isaiah. However, in the later sections, such judgment yields to a portrayal of God who announces comfort and sends his servant, "my chosen, in whom my soul delights; I have put my spirit upon him" (42:1; cf. Mark 1:10–11). This servant, who hears God's word while suffering mockery and abuse (50:5–6), "was wounded for our transgressions, crushed for our iniquities" (53:5), and "was cut off from the land of the living, stricken for the transgression of my people" (53:8); "through him the will of the LORD shall prosper" (53:10) and he will be receive "a portion with the great" (53:12).[48]

The Gospel of Mark follows the same pattern, especially when the Galilean ministry of Jesus ends. Then, not only do the opponents of Jesus have eyes that do not see (4:10–12), but also the disciples in their desire for power exhibit having ears that do not hear (8:17–18). As such, the latter are not able to hear the voice of Jesus the "servant" who, in contrast to the tyranny and overweening power of Gentile rulers, proclaims that "the Son of Man came not to be served but to serve, and to give his life a ransom for many."[49] With startling insight,

---

48. See Donahue and Harrington, *Gospel of Mark*, 315: "The allusion probably evoked other phrases from Isaiah 53: 'a man of suffering...has borne our infirmities....' Rather than being a foreign body attached to the end of Mark 10:41–45, the 'ransom' saying provides the key to the whole passage and to Mark's Gospel as a whole."

49. Whether the Suffering Servant of Isaiah is alluded to in Mark 10:45 has long been a subject of debate. An earlier consensus that Mark 10:45 alludes to Isa 53 was challenged by C. K. Barrett, "The Background of Mark 10:45," in *New Testament Essays:*

Marcus notes that "in the canonical context of Isaiah, significantly, the suffering of the Lord's Servant fits into a larger context of joyful redemption. Within Isaiah 52 — 53 itself, the sufferer is an enlightened one who illuminates others and thus reverses the sentence of blindness pronounced on the people in Isaiah 6:9–10."[50] So, too, Jesus, Son and Servant, reverses the sentence of Mark 4:10–12. Significantly, at the end of Mark's "way section" (8:22 — 10:52), Bartimaeus "regained his sight and followed him on the way," a way first proclaimed in Mark 1:2–3.[51]

Though I have centered on certain explicit quotations of Isaiah in Mark, and called attention to particular theological perspectives and themes in both works, the challenge remains to continue to read with "stereo-vision" the "Fifth Gospel"[52] and Mark's proclamation of "the good news of Jesus Christ, the Son of God, as it is written in the prophet Isaiah."

Studies in Memory of Thomas Walter Manson, 1893–1958 (ed. A. J. B. Higgins; Manchester, UK: Manchester University Press, 1959), 1–18. Barrett (15) refers to Manson as typifing the earlier consensus in *The Servant-Messiah: A Study of the Public Ministry of Jesus* (Cambridge, UK: Cambridge University Press, 1953), 73. In strong agreement with Barrett is Morna D. Hooker, *A Commentary on the Gospel according to St. Mark* (BNTC; London: A & C Black, 1991), 248–51; restated in eadem, "Isaiah in Mark's Gospel," 48. Recently the pendulum has swung back to the earlier view that Jesus as a servant "who gave his life as a ransom for many" reflects the Servant of Isa 53. See, e.g., Rikki Watts, "Jesus' Death, Isaiah 53 and Mark 10:45: A Crux Revisited," in *Jesus and the Suffering Servant: Isaiah 53 and Christian Origins* (ed. W. H. Bellinger Jr. and W. B. Farmer; Harrisburg, PA: Trinity Press International, 1998), 125–51; and idem, "Mark," 203–6.

50. Joel Marcus, *Mark 8 — 16* (AYB 27A; New Haven: Yale University Press, 2009), 757.

51. Ibid.

52. John F. Sawyer, *The Fifth Gospel: Isaiah in the History of Christianity* (Cambridge, UK: Cambridge University Press, 1996).

12

Acts 28—Game Over?

Isaiah, Baseball, Jews, and Luke

Christopher R. Matthews
(BOSTON COLLEGE SCHOOL OF
THEOLOGY AND MINISTRY)

In this paper in honor of my colleagues of nearly three decades, I will concentrate on the New Testament side of things, intersecting to a degree with some concerns evident throughout Dan Harrington's scholarly work (the Jewishness of Jesus), and also fitting with respect to his contributions to interreligious understanding (Jewish-Christian dialogue). In connection with this endeavor, and in line with the theme of this volume, I focus below on the appearance at the end of the Book of Acts of a passage from the Book of Isaiah, which will do double duty as an appropriate tie-in for an area of Dick Clifford's work. I also want to acknowledge Dan's great love of sports; therefore, I will show how baseball can serve as an instructive analogue for how we should read a particularly controverted New Testament text employing an Old Testament text, and thereby illustrate how salvation history works both contrary to, yet in line with, expectations. Really!

PAUL, ISAIAH, AND
THE JEWS OF ROME

The text under view here is the penultimate scene in Acts, the dramatic encounter in 28:23–28 between Paul and the local leaders of the Jews at Rome (specified at Acts 28:17), and perhaps other members of the Jewish community (the "great numbers" of 28:23). In this vignette, we learn that Paul conducts an all-day seminar of sorts in an attempt to persuade his Jewish audience about Jesus on the basis of the Law and the Prophets. The results are mixed: some are persuaded, while others refuse to believe. As the meeting is breaking up, Paul underlines his argument with a final scriptural salvo—he quotes the judgmental words of Isa 6:9–10 and announces that the "salvation of God" referred to in this text has now been sent to receptive Gentiles:

> So they disagreed with each other; and as they were leaving, Paul made one further statement: "The Holy Spirit was right in saying to your ancestors through the prophet Isaiah,
> 'Go to this people and say,
> You will indeed listen, but never understand,
>   and you will indeed look, but never perceive.
> For this people's heart has grown dull,
>   and their ears are hard of hearing,
>   and they have shut their eyes;
>   so that they might not look with their eyes,
>   and listen with their ears,
> and understand with their heart and turn—
>   and I would heal them.'
> Let it be known to you then that this salvation of God has been sent to the Gentiles; they will listen" (Acts 28:25–28, NRSV).

It is no secret that this denouement of Luke's "history" of the church in Acts has exercised great influence on Christian self-perception vis-à-vis Judaism through the ages. In concert with various other texts in the New Testament (e.g., the portrayal of the Jews in the

191

Gospel passion narratives and in much of the Fourth Gospel), it has been taken by various interpreters to indicate a decisive divine abandonment of the Jews. In such readings, Luke is understood to have documented through the course of his second volume Paul's strenuous efforts in synagogue after synagogue to convince Jews of the truth of the gospel message, while simultaneously revealing this unreceptive audience's uncompromising rejection of the message, resulting in a self-disqualification from salvation as forecast long ago by Isaiah.

There are various problems, however, both with this general construal of the implication of the narrative course of Acts, and the specific interpretation of the scene containing Paul's final words to "the Jews" in Acts, especially concerning how the citation of Isa 6 embedded in it should be understood to function. For anyone familiar with modern-day academic biblical studies, it should come as no surprise that there is voluminous discussion of this climactic scene in Acts in the commentaries and other scholarly literature. Among this research are many contributions that seek to show, some more successfully than others, that what Luke aims to communicate with his overall narrative construction is something well short of a clear break between the God of Israel and the Jews.[1] While it is difficult to find anything to add to this well-documented discussion, here I hope to indicate how the larger narrative perspective of Luke-Acts, which has been carefully constructed by the author, suggests, somewhat strongly and insistently, how we are to interpret the pivotal scene before us. After summarizing the points I have in mind for such a reading of the text and acknowledging the prominent reuse of the passage from Isaiah that occurs within it, I will show how baseball and biblical narrative share a few rules of play. But first, I wish to illustrate the perception of the function of the quotation of Isa 6 in Acts 28 found in several major commentaries on Acts.[2]

---

1. See, for example, the essays by Jacob Jervell, David L. Tiede, David P. Moessner, Marilyn Salmon, Robert C. Tannehill, and Michael J. Cook in *Luke-Acts and the Jewish People: Eight Critical Perspectives* (ed. J. B. Tyson; Minneapolis: Augsburg, 1988).

2. My coverage is necessarily very selective and makes no claim to cover all aspects of this disputed passage; even a monograph on the topic would be hard-pressed to offer more than representative coverage of the scholarly output on this passage.

ISAIAH—THE CLOSER IN
THE NINTH INNING?

In his often insightful treatment of Acts, Ernst Haenchen typifies a line of interpretation that views the Isaiah citation at the end of Acts as the climactic judgment of rejection of the Jews in favor of the Gentiles. Already, with respect to Acts 28:24, Haenchen somehow knows that with the narrator's report that "some were persuaded" (*hoi men epeithonto*), "there is no thought of a real conversion."[3] He identifies the Isaiah passage as "a prophecy of obduracy" that "prepares for v. 28."[4] He disallows the possibility that *mēpote* in the quote from Isa 6:10 (rendered "So that they might not" in the NRSV) could have the meaning "unless perhaps," explaining that the "prophecy describes here only the actual stubbornness and not its possible cessation."[5] Lest we be inclined to some uncertainty about these conclusions, Haenchen notes, with reference to Mark 4:12 and parallels as well as John 12:40, that "Isa. 6.9f. was understood in the Hellenistic community purely as God's judgement of rejection."[6] Thus he can stress the agreement of Acts 28:28 with the similar "pronouncements" in 13:48 (at Pisidian Antioch) and 18:6 (at Corinth), and conclude that with Acts 28:28, "the reason is given for the transfer of the saving proclamation from the Jews to the Gentiles."[7] Hans Conzelmann's brief analysis of the passage confirms Haenchen's judgment: The Gentile "church has taken possession of the inheritance of Israel. The schema is completed. This third declaration about turning away from the Jews and turning toward the Gentiles...is final."[8]

---

3. Ernst Haenchen, *The Acts of the Apostles: A Commentary* (trans. Bernard Noble and Gerald Shinn; trans. rev. R. McL. Wilson; Philadelphia: Westminster, 1971), 723.

4. Ibid., 724.

5. Ibid.

6. Ibid., n1, adding: "We may not confound this theological interpretation with Rom. 11.26."

7. Ibid. "The last chapter also is thus completely integrated into the total work in that it bases the justification of the Gentile mission on the refusal of the Jews" (ibid., 730).

8. Hans Conzelmann, *Acts of the Apostles: A Commentary on the Acts of the Apostles* (trans. J. Limburg et al.; Hermeneia; Philadelphia: Fortress, 1987), 227.

C. K. Barrett observes that "many take the view that Luke (cf. 13.46; 18.6) considers the mission to the Jewish people as a whole to be at an end," and judges this "to be too simple an analysis of Acts."[9] He problematizes Haenchen's facile dismissal of the implication of the verb *epeithonto* ("they were persuaded"), noting that "πείθεσθαι ['be persuaded'] is the opposite of ἀπιστεῖν ['disbelieve'], that is, it means *to believe*."[10] He contextualizes Luke's employment of Isa 6:9–10 within the wider recourse to this passage in the New Testament,[11] and suggests that Luke's message is that "the unbelief of Israel is not an unhappy accident but part of God's intention."[12] He believes that "Luke is not dealing with the more remote consequence of the ultimate destiny of Israel….If the Jews vacate their place, the Gentiles will take it…but [this] does not imply that salvation is no longer available to Jews."[13]

Barrett's observations tempering the "finality" of a common reading of Acts 28:23–28, typified here by Haenchen and Conzelmann, acknowledge a debt to the perspective emphasized in Jacob Jervell's work on Luke-Acts, which stresses the existence of a "mighty minority" of Jewish Christians in the church of Luke's day.[14] Stephen Wilson

---

9. C. K. Barrett, *A Critical and Exegetical Commentary on the Acts of the Apostles* (2 vols.; ICC; London: T & T Clark, 1994–98), 2:1246.

10. Ibid., 2:1244, emphasis original.

11. Ibid., 2:1237; the passages in question are Mark 4:12; Matt 13:14–15; Luke 8:10; John 12:40; and Rom 11:8.

12. Ibid., 2:1245.

13. Ibid., 2:1246.

14. Ibid. For Jervell's positions, see esp. Jacob Jervell, "The Divided People of God: The Restoration of Israel and Salvation for the Gentiles," in idem, *Luke and the People of God: A New Look at Luke-Acts* (Minneapolis: Augsburg, 1972), 41–74, originally published in 1965 in German and Norwegian versions (see 62–64 on Acts 28); idem, "The History of Early Christianity and the Acts of the Apostles," in idem, *The Unknown Paul: Essays on Luke-Acts and Early Christian History* (Minneapolis: Augsburg, 1984), 13–25; and idem, "The Mighty Minority," in *Unknown Paul*, 26–51, first published in 1980. See Barrett's (and others') contribution(s) to the Jervell *Festschrift*: C. K. Barrett, "What Minorities?" in *Mighty Minorities?: Minorities in Early Christianity—Positions and Strategies. Essays in Honour of Jacob Jervell on His 70th Birthday, 21 May 1995* (ed. D. Hellholm, H. Moxnes, and T. K. Seim; Oslo: Scandinavian University Press, 1995), 1–10.

offers an assessment of the dueling positions of Haenchen and Jervell on this passage in his 1973 monograph.[15] After reviewing Jervell's evidence for his claim that it is Jewish acceptance and not rejection that leads to the Gentile mission, and crediting Jervell with "a useful corrective," Wilson finds that "Jervell's overall conclusions must remain in doubt."[16] Wilson observes that "it is generally agreed that the programmatic statements in 13:46, 18:6 and 28:28 are Luke's own summary of the events in the Church's mission…[and] represent Luke's own interpretation of the Jew-Gentile question."[17] Thus Wilson concludes that Jervell "undervalues the importance" of the passages in 13:46, 18:6, and 28:28, while overemphasizing passages indicating Jewish belief (13:43, 46; 28:24, 28).[18] Wilson sorts out the discrepancy in Luke's narrative by viewing those passages that portray a positive Jewish response to the gospel as reflecting Luke's historical interests (i.e., what happened in the apostolic age), while those narrating Jewish rejection of the gospel are taken as reflecting the situation of the church in Luke's day.[19] Whether this represents a correct assessment of Luke's narrative construction, however, is still open to interpretation. But Wilson puts his finger on an important issue, with significant consequences for the debate over the meaning of Acts 28:23–28, when he observes that "one problem is that Luke seems to use the word 'Jews' loosely: the implication of 13:46, 18:6 and 28:28 is that all Jews are meant, whereas 13:43 and 28:24 show that this cannot be so."[20] I will return to this issue of Jewish "definition" or "identity" presently.

More recently, Richard Pervo has doubled down on the view exemplified by Haenchen and Conzelmann. The scene in Acts

---

15. Stephen G. Wilson, *The Gentiles and the Gentile Mission in Luke-Acts* (SNTSMS 23; Cambridge, UK: Cambridge University Press, 1973), 226–33. Note that this volume is based on Wilson's PhD thesis directed by Barrett and accepted by Durham University in 1969.

16. Ibid., 228–29.

17. Ibid., 232.

18. Ibid., 229, 232.

19. Ibid., 232–33.

20. Ibid., 232.

28:23–28 is "the third and climactic time" that Paul "announces a turn to the gentiles."[21] For Pervo, this means that "the entire Greek-speaking Diaspora has rejected the offer of salvation. The Jewish people had their chance, but failed to exploit it. Luke knew as much about 'the rule of three' as anyone, and he exploited it vigorously."[22] While Pervo refers to a literary rule, in baseball terms "the rule of three" means three strikes and you're out! Pervo contends that both structurally and through small details of the text, Luke portrays a final rejection. Thus the use of Isa 6:9–10 here forms an *inclusio* with the use of Isa 49:6 at Acts 13:47, the initial "turn to the Gentiles" in the series of three. And with regard to detail, Paul's reference to "your ancestors" (Acts 28:25) significantly echoes Stephen's same style of address at the end of his speech (7:52). This leads Pervo to observe that in Acts 28, "the Jewish people in general are once more and finally labeled as 'the other.'"[23]

GAME OVER = SEPARATE RELIGIONS?

No matter how one ultimately understands the portrayal of Paul's meeting with the Roman Jews in Acts 28, the sudden invocation of Isa 6:9–10 in verses 26–27 comes "as a shock after the mixed reception reported in v. 25."[24] Pervo understands its use here to be in accord with its use elsewhere in the New Testament "as an explanation of missionary failure."[25] But more ominously, he detects here "a shift toward invok-

---

21. Richard I. Pervo, *Acts: A Commentary* (Hermeneia; Minneapolis: Fortress, 2009), 681.

22. Ibid., adding: "This third example of the formula comes at the very end of the book and 'carries special narrative weight.' All of the attempts to mitigate the impact of this final utterance have to row against the powerful current of this narrative weight." Pervo cites the observation on "special narrative weight" from Joseph B. Tyson, *Images of Judaism in Luke-Acts* (Columbia: University of South Carolina Press, 1992), 177. Tyson further elaborates (178): "The announcements at Pisidian Antioch and Corinth now turn out to be anticipations of this final proclamation of the termination of the Pauline mission to the Jews."

23. Pervo, *Acts*, 684.

24. Ibid.

25. Ibid., 685; he cites Mark 4:12 and Luke 8:10, and refers also to John 12:39–40.

ing the passage to condemn the Jews in general," and contrasts this with Paul's view: "For Paul this rejection was provisional; Luke viewed it as final and the grounds for the existence of (in modern terms) *a separate religion*."[26] Pervo's interpretation is framed by a particular understanding of Luke's context. In his view, "Judaism and Christianity began to emerge as *clearly distinct entities* c. 90 CE. A generation later, Luke was engaged in retrojecting this separation to the 'primitive' period." Thus he claims that "those of Jewish background who adhere to the church are *no longer 'Jews*,' certainly not to be numbered among 'the Jews,' which is the preferred word for 'the other.'"[27] In this analysis, an important issue arises that affects one's interpretation of this and other passages in Luke-Acts in decisive ways, namely: What period is Luke primarily concerned with in the framing of his account: the church "back there," or the church of Luke's own day? Pervo sets out the main alternatives in his treatment of the interaction between Paul and the Roman Jews: "The question for interpreters is whether this conversation deals with contemporary problems of Luke's time, or, as this commentary holds, attempts to justify the separation that has taken place."[28] Below, I will move in the opposite direction and suggest that Luke primarily aims his narrative at the concerns of his own time.

The notion of an early, definitive separation of Judaism and Christianity is still widely held, and exceptions are often taken to prove the rule. Joel Marcus has recently highlighted Hippolytus as "part of a small but significant minority of ecclesiastical thinkers who preserved the heritage of Romans 11 in ascribing to the Jews a continuing and positive role in salvation history."[29] As a prelude to his sur-

---

26. Ibid., emphasis added.

27. Ibid., emphasis added. Pervo dates Acts to about 115 CE (ibid., 5).

28. Ibid., 683. Objecting to Robert C. Tannehill's view, expressed in various writings (e.g., "Rejection by Jews and Turning to Gentiles: The Pattern of Paul's Mission in Acts," in Tyson, *Luke-Acts and the Jewish People*, 83–101), that the end of Acts presents the story of Israel as a tragedy, Pervo insists (*Acts*, 681n10) that Luke "presents the story of contemporary Judaism vis-à-vis Christianity as a melodrama in which the Jews receive the punishment they thoroughly deserve."

29. Joel Marcus, "Israel and the Church in the Exegetical Writings of Hippolytus," *JBL* 130 (2011): 403.

vey of the writings of Hippolytus as evidence for "a soteriology inclusive of Israel," Marcus notes other texts that provide evidence for early Christians who held to an "inclusive theology," namely, the *Testaments of the Twelve Patriarchs*, the *Didascalia Apostolorum*, and the Pseudo-Clementine *Homilies* and *Recognitions*. The *Epistle of Barnabas* comes into play too, revealing in its polemic (*Barn.* 4.6–7) those "who claim that both Jews and Christians enjoy a covenantal relationship with the God of Israel."[30] But Marcus himself observes that "most of the Christians we know about from the early centuries concur with Barnabas that Israel has lost its status as God's covenant people and has been replaced by the church." He goes on to observe that the "theology of Christian replacement of Judaism…has deep roots in the NT," and includes Acts 28:25–28 among the texts he cites to back up this claim.[31]

TWO ISSUES

This is enough to establish the contours of a well-represented way of reading the Isaiah quote and the depiction of Paul's meeting with the Jews of Rome in Acts 28. There are two principal issues I wish to raise about the construal of this scene as a final rejection of the Jews. First, I want to note briefly various contraindications to this interpretation already built into the narrative of Luke-Acts, items noted by Jervell, Robert Tannehill, and many others, that lead us to ask the sensible literary-critical question: Why are such details given space in the narrative, unless they serve some meaningful purpose with regard to the delivery of the author's overall message? Second, I want to underline how much the "traditional" view of the ending of Acts assumes the existence of "Christianity" and "Judaism" and their interrelation (or lack thereof) around the end of the first and beginning of the second century. Such assumptions may fundamentally be no better than guesses, or at worst, impositions, that is, positions that are clearly prob-

---

30. Ibid., 385.

31. Ibid., 386.

lematic in view of other evidence that survives from the ancient world. It is widely assumed that we know what Luke means when he refers to "the Jews," but there are possibilities of reference, even intra-Jewish reference, that are not adequately considered by many interpreters.

GENTILES IN JEWISH CLOTHING

In a recent essay, I attempted to highlight "significant counter-indications throughout the text of Luke and Acts that call into question Luke's intent to offer a straightforward story of the replacement of Israel/Judaism by the church/Christianity."[32] Here I can do no more than indicate in very schematic fashion some texts in Luke and Acts that are quite suggestive of Luke's and the Lukan community's continuing interest in things "Jewish." Among such passages are the narrator's notice at Acts 6:7 that "a great many of the priests became obedient to the faith"; the observation at Acts 21:20 about "how many thousands of believers there are among the Jews"; the message communicated by the infancy narrative in Luke 1—2 that "salvation is a participation in the hope that the God of Israel will redeem his people";[33] the "seemingly impossible benefaction of a Roman centurion who demonstrates his love for the Jewish people by building a synagogue at Capernaum (Luke 7:5)";[34] the devout Cornelius of Acts 10:2, who "prayed constantly to God"; the proselytes and God-fearers who respond to Paul's mission (Acts 13:16, 26, 43; 16:14; 17:4, 17; 18:7); the elements of the so-called apostolic decree (Acts 15:20, 29; 21:25) that "fit well among the laws cataloged in Leviticus 17—18 that apply to Gentiles living in Israel";[35] and Simeon's oracle at Luke 2:32, which shows that "the turn to the Gentiles is not a turn away from the glory of Israel."[36]

---

32. Christopher R. Matthews, "'We Had Hoped That He Was the One to Redeem Israel': The Fragility of Hope in Luke-Acts," in *Hope: Promise, Possibility, and Fulfillment* (ed. R. Lennan and N. Pineda-Madrid; New York: Paulist, 2013), 57–69.

33. Ibid., 60.

34. Ibid.

35. Ibid., 66.

36. Ibid., 67.

The interest that we see in the narrative of Luke-Acts for things Jewish emerges naturally in Luke's characterization of the first Gentile convert, Cornelius, as one who practices a style of Jewish piety (i.e., praying and giving alms). Though this may be a strange, limited, or liminal type of "Judaism" measured by later, rabbinic standards, can we really say that it is not a possible formulation of a Judaism at this point in history (turn of the first century)? One problem with the readings of Haenchen, Pervo, and others who take the placement of the Isaiah citation on Paul's lips in Acts 28 to signal a final rejection of Judaism is that they appear to locate some definitive "parting of the ways" much too early. In addition, they operate with the problematic assumption that "Judaism" and "Christianity" are known entities at this early date. In recent years, some scholars of ancient Christianity and Judaism have recognized that such an understanding of our historical evidence is suspect.[37]

WHO IS A JEW (OR A CHRISTIAN)?

Daniel Boyarin is a notable proponent of the idea that the emergence of "Christianity" and "Judaism" is better considered a fourth-century phenomenon:

> The question of when Christianity separated from Judaism is a question whose answer is determined ideologically. We need always to ask: Whose Judaism?; whose Christianity? Shall we make the determining point an act of inner-Jewish hostility to certain authorities that we choose now to name

---

37. See, e.g., Annette Yoshiko Reed and Adam Becker's discussion of the "problems with the 'parting' model," and the proposal to move beyond it, in the introduction to *The Ways That Never Parted: Jews and Christians in Late Antiquity and the Early Middle Ages* (ed. A. H. Becker and A. Y. Reed; TSAJ 95; Tübingen: Mohr Siebeck, 2003), 16–24. They observe: "Even after the second century, the boundaries between 'Jewish' and 'Christian' identities often remained less than clear, consistent with the ambiguities in the definition of both 'Jew' and 'Christian.'... Accordingly, a growing number of scholars have begun to challenge the 'Parting' model, citing its methodological paucity, its inadequacy as an historical account, and its inability to explain much of our primary evidence" (ibid., 2).

"the Jews," or are we looking for something else, and if so, what?[38]

After affirming Judith Lieu's observation that we might think about the separation of Christianity and Judaism only in the fourth century, Boyarin continues: "There seems to be no absolute point, theological or otherwise, at which we could say for this early period [as early as the first century]: It is this that marks the difference between Judaism and Christianity."[39] Boyarin proposes various metaphors to move away from the "older theory" of a "family tree" or "opposition" model for a "parting of the ways," to an understanding of a "spectrum" or "wave theory account of Christian-Jewish history," in which Christianity and Judaism are "not strictly bounded and differentiated from each other but instead shade one into the other."[40] Referring to his own earlier work, Boyarin suggests that "we might think of Christianity and Judaism in the second and third centuries as points on a continuum from the Marcionites…to many Jews on the other end for whom Jesus meant nothing. In the middle, however, there were many gradations which provided social and cultural progression across this spectrum."[41]

My suggestion is that Luke-Acts emerges from a group located more toward the center of such a continuum, during a period prior to the imposition of "border lines," to use Boyarin's terminology.[42] Boyarin

---

38. Daniel Boyarin, *Border Lines: The Partition of Judaeo-Christianity* (Divinations: Rereading Late Ancient Religion; Philadelphia: University of Pennsylvania Press, 2004), 6.

39. Ibid., 7. He refers to Judith M. Lieu's comments on "Judaism" and "Christianity" eluding "our conceptual grasp" in her essay, "'I Am a Christian': Martyrdom and the Beginning of 'Christian' Identity," in eadem, *Neither Jew Nor Greek?: Constructing Early Christianity* (Studies of the New Testament and Its World; London: T & T Clark, 2002), 227, where she also asks what makes the New Testament non-Jewish.

40. Boyarin, *Border Lines*, 18.

41. Ibid., 17–18.

42. At the outset of his volume, Boyarin "insist[s] that the borders between Christianity and Judaism are as constructed and imposed, as artificial and political as any of the borders on earth…. Rather than a natural-sounding 'parting of the ways,' such as we usually hear about with respect to these two 'religions,' I will suggest an imposed *partitioning* of what was once a territory without border lines" (ibid., 1, emphasis original).

connects the latter development with "heresiology,"[43] and in terms of an identifiable figure, with Justin Martyr.[44] I think it is more than fair to say that the author of Luke-Acts is not involved, formally or otherwise, in the production of heresiological literature,[45] and that his theological concerns are significantly distinguishable from Justin's both in form and content. Rather, the circle of readers for whom Luke writes seems to be heir in some sense to the Pauline communities established around the Aegean Sea. I take the heroic portrayal of Paul in Acts to be a basic indicator of this understanding. And just as Paul's own activities involved a collaboration among Jews and non-Jews, it is not far-fetched to assume that, several generations later, a similar social sensibility was still operative among those in a particular "Christ group" that understood itself to be devoted to the God of Israel. That is, they perceived themselves as in some sense "Jewish," but in a manner that did not necessarily exclude other Jews,[46] perhaps in line with a scenario such as Paul himself outlines in Rom 9—11.

My understanding of the contours of the "Lukan community" has been shaped in light of Philip Esler's perceptive study of the Lukan works.[47] He offers a persuasive case that in Acts "the crucial

---

43. "Early Christian heresiology, whatever else it is, is largely the work of those who wished to eradicate the fuzziness of the borders, semantic and social, between Jews and Christians and thus produce Judaism and Christianity as fully separate (and opposed) entities—as religions, at least in the eyes of Christianity" (ibid., 2).

44. Ibid., 4.

45. Thus I am not persuaded by Joseph B. Tyson's contention (*Marcion and Luke-Acts: A Defining Struggle* [Columbia: University of South Carolina Press, 2006]) that Luke-Acts has been designed to oppose Marcionite Christianity. His case involves numerous suppositions; but a coherent reading of Luke's narrative in the manner presented here is possible without such assumptions.

46. See the critique of the view that early Christianity was a sect within Judaism in Eyal Regev, "Were the Early Christians Sectarians?" *JBL* 130 (2011): 771–93. Note his conclusion (ibid., 793, emphasis original): "The evidence collected here suggests not only that the early Christian communities were not sects in the pure sociological sense of the term but also that they were still in the early process of *social formation and institutionalization*. This fluid social organization of the early Christian communities may have been closely related to the reluctance of many of them to dissociate themselves from the Jewish society at large."

47. Philip F. Esler, *Community and Gospel in Luke–Acts: The Social and Political Motivations of Lucan Theology* (SNTSMS 57; Cambridge, UK: Cambridge University Press, 1987).

development in the spread of the mission throughout the Diaspora is to be the establishment of Christian communities containing both Jews and Gentile God-fearers."[48] He observes that after the Cornelius narrative in Acts 10—11, there are some twenty conversion accounts whose "prominent feature is that Luke portrays Christian evangelism as having been successful almost entirely among Jews and God-fearers attending synagogues where the Gospel was first preached."[49] As Esler goes on to note, the Lukan pattern appears to be contrary to the evidence available in Paul's own letters with regard to his evangelistic activities. He concludes:

> Luke's programmatic bias in favour of Gentile God-fearers and almost total omission of ex-idolaters from the early congregations are most plausibly explained as a modification of the historical facts, designed to accord with the composition of his own community, in particular with the fact that its Gentile members, or a significant proportion of them, had been adherents of Yahweh and synagogue-attenders prior to their becoming Christians.[50]

All that is needed to update this attentive reading of the narrative of Acts is to take the emphasis off the notion that "becoming Christians" somehow means leaving "Judaism." In line with the observations of Boyarin and others who stress the fluidity of these concepts in the early centuries of the Common Era, the members of the Lukan community described by Esler cannot be clearly placed on one side or the other of some hypothetical Jewish/Christian divide.[51] That Luke's text can

---

48. Ibid., 39.

49. Ibid., 38.

50. Ibid., 44.

51. As Boyarin notes (Daniel Boyarin, "Rethinking Jewish Christianity: An Argument for Dismantling a Dubious Category [to Which Is Appended a Correction of My *Border Lines*]," *JQR* 99 [2009]: 28), "Everything that has traditionally been identified as Christianity in particular existed in some non-Jesus Jewish movements of the first century and later as well. I suggest, therefore, that there is no nontheological or nonanchronistic way at all to distinguish Christianity from Judaism until institutions are in place that make and enforce this distinction, and even then, we know precious little about what the nonelite and nonchattering classes were thinking or doing."

be used later to insist on the existence of such a division is a matter of reception; but when this perception is imported back to the time of the text's origination, it may be identified as a misreading of the text. Thus Esler's observations on the Lukan community substantiate the view that Luke's portrayal in Acts 28 speaks to the situation of Luke's own time and is not a historian's attempt to justify a separation that has taken place.

PROPHETIC REPROOF

It is time to return to the Isaiah text in Acts 28 that has fomented all of this discussion. How would Luke's ideal readers have understood this text? It seems fair to assume that Luke was quite familiar with the Septuagint version of Isaiah, given its extensive use throughout Luke-Acts, both by way of citation and allusion.[52] For this frequent intertextual employment of the prophet to be effective, we might also assume a commensurate familiarity among Luke's first readers. Thus it seems reasonable to presume both Luke's and his audience's broad knowledge of Isaiah. With regard to the "harsh commission" of Isa 6:9–10, Gene Tucker notes that in the immediate context of Isa 6, ending with verse 13, "the editors of the book, if not Isaiah or the earliest tradents, saw that the national disaster could be a cleansing punishment and that new life could grow out of it."[53] Surely we should not assume that Luke and his readers were incapable of reading such a text for what it was in its more ancient formulation, namely, a prophetic reproof. Huub van de Sandt proposes that Luke uses Isa 6:9–10 to craft a somewhat more extended reproof that includes verse 25c and verse 28.

---

52. Peter Mallen (*The Reading and Transformation of Isaiah in Luke-Acts* [LNTS 367; London: T & T Clark, 2008], 2–3) notes that Luke "includes more extended quotations from Isaiah than from any other scriptural book. Overall in Luke's writings there are nine explicit quotations from Isaiah and, according to the list supplied in NA[27], more than one hundred verbal allusions."

53. Gene M. Tucker, "The Book of Isaiah 1–39: Introduction, Commentary, and Reflections," *NIB* 6:104. In Isaiah's context, the disaster is the threatened Assyrian domination of Judah.

"The whole of vv. 25c–28…represents a prophetic reproof, modelled upon the passages of severe criticism in Isaiah and Ezekiel, and is intended to incite the Roman Jews to convert. The statement in v. 28, therefore, does not imply God's abandonment of Israel as a people."[54] Whether or not one accepts the details of van de Sandt's proposal, he provides a reasonable explanation of the function of a prophetic reproof in a Jewish context. As we have seen, there is no reason to disassociate Luke and his readers from such a context. At the same time, it is not necessarily the case that "the Jews" Luke is particularly concerned about are non-Jesus-believing Jews. As John Gager has provocatively suggested, "the Jews" of Acts may be, to use our problematic terminology, "Jewish Christians."[55] The bottom line is that there is no reason to see Luke's narrative ending or the citation of the reproof from Isaiah as anything other than an intra-Jewish conversation or dispute.

WHEN A THIRD STRIKE IS NOT STRIKE THREE

So how does baseball help with determining the nature of Paul's third "turn to the Gentiles"? Whatever the correct configuration of the social situation behind Luke's narrative scene in Acts 28 might be, one must recognize that sometimes a third strike does not equal a strikeout. A particularly memorable example of this was an at bat by the

---

54. Huub van de Sandt, "Acts 28,28: No Salvation for the People of Israel?: An Answer in the Perspective of the LXX," *ETL* 70 (1994): 358.

55. John G. Gager, "Where Does Luke's Anti-Judaism Come From?" in *Heresy and Identity in Late Antiquity* (ed. E. Iricinschi and H. M. Zellentin; TSAJ 119; Tübingen: Mohr Siebeck, 2008), 207–11. See my brief sketch of the struggle I see in "Luke's own day between the Christian type of Judaism that Luke knows and espouses, and another form of Jewish Christianity," and my appreciation of Gager's proposal, as well as my demurral about his precise delineation of the idea, in Matthews, "We Had Hoped," 68, 69n4. Also see the earlier study by E. Leigh Gibson, "The Jews and Christians in the *Martyrdom of Polycarp*: Entangled or Parted Ways?" in Becker and Reed, *Ways That Never Parted*, 145–58, where she finds the relevant social context "not between a Christian community fully opposed to a Jewish community but within a Jesus-following community struggling with its Jewish inheritance" (158).

Dodgers' Alex Cora in 2004, during which he fouled off fourteen straight pitches—before hitting a home run![56] Luke may not be sanguine about a home run bringing the situation about which he writes to a resolution, but his ending does communicate the ongoing nature of an issue of concern to him and his readers. Such an open-ended conclusion is consistent with how a prophetic reproof might be expected to operate. A home run might be a much unexpected result; but isn't this exactly what Paul himself envisaged in Rom 11:26?

---

56. See http://mentalfloss.com/article/25285/6-epic-bats#ixzz2eUoq8xTc, accessed 26 September 2013.

13

Constructing Matthew

The Convergence of Context, Sources, and Traditions That Shaped the Gospel

Donald Senior, CP
(CATHOLIC THEOLOGICAL UNION)

It is a great personal pleasure for me to be part of a tribute to Richard Clifford, SJ, and Daniel Harrington, SJ, two exceptional Catholic biblical scholars and gracious colleagues and friends. The overall theme of this volume—illustrating how biblical texts employ and adapt prior traditions—is most apt for the work of each of these scholars. My focus will be on the Gospel of Matthew, one of the centerpieces of Dan Harrington's many contributions to New Testament studies.

Harrington provided the inaugural volume of the Sacra Pagina series, of which he himself was the general editor, a commentary on the Gospel of Matthew.[1] True to both his own scholarly expertise and the nature of Matthew's Gospel, his commentary stressed the Jewish character of the First Gospel. He identified the context of the Gospel as written for a mainly Jewish community in the critical period after 70 CE and the destruction of the Jerusalem Temple and its attendant impact on both Judaism and Jewish Christianity. As he notes,

---

1. Daniel J. Harrington, *The Gospel of Matthew* (SP 1; Collegeville, MN: Liturgical Press, 1991).

Matthew's Gospel should be read as one of several Jewish responses to the destruction of the Jerusalem Temple in AD 70. The Matthean community still existed within the framework of Judaism but in tension with other Jewish groups—especially the early rabbinic movement. Matthew's theological program should be viewed as an attempt to show how the Jewish tradition is best preserved in a Jewish-Christian context.[2]

Matthew's Gospel, however, was not created out of whole cloth. Harrington joins a majority of contemporary biblical scholars in affirming that Matthew used the Gospel of Mark as a major source, and also had access to a collection of the sayings of Jesus known as "Q," as well as some traditions special to his own Gospel.[3] From the Gospel of Mark, Matthew drew his basic narrative structure, with its emphasis on the Galilean ministry of Jesus, the dramatic single journey to Jerusalem, and the dominating presence of the passion story. From Q, Matthew drew an abundance of sayings and additional parables of Jesus, which were integrated into Matthew's story through the construction of five great discourses (chs. 5—7; 10; 13; 18; 24—25). Special material both amplifies some of the Markan narrative and gives the Gospel its distinctive beginning and end.

On both the ascribed context of Matthew's Gospel and the hypothesis about its sources, Harrington's perspective continues to be shared by the majority of Matthean scholars. In terms of context, there is some divide along the fault line of whether Matthew's community considered itself as a dissident community yet still within the orbit of Judaism, or whether the alienation of Matthew's community had become sufficient to lead to a recent break with the Jewish community and a more determined move into the Gentile world.[4] In any case, there

---

2. Ibid., 17.

3. Donald Senior, *What Are They Saying about Matthew?* (rev. ed.; New York: Paulist, 1996), 21–25; see also idem, "Direction in Matthean Studies," in *The Gospel of Matthew in Current Study: Studies in Memory of William G. Thompson, S.J.* (ed. D. E. Aune; Grand Rapids: Eerdmans, 2001), 5–21.

4. Authors who believe that Matthew and his community remained within Judaism and anticipated only that some Gentiles would come into the community on Jewish-

is a strong consensus that Matthew's most important frame of reference is the relationship with Judaism.[5] While some recent scholarship has insisted that attention must also be paid to Matthew's response to the surrounding Roman imperial context, this perspective is, at best, quite secondary to Matthew's concern about the relationship of Jesus and his teaching and mission to Judaism.[6] As Peter Oakes has noted, engagement with Roman officials is very sparse in Matthew, especially compared with the multiple interactions with Jewish religious leaders. The ensemble of New Testament writings suggests a variety of reactions to Roman authority—some highly critical, such as the Book of Revelation; but others evidencing even respect for Roman law and authority, such as Paul's own writings and some aspects of Luke-Acts.[7] Likewise, Dorothy Weaver has observed that the Roman characters in Matthew's Gospel are "complex" and not one-dimensional. The centurion at Capernaum (8:5–13) and Pilate's wife (27:19) are presented sympathetically, while Pilate is portrayed as weak and vacillating. The Roman soldiers at the crucifixion ultimately acclaim Jesus as "Son of God." She concludes that the portrayal of the Roman characters in the

---

Christian terms alone include Anthony J. Saldarini, *Matthew's Christian-Jewish Community* (CSHJ; Chicago: University of Chicago Press, 1994); and J. Andrew Overman, *Matthew's Gospel and Formative Judaism: The Social World of the Matthean Community* (Minneapolis: Fortress, 1990). Others hold that Matthew's community had already experienced a clean break with Judaism; see, e.g., Graham Stanton, *A Gospel for a New People: Studies in Matthew* (Edinburgh: T & T Clark, 1992), 157–68; and Ulrich Luz, *Matthew 1—7: A Commentary* (Hermeneia; Minneapolis: Fortress, 2007), 45–56. For further discussion, see Donald Senior, "Between Two Worlds: Gentiles and Jewish Christians in Matthew's Gospel," *CBQ* 61 (1999): 1–23.

5. See the recent discussion in Donald Senior, ed., *The Gospel of Matthew at the Crossroads of Early Christianity* (BETL 243; Leuven: Peeters, 2011), esp. 3–24.

6. See, e.g., Warren Carter, *Matthew and Empire: Initial Explorations* (Harrisburg, PA: Trinity Press International, 2001); and his commentary, *Matthew and the Margins: A Sociopolitical and Religious Reading* (The Bible & Liberation; Maryknoll, NY: Orbis, 2000). Similarly, David C. Sim, "Rome in Matthew's Eschatology," in *The Gospel of Matthew in Its Roman Imperial Context* (ed. J. K. Riches and D. C. Sim; JSNTSup 276; Early Christianity in Context; London: T & T Clark, 2005), 91–106.

7. Peter Oakes, "A State of Tension: Rome in the New Testament," in Riches and Sim, *Matthew in Its Roman Imperial Context*, 75–90.

Gospel is not ideological but complex, not unlike the portrayal of the disciples themselves![8]

Regarding sources, among those who affirm the classic Two Source theory, there is debate about the special material in Matthew. Much of this material may in fact be attributed to the redactional activity of the evangelist, and only in some cases does Matthew draw on unique preexisting source traditions available to his community.[9]

The general working consensus about the broad circumstances of Matthew's community and the sources of his Gospel enables us to understand more profoundly the structure or "anatomy" of Matthew's narrative and its theological implications. It is that analysis that will be the focus of this contribution.

CIRCUMSTANCES AND CONTEXT

There is clear evidence in Matthew's Gospel of the tension between Matthew's Jewish-Christian community and other Jews seeking a way to reaffirm their identity in the wake of the destruction of the temple. Matthew's sharp critique of the Jewish leaders as found, for example, in the woes of chapter 23 reflects, in the view of virtually all commentators, not only debates about law observance flowing from the ministry of the historical Jesus, but also the attempt to delegitimize the competing religious authority of the Jewish religious leaders who were in tension with the Matthean Jewish-Christian community.[10] Similarly, both the explicit affirmation of the privileged role of Israel in the mission of Jesus (see 10:5 and 15:24), and the anticipations of a

---

8. See Dorothy Weaver, "'Thus You Will Know Them by Their Fruits,'" in Riches and Sim, *Matthew in Its Roman Imperial Context*, 107–27.

9. See Donald Senior, "Matthew's Special Material in the Passion Story," *ETL* 63 (1987): 272–94; and Stephenson H. Brooks, *Matthew's Community: The Evidence of His Special Sayings Material* (JSNTSup 16; Sheffield, UK: JSOT Press, 1987).

10. Saldarini (*Matthew's Christian-Jewish Community*, 107–16;) characterizes Matthew's community in sociological terms as "deviant" vis-à-vis the dominant Jewish majority; similarly, Dennis Duling, "Ethnicity, Ethnocentrism, and the Matthean Ethos," *BTB* 35 (2005): 125–43, who speaks of Matthew's situation in terms of "marginality."

future mission to the Gentiles (e.g., the homage of the Magi, 2:1–12; the faith of the centurion, 8:5–13; and that of the Canaanite woman, 15:21–28), reflect the inner-community debate about the identity of the Christian community itself and the conditions under which Gentiles could legitimately be admitted to it. It is clear, as we will see by an examination of its structure, that Matthew's Gospel wanted to strongly affirm the roots of Christian faith in the history of Israel and God's revelation to Israel. The Jesus of Matthew's Gospel is deeply embedded in the history of his people, reverences the law, and concentrates his mission on Israel. At the same time, however, the structural momentum of the Gospel and its components move the reader toward the full legitimization of the Gentile mission at the conclusion of the Gospel. In many ways, Matthew's Gospel is intended not only to affirm the Jewish roots and ethos of Jesus and his teaching, but also to show that the eschatological horizon of Jesus' mission was the extension of the mission of salvation to the whole Gentile world.[11] Thus Matthew's Gospel intends to show that the outflowing of salvation to the whole world was not simply an accident or a rebound from the failure of Israel to respond, but part of God's intent from the beginning.

Matthew's frequent use of biblical quotations introduced with the fulfillment formula and applied to specific circumstances of Jesus' mission are also part of this scheme.[12] The entire span of Jesus' mission — from his conception and birth through the advent of his Galilean ministry, his miracles, the opposition to his ministry, and his suffering and death — falls within the scope of God's prophetic word expressed in the Scriptures and brings that word to fulfillment. In this sense, the keynote statement of Jesus in 5:17 expresses a fundamental perspective of Matthew's entire Gospel — "Do not think that I have come to abolish the law or the prophets; I have come not to abolish but to fulfill."

---

11. See the important study of Matthias Konrad, *Israel, Kirche, und die Völker im Matthäusevangelium* (WUNT 215; Tübingen: Mohr Siebeck, 2007).

12. See Matt 1:15, 22; 2:5, 15, 17; 4:14; 8:17; 12:17; 13:14, 35; 21:4; and 26:56. On the function of the fulfillment texts in Matthew's theology, see Donald Senior, "The Lure of the Formula Quotations: Re-assessing Matthew's Use of the Old Testament with the Passion Narrative as Test Case," in *The Scriptures in the Gospels* (ed. C. M. Tuckett; BETL 131; Leuven: Leuven University Press, 1997), 89–115.

CONSTRUCTING THE GOSPEL

The preceding sketch of the context of Matthew's Gospel and some of its major theological concerns finds confirmation in an analysis of three "building blocks" of Matthew's narrative: (1) his introduction and ending, (2) his reordering of materials in 4:23—11:30, and (3) his insertion of discourses. It is at these points in particular that Matthew deviates from his primary source, Mark.

1. THE BEGINNING AND THE END

Matthew's title (1:1) succinctly lays out the entire program of the Gospel: "the book of the origins (or genealogy) of Jesus Christ, the son of David, the son of Abraham." Jesus' identity as "Son of David" will be reaffirmed in the Gospel in the genealogy (1:6), in his conception and birth in Bethlehem, and particularly in some of the healing stories (see, e.g., 9:27; 12:23; 15:22; 20:30–31). The crowds will acclaim Jesus as "Son of David" upon his entry into Jerusalem (21:9, 15). With this title Matthew obviously affirms the strong Jewish roots and identity of Jesus as the Davidic Messiah. At the same time, he is the "Son of Abraham," signaling the universal scope of the Christian mission by citing the name of the "father of all nations"—an important role for Abraham in early Christian literature.[13]

The opening genealogy (1:2–18) amplifies the affirmations of the title, tracking Jesus' Jewish lineage from Abraham through David and on to the birth of Jesus through Joseph's Davidic heritage. The coherent scope of the genealogy is explicitly noted by Matthew in the summary of 1:17–18. At the same time, references to the women (Tamar, Rahab, Ruth, Bathsheba, and Mary herself), who share a common trait of being "outsiders" or those for whom inclusion into the messianic lineage is under unusual circumstances (including Jesus' own conception by the Holy Spirit), form a subtle but evident harbinger of the advent of the Gentiles into the realm of Israel's sal-

---

13. See Paul's reflections on Abraham as justified through faith before the law and his designation as "the father of many nations" in Rom 4:1–25.

vation history—an anticipation that will also take place in the later stories of the Gentile centurion (8:5–13) and Matthew's version of the Canaanite woman (15:21–28).

The contents of the infancy narrative both affirm Jesus' identification with Israel and the recapitulation of its history, as well as anticipate the future events of the Gospel. The threats to Jesus and his family from the despot Herod, their flight into Egypt under the guidance of a Joseph who is instructed through dreams (2:13–14), and their call to return to Israel (2:15) recapitulate the travails and triumphs of Israel in the Joseph stories of Genesis and Exodus. The threat posed by Archelaus leads the family of Jesus to be exiled from their ancestral home, recalling another chapter of Israel's history (2:22–23). At the same time, the visit of the Magi and their homage (in contrast to the treachery of Herod and his Jerusalem court) is another harbinger of the future inclusion of the Gentiles (2:1–12), just as the threat to Jesus' life anticipates the suffering of the passion.

Thus Matthew, in distinction from Mark, begins his narrative with the reader's attention, as it were, drawn to Jesus' intimate connection with God's people Israel, but at the same time there are hints of the discontinuity to come.

The end of Matthew's Gospel also is distinctive in comparison with Mark's Gospel. Matthew adds the commissioning story in contrast to the conclusion of Mark's Gospel, which finishes with the discovery of the empty tomb, the announcement of Jesus' resurrection to the women witnesses, and the instruction that they carry the resurrection message to Jesus' disciples who will see him in Galilee (Mark 16:1–8)—an encounter promised but not narrated. Matthew alters this ending in a pronounced way by including an appearance of the risen Jesus to the women as they leave the tomb (Matt 28:8–10), and, even more significantly, by narrating the appearance of the risen Christ to the Eleven in Galilee (28:16–20). This account presents the risen Christ, filled with "all power in heaven and on earth," commissioning the apostles to extend his mission by "making disciples of all nations." To that is added the promise of the abiding presence of Christ with his community "until the end of the age" (28:20), thus completing the resonance of the name given to Jesus at the outset of the Gospel—"they shall name him Emmanuel, which means, 'God is with us'" (1:23). Therefore Matthew conceives of the outcome of the mission of Jesus as the extension of God's salvation to all nations—the ultimate eschatological goal, in Matthew's view, of the entire plan of God.

If at the beginning of the Gospel the reader is, in effect, turned back to the story of Israel and Jesus' profound connection with and recapitulation of Israel's experience, at the end of the Gospel the reader is turned in a different direction—toward the nations where the gospel must be preached, and to the end of time when all will be fulfilled. Turning to "all nations" and to the "end of the age" need not mean that Israel is now abandoned. The saying of Jesus in 23:39 implies that in Matthew's view (not unlike that of Paul in Rom 9—11), Israel, too, will ultimately acclaim Jesus as the Messiah: "I tell you, you will not see me again until you say, 'Blessed is he who comes in the name of the Lord.'" Thus the historic privilege of being God's chosen people remains and is honored by Jesus in his earthly mission (see 10:5; 15:24), but in the advent of the new age, God's offer of salvation is now extended to all the nations, forging a new people composed of Jew and Gentile.

2. THE REORDERING OF SOURCES IN MATTHEW 4:23—11:30

A section of the Gospel of Matthew that draws on both Markan and Q material but imposes its own coherent structure is found in Matt 4:23—11:30. The structural intricacies of this section and its relationship to Matthew's sources was first studied in detail by my late Doctor Father, Frans Neirynck, in his seminal article, "La rédaction Matthéenne et la structure du premier évangile."[14] As he noted, Matthew uses Mark's first reference to Jesus' teaching at Mark 1:21 as the point for the insertion of a whole section stretching from the introduction to the Sermon on the Mount in Matt 4:23 to the conclusion of chapter 11. One of the key structural elements in this section is the

---

14. *ETL* 43 (1967): 41–73.

summary of Jesus' ministry of teaching and healing found in 4:23: "He went around all of Galilee, teaching in their synagogues, proclaiming the gospel of the kingdom, and curing every disease and illness among the people." This verse announces the organizational motif of the next several chapters, with the foundational summary of Jesus' teaching in the Sermon on the Mount in chapters 5—7 and a collection of miracle stories in chapters 8—9.

The cogency of this section is apparent in Matthew's repetition of the same thematic verse at the end of chapter 9: "Jesus went about to all the towns and villages, teaching in their synagogues, proclaiming the gospel of the kingdom and curing every disease and illness" (9:35). Thus chapters 5—9 present a broad portrayal of Jesus' messianic ministry of teaching and healing. Other motifs are woven through this section, such as the call to discipleship (9:9–13; see also 8:18–22) and an important anticipation of the ultimate universal mission of the community in the story of the healing of the centurion's servant (8:5–13).

The conclusion of chapter 9 prepares for the mission discourse of chapter 10. The same crowds that flock to Jesus from all the points of the compass in 4:24–25 and trigger the Sermon on the Mount reappear in 9:36–38, where they now prompt Jesus to commission his disciples to go on mission "to the lost sheep of the house of Israel," thus leading into the mission discourse of 10:1–42. Chapter 11, in turn, introduces the motif of opposition (a motif that begins in Mark already at 2:1—3:6). John the Baptist is in prison and sends his disciples to question Jesus about his identity, leading to the summary of 11:4–6. The rest of the chapter deals with opposition to Jesus and Jesus' own affirmation of both his mission and his intimacy with the Father (11:25–30). Stories of healing and opposition continue in chapter 12, as Matthew rejoins the thread of Mark's narrative.

In this key section of the Gospel, the evangelist has laid out for the reader both his grand portrayal of the mission of Jesus as teacher and healer, as well as the mission of the community that is to continue preaching and healing in Jesus' name.

3. INSERTION OF THE DISCOURSES

One of the well-known features of Matthew's Gospel is its presentation of five great discourses. Along with some Markan source material, Matthew draws heavily on Q for the content of these discourses. They are typically punctuated by a formula that concludes the discourse and connects it back to the ongoing narrative. Thus the mission discourse concludes as follows at 11:1: "When Jesus finished giving these commands to his twelve disciples, he went away from that place to teach and to preach in their towns" (cf. 7:28; 13:53; 19:1; 26:1). Moreover, the discourses are inserted into the narrative in connection with prompts found in Mark's narrative. For example, the summary reference to Jesus' teaching in Mark 1:21 aligns with the Sermon on the Mount in Matt 5—7; the call of the Twelve in Mark 3:13–19 with the mission discourse in Matt 10; the parable chapter in Mark 4 with the parables discourse in Matt 13; the disciples' discussion about greatness in Mark 9:33–37 with the community discourse of Matt 18; and Mark's scene of Jesus teaching in the temple (Mark 11—12) and the eschatological discourse on the Mount of Olives (Mark 13) with the eschatological discourse of Matt 24—25.

The content of these discourses reveals again the impact of Matthew's context and purpose. The Sermon on the Mount should not be considered as simply one discourse among a series of five, but as foundational for all the rest. At the beginning of the Sermon, Jesus declares the motif of continuity and fulfillment that is fundamental to Matthew's theological perspective: "Do not think that I have come to abolish the law or the prophets; I have come not to abolish but to fulfill" (5:17). The so-called antitheses or contrast statements that follow in 5:21–48, which form the heart of Jesus' ethical teaching, illustrate what is meant by the "greater righteousness" that is to be exemplified by Jesus' disciples. This is in contrast to the righteousness of the "scribes and Pharisees" (5:20), the stereotypical opponents of Jesus and the prime examples of religious hypocrisy and lack of integrity (see 23:1–39). In each instance, Jesus' teaching is rooted in the Torah but extends what is found there in a more profoundly interior way and with a more radical ethical demand, revealing from the perspective of the gospel the ultimate intent of the law. The latter section of the Sermon (6:1–18) uses the classical components of Jewish piety—almsgiving, prayer, and fasting—to illustrate again the religious integrity and intensity required of the follower of Jesus. The Sermon concludes (7:21–29) with exhortations to put words into action, a recurring emphasis of Jesus' teaching in Matthew's Gospel (see, e.g., the parable of the two sons in 21:28–32, and the emphasis on judgment in chs. 24—25). The scribes and the Pharisees, by contrast, are characterized by Matthew as hypocrites who "preach but do not practice" (23:3).

The mission discourse of chapter 10 abides by the restriction given during Jesus' lifetime—prior to the universal commission of 28:16–20—to go only "to the lost sheep of the house of Israel." Yet within the body of the discourse, the ultimate mission to the world is anticipated in the warnings about being led before "governors and kings for my sake as a witness before them and the pagans" (10:18). Thus long before the apocalyptic events that erupt at Jesus' death (27:51–53) and resurrection (28:2–4) that signal the coming of the eschaton and the falling away of previous restrictions, Matthew's Gospel has one eye on the Gentiles and on the climactic nature of the universal mission as the ultimate goal of the gospel story.

In the parables discourse, Matthew characteristically adds to Mark's repertoire additional parables about judgment, such as the parable of weeds among the wheat (Matt 13:24–30, with its explanation in 13:36–43) and the parable of the net (13:47–49).

The community discourse of chapter 18 is one of the most compelling of the Gospel's discourses. Matthew draws on Mark's implied critique of the disciples' ambitions found in Mark 9:33–37, following the second passion prediction (Mark 8:30–32), and also utilizes the sayings about scandal in Mark 9:42–48 (see Matt 18:6–9). But Matthew shapes the discourse around two parables and key sayings of Jesus. The Q parable of the lost sheep (found also in Luke 15:4–7) is given a new interpretation as it is applied to erring members of the community. Even one lost sheep is to be sought out and rejoiced over when recovered. The saying of Jesus in 18:14 drives home the ecclesial meaning of the parable. A procedure for dealing with disputes—

echoing a similar procedure found in Qumran's *Manual of Discipline* (1QS V, 24–VI, 2; CD IX, 2–3) — also signals a note of seeking reconciliation and the role of the community in ensuring good order and justice within the *ekklēsia*. This gathering is empowered by the presence of the Risen Christ in its midst (18:19–20), taken by most commentators as a reprise of the "Emmanuel" motif of 1:23 (see also 28:20). The second half of the discourse is commandeered by the parable of the unforgiving servant and the saying of Jesus in 18:35 that reinforces the need for forgiveness "from the heart." The parable, which is found only in Matthew, is an example of special material that may be the result of the redactional activity of the evangelist. It seems to be a coda on the injunction of the Lord's Prayer about forgiveness (see Matt 6:12), and is filled with characteristic Matthean vocabulary, style, and moral interest. The discourse as a whole reflects not only Matthew's interest in the makeup and comportment of the post-Easter community, but also the stress on forgiveness and reconciliation already emphasized in Jesus' teaching in the Sermon the Mount (see, e.g., 5:21–26, 36–42, and the climactic 5:43–48). It is not impossible that such an emphasis is prominent in Matthew's Gospel because of tensions within the community over the issue of how to envision the Gentile mission.

Finally, the eschatological discourse of chapters 24—25 is an extension of Mark's final polemical scenes in the temple (chs. 11—12) and his discourse at the end (ch. 13). Besides absorption of Mark's material about the end-time, Matthew adds four judgment parables: the faithful or unfaithful servant (24:45–51), the ten virgins (25:1–13), the talents (25:14–30), and the judgment of the nations (25:31–46). The parables of the faithful or unfaithful servant and the talents are drawn from Q and have parallels in Luke's Gospel (Luke 12:41–46; 19:12–27); the other two parables, the ten virgins and the judgment of the nations, are unique to Matthew and are reflective of his style and theology. In many ways, Matthew's emphasis on judgment is a rhetorical follow-through of his emphasis on the importance of doing good deeds rather than simply saying the right words. The parable of the judgment of the nations is a classic expression of this perspective.

Thus, Matthew successfully incorporates this extensive selection of parables and other sayings material into his narrative through the device of "discourses." In effect, the rapidly advancing and breathless pace of Mark's narrative is slowed from time to time to allow Jesus to teach, and then the narrative again picks up the pace. The content and ordering of this teaching material has given Matthew's Gospel its traditional "catechetical" tone and accounts for its popularity in the early church.

CONCLUSION: CONSTRUCTING MATTHEW

In concluding our study of the "anatomy" of Matthew's Gospel, we can turn again to its context. Matthew absorbs his primary source, the Gospel of Mark, which serves as the narrative backbone of his own Gospel. But prompted by the compelling circumstances of his post-70 context and with access to additional discourse material, Matthew reworks Mark's account into a new story that grapples with the complex relationship of his community's Jewish roots and the formation of its Christian identity. For the sake of his mainly Jewish-Christian community, this new story composed by Matthew must address the legitimate claim of Jewish Christians to their deep roots in Judaism and their membership in God's chosen people. Faith in Jesus as the Messiah and Son of God did not violate that sacred heritage, but rather brought it to its ultimate goal and complete fulfillment. At the same time, attacks by the community's religious opponents—themselves concerned with community identity following the destruction of the temple—had to be refuted and discredited. Matthew attempts this by characterizing the religious leadership of the dominant majority as lacking integrity and as hypocritical, and thereby functioning to lead astray their own people.

Key to all of this is Matthew's strong Christology. It is the faith of the community in Jesus' identity as the Messiah, the Son of David, and above all as the beloved Son of God that enables it to see Jesus' teaching and healing actions as not opposed to the law but as its fulfillment and completion. The community will never be abandoned or confounded because in its midst dwells the Risen Christ, who comes back to them in the final scene of the Gospel and thus fulfills the promise of his name "Emmanuel—God-with-us."

In the conclusion to his masterful multivolume commentary on the Gospel of Matthew, Ulrich Luz speculates on the sequence of events that led to this new version of the Gospel.[15] He suggests that the origin of Matthew's community was to be found somewhere in upper Galilee or Syria, in a thoroughly Jewish-Christian community that had access to a treasury of sayings and teachings of Jesus and was immersed in a mission to their fellow Jews. In the chaotic aftermath of the Jewish revolt and its tragic conclusion with the destruction of the temple and the subsequent scattering of the Jerusalem Christian community, Matthew's Jewish-Christian community drifted farther north, ultimately settling in the region of Antioch, the third largest city in the Roman Empire and the location of both Jewish-Christian and Gentile-Christian adherents (as the testimony of Acts suggests). Here they encountered Mark's Gospel, which focused on the healings and exorcisms of Jesus and his giving of his life on the cross. In this key area of Antioch—which according to the Acts of the Apostles had become the incubator for the Gentile mission under Paul and Barnabas—Matthew's community, through the instrumentality of the anonymous evangelist we call "Matthew," fused Mark's Gospel with the additional sayings material and other distinctive traditions available to this Jewish-Christian community. And here, too, the mission to the Gentiles, already a key pastoral question for the early church, became a new and compelling challenge for Matthew's community.

From this convergence of context, sources, and interpretative traditions, the Gospel of Matthew was born, thus exemplifying at the very outset of the Christian movement a creative and pastorally effective reinterpretation of a community's heritage.

---

15. Ulrich Luz, *Matthew 21—28: A Commentary* (Hermeneia; Minneapolis: Fortress, 2005), 637–44.

14

Flesh and Spirit in John and Qumran Revisited[1]

Harold W. Attridge
(Yale Divinity School)

The topic of the relationship between John and the Dead Sea Scrolls has generated a mountain of scholarly literature. Scholars began with initial enthusiasm about potential parallels and hoped to draw genetic connections between the Scrolls, their presumed Essene authors, and the Fourth Gospel. This turn in Johannine scholarship marked a decisive shift from older attempts to situate the Gospel in a Hellenistic or gnostic milieu and to find its roots instead in the soil of Palestinian Judaism. Although that development usefully corrected previously widespread assumptions, the precise connections between the Scrolls and the Fourth Gospel, especially in regard to their "dualism," proved elusive, and scholars in recent decades have been increasingly cautious about making a firm connection between the Gospel and the Scrolls.[2] Nonetheless, even skeptical scholars or scholars not particularly interested in issues of the Gospel's religiohistorical background recognize at

---

1. A version of this paper was presented at the meeting of the Studiorum Novi Testamenti Societas in 2010. I am happy to offer it here in tribute to Daniel Harrington and Richard Clifford, colleagues who have made significant contributions to the study of the literature of ancient Israel and its impact on early Christianity.

2. See Harold W. Attridge, "The Gospel of John and the Dead Sea Scrolls," in *Text, Thought, and Practice in Qumran and Early Christianity* (ed. R. Clements and D. R. Schwartz; STDJ 84; Leiden: Brill, 2009), 109–26, referring to earlier literature. More generally, see Mary L. Coloe and Tom Thatcher, eds., *John, Qumran and the Dead Sea*

least phenomenological parallels and have attempted to make use of them in interpreting the Gospel.[3] This paper will argue that the fourth evangelist shaped his treatment of "flesh" and "spirit" to stake a claim quite different from that of the Scrolls.

FLESH AND SPIRIT IN THE SCROLLS

While attempts at comparison between John and the Scrolls continue to be debated, the analysis of the Scrolls themselves has progressed considerably, driven largely by the publication of the fragmentary materials from Cave IV, as well as the analysis of the redactional development of important Scrolls such as 1QS. For our purposes, the most interesting result of that line of investigation has been the focus on the sapiential texts labeled 1Q/4QInstruction (1Q26; 4Q415–418a; 4Q423).[4] Jörg Frey's analysis of critical passages

---

Scrolls: Sixty Years of Discovery and Debate (Atlanta: Society of Biblical Literature, 2011); and Paul Anderson, *The Riddles of the Fourth Gospel* (Minneapolis: Fortress, 2011), esp. 36–38, 187–90, distinguishing between prescriptive and reflective dualism.

3. Francis J. Moloney (*The Gospel of John* [SP 4; Collegeville, MN: Liturgical Press, 1998]), at the literary end of the spectrum of Johannine scholarship, cites well-known passages from CD 1, 1QS, the Copper Scroll, and 4QFlor. On the other hand, Hartwig Thyen (*Das Johannesevangelium* [HNT 6; Tübingen: Mohr Siebeck, 2005]) makes little use of Scrolls material. Similarly Craig Keener (*The Gospel of John: A Commentary* [2 vols.; Peabody, MA: Hendrickson, 2003]) devotes considerable attention to the relevance of rabbinic literature for interpreting John (1:185–94), but little to the question of the relevance of the Scrolls, although the commentary frequently cites them.

4. For a review of the literature and an analysis of the important texts, see Jörg Frey, "Flesh and Spirit in the Palestinian Jewish Sapiential Tradition and in the Qumran Texts: An Inquiry into the Background of Pauline Usage," in *The Wisdom Texts from Qumran and the Development of Sapiential Thought* (ed. C. Hempel, A. Lange, and H. Lichtenberger; BETL 159; Leuven: Peeters, 2002), 367–404. See also idem, "Das paulinische Antithese von Fleisch und Geist und die palästinische-jüdische Weisheit Tradition," ZNW 51 (1999): 45–77; idem, "The Notion of 'Flesh' in 4QInstruction and the Background of Pauline Usage," in *Sapiential, Liturgical, and Poetical Texts from Qumran* (ed. M. Baillet et al.; STDJ 34; Leiden: Brill, 2000), 197–226; and idem, "'Licht aus dem Höhlen?' Der 'johanneische Dualismus' und die Texte von Qumran," in *Kontexte des Johannesevangeliums: Das vierte Evangelium in religions- und traditionsgeschichtlicher Perspektive* (ed. J. Frey and U. Schnelle; Tübingen: Mohr Siebeck, 2004), 81–116. See also Eibert Tigchelaar, "'Spiritual People,' 'Fleshly Spirit,' and 'Vision of Meditation': Reflections on *4QInstruction* and 1 Corinthians,"

in these texts[5] demonstrates the early development of a distinctive use of the term "flesh," unparalleled in traditional biblical language. "Flesh" in this usage refers to the condition of humankind mired in sin and alienated from God. The usage is echoed in some of the major Scrolls, such as 1QH[a] V, 30–33, which refers to the "spirit of flesh" (*rwḥ bśr*); 1QH[a] VII, 34–35, which opposes flesh and spirit; and 1QH[a] XII, 30–31, which emphasizes the connection of flesh and sin. Similar uses appear in the hymnic material at the conclusion of the Scroll of the Rule, 1QS XI, 7, where *bśr* seems to have a social referent to the people outside the community, and 1QS XI, 9–10, where the connection of flesh with evil, faithlessness, iniquity, sin, and depravity is emphasized. As Frey argues, it seems likely that the innovative usage emerged in sapiential circles prior to the development of the sectarian community represented by 1QS and related documents. Moreover, the further dualistic schemes, with their cosmic and psychological dimensions that are found in the "Treatise on the Two Spirits" (1QS III, 13–IV, 26) embedded in one redaction of 1QS, present a framework for making sense of the anthropology implied in the new assessment of "flesh."[6] The contention that the basic usage is a development of presectarian Jewish sapiential reflection may be confirmed by the presence of the negative attitude toward "flesh" in other texts of Second Temple Judaism such as *T. Judah* 19.4; *T. Zebulun* 9.7–8; and *Life of Adam and Eve* 25.3.[7]

Tracing the development of this usage as a way of describing the condition of sinful humanity is intrinsically interesting, but may also provide some useful background for developments in early Christianity. Frey, at least, argues that the distinctive use of "flesh" in Paul as a way of referring to humanity in its sinfulness (e.g., Gal 5:16–17; Rom 8:5–8)

---

in *Echoes from the Caves: Qumran and the New Testament* (ed. F. Garcia Martinez; STDJ 85; Leiden: Brill, 2009), 103–18.

5. 4Q418 81 1–2; 4Q416 1 10–13; 4Q417 1 I 6–7; 4Q416 1 16, associated with *ysr bśr*.

6. For another analysis of the relationship between 1Q/4Q Instruction and probably later sectarian documents from Qumran, see Shane Alan Berg, "Religious Epistemologies in the Dead Sea Scrolls: The Heritage and Transformation of the Wisdom Tradition" (Ph.D. diss., Yale University, 2008).

7. See Frey, "Flesh and Spirit," 400–2.

derives from Jewish sapiential usage, to which Paul may have been exposed as a student in Jerusalem.[8] A direct link from Paul to Essene sectarians attested at Qumran need not therefore be assumed, but the texts of the Dead Sea Scrolls may indeed be relevant to one distinctive expression of early Christianity. Can we find any analogous connections to the Fourth Gospel?

FLESH IN JOHANNINE LITERATURE

In order to test that possibility, we need first to review the ways in which the Fourth Gospel and other Johannine literature use "flesh" (*sarx*). A dozen passages in the Gospel and two in the first Johannine epistle are relevant.[9] Two appear in the Prologue of the Gospel, one referring to ordinary human birth (1:13), "from the will of the flesh" (*ek thelēmatos sarkos*), and one to the incarnation of the Logos (1:14), "the Word became flesh" (*logos sarx egeneto*). Reference to birth appears again in the dialogue with Nicodemus (3:6) where the flesh-spirit contrast emerges most clearly: "What is born of flesh is flesh, what is born of spirit is spirit."

The next collection of references to *sarx* appears in the Bread of Life discourse (6:51–58), beginning with the proclamation that the "bread from heaven" that Jesus gives is his flesh for the life of the world (6:51). To the Jews' question about how Jesus can give his flesh to eat (6:52), he responds that his disciples must eat his flesh and drink his blood if they are to have life (6:53, 54); his flesh is true food (6:55); and by consuming it one abides in Jesus, and Jesus in the consumer (6:56). The following story about a division among the disciples over Jesus' words draws a sharp contrast between the life-giving spirit, associated with the words that Jesus speaks, and the flesh, "which is of no use" (*hē sarx ouk ōphelei ouden*; 6:63).

The next reference occurs in a polemical context in the midst of a discourse where Jesus proclaims himself the true light of the world

---

8. Ibid., 402–4, relying on Acts 22:3 and 26:4–5 for Paul's academic career.

9. See the handy summary in Thyen, *Johannesevangelium*, 193–94.

(8:12). The Pharisees respond and reject his testimony as untrue (8:13). He rejoins that they are ignorant of his true origin and that they "judge according to the flesh," while he judges no one (8:15). Finally, in his final solemn prayer asking to be "glorified," he suggests, as a basis for the request, the fact that the Father has given him "power over all flesh" so that he might give them eternal life (17:2).

The first reference to "flesh" in 1 John is 2:16, part of an admonition not to "love the world" because what is in the world is not of the Father but of the world. This includes "the desire of the flesh" (*epithymia tēs sarkos*), and "the desire of the eyes" and "arrogant living." The second reference in the epistle appears in 1 John 4:2 as part of a confessional formula. Every spirit that confesses that Jesus Christ came in flesh (*en sarki elēlythota*) is of God.

GENERAL OBSERVATIONS

The first thing to observe about these references to the "flesh" is how different they appear to be from what occurs in Paul, as well as from the sapiential materials from Qumran and the texts that are related to them. The closest parallel to the tradition that seems to view "flesh" as the condition of sinfulness is perhaps 1 John 2:16. Both the connection with "desire" and the juxtaposition of fleshly desire with "desire of the eyes" and "arrogant living" point in that direction. The latter two phrases define and make specific what the "desire of the flesh" is about, covetousness and prideful arrogance. Nothing quite so specifically related to sin appears in any of the other Johannine texts, except the first appearance of "flesh" in the Prologue of the Gospel, with its disparagement of "will (*thelēmatos*) of flesh." We shall return to both passages in due course.

Several texts offer rather conventional usages. The reference in John 8:15 to judging "according to the flesh" is equivalent to saying "judge in a human fashion," with all the potential for failure that such judgment carries. The implied antithesis is "judge according to the truth." Not much is made of the antithesis at this point, but it is cer-

225

tainly a part of the theme of right judgment that runs through the Gospel, from the dispute over healing on the Sabbath, which offers a mini-trial of Jesus (5:10–24),[10] through the confrontation with Pilate (18:28–19:16).[11]

The reference to "all flesh" in the prayer of John 17:2 refers first and foremost to humankind, which is the object of the beneficent action of the Father and Son who provide eternal life. The condition of the human recipients of eternal life is not specified. Presumably they need to have sins taken away (1:29), however that expiation is understood.[12] They may need to be freed from ignorance by knowledge of the truth (8:32), however that relates to the removal of their sins. They certainly need to have the spirit infused in them, as Jesus insisted in his dialogue with Nicodemus (3:5) and in his response to controversy over the Bread of Life discourse (6:63). Whatever the condition that obtains for fleshly human beings, they *in their fleshiness* will be given eternal life. In comparison with the life-giving spirit, flesh may be useless, but it is not the source or locus of sin.

The final prayer of Jesus in John 17 may imply an eschatological hope not unlike that of Rom 8:22–23, where Paul describes the "groaning" of all creation as it awaits the "redemption of our bodies," but the difference is worth noting as well. In Paul, the body will be redeemed, and presumably given eternal life. In John the "flesh" will gain eternal life, even if the term is simply a metonymy for the collectivity of saved humanity.

Several passages operate within an antithetical framework, which invites a comparison with the Gospel's other antitheses. That is most clearly the case in John 3:6, in the middle of the Nicodemus dis-

---

10. On the forensic rhetoric in this chapter, see Harold W. Attridge, "Argumentation in John 5," in *Rhetorical Argumentation in Biblical Texts* (ed. A. Eriksson, T. H. Olbricht, and W. Übelacker; ESEC 8; Harrisburg, PA: Trinity Press International, 2002), 188–99.

11. On the theme in general, see Andrew T. Lincoln, *Truth on Trial: The Lawsuit Motif in the Fourth Gospel* (Peabody, MA: Hendrickson, 2000).

12. On the understanding of sin in the first century, see Gary Anderson, *Sin: A History* (New Haven: Yale University Press, 2009), 207n1. Anderson notes that the Johannine use reflects biblical notions of sin as a burden.

course, where Jesus proclaims the need to be "born (*anōthen*)" (3:3), that is "of water and spirit," in order to enter the kingdom of God (3:5). The wordplay that Nicodemus famously misunderstands implies a sharp distinction between above and below, between heaven and earth. That dichotomy will resurface later in the discourse (3:11–13) to define the origin and destiny, and therefore the significance, of Jesus. The distinction between heaven and earth is immediately correlated with the distinction between spirit and flesh. "What is born of flesh is flesh, what is born of spirit is spirit" (3:6). The tautology seems to function as a rebuke to Nicodemus. Look, Jesus seems to say, there are clearly two kinds of "birth," the natural, fleshly one that you had in mind in hearing my claim about being born *anōthen*, and another one. That second one has an element of mystery to it, like the mystery of the source of the wind, which blows where it wills (3:8), but in that mystery you find the kingdom of God.

The explanation does not particularly help Nicodemus, who still wants to know how all this can happen (3:9). The next stage of the dialogue suggests that Nicodemus needs to understand more than anything who it is that is speaking to him, but we can leave the christological point and return to the spirit-flesh dichotomy. The passage suggests that what pertains to the realm above, to the realm of spirit, is ultimately of God. The Gospel will soon affirm that God is spirit and is to be worshiped in spirit and truth (4:23–24). More could be said on the theme of the spirit,[13] but the antithesis of John 3 establishes an important point. There is a clear distinction between the realms of spirit and flesh, but the distinction is not necessarily one of antagonistic opposition. The realms operate in distinct ways, one "natural," straightforward, and easily comprehensible, and one mysterious. To be "born" of one or the other has implications for what one is, but the implication of the whole discourse is that one may be "born" of both. One already born of "flesh" may be born *anōthen*, "again" and "from above," by the action of "water and spirit," perhaps alluding to

---

13. For reading the Johannine "spirit" through a Stoic lens, see Gitte Buch-Hansen, *"It Is the Spirit That Gives Life": A Stoic Understanding of Pneuma in John's Gospel* (BZNW 173; Berlin: de Gruyter, 2010).

baptism. Given that understanding, it is not at all surprising that Jesus can later pray (17:2) about the power given him to provide eternal life to all flesh.

The rather sharp spirit-flesh dichotomy of John 3:6, echoed in 6:63, despite its correlation with the antitheses between above and below, old and new, and God and world, points to an interesting and important feature of Johannine "dualism." It is not a fixed metaphysical scheme, but a set of oppositions to be overcome.

FLESH IN THE PROLOGUE

It is now appropriate to turn to the Prologue for the last two, but perhaps most influential, texts referring to flesh. The first, John 1:13, exhibits some thematic connection with the Nicodemus episode in the use of "birthing" language to refer to a relationship with God. The simplest way of taking the verse is to see it making something of the same point that is scored by John 3:6. There are "natural" human things associated with birth, the "bloods" (*haimatōn*) of semen and menses, the "desire of flesh" that arouses sexual activity, and the whole activity generated by "the desire of the male" (*thelēmatos andros*). Contrasted to all that stands the possibility of birth "from God" (*ek theou*).[14] Exactly how the birth "from God" is to be understood is not at all clear, but that is hardly surprising in the context of this tantalizing prelude to the Gospel as a whole. One might also suspect that the distinction between the natural and the divine "birthings" implies negative value judgments about human activity, especially connected with the "flesh." But how negative should those value judgments be? John 6:63 suggests the answer that the activities of the "flesh" are not of any value for the relationship to God, but they are not necessarily inimical to it. To read more into the text is probably to import from Paul or Qumran an association of the "flesh" and "sin," which does not seem to be borne out in the rest of

---

14. A reader with a preference for a deterministic reading of Johannine anthropology might find grounds for different classes of human beings here, all mired in particular kinds of sin, as opposed to those predestined by God for salvation.

the Gospel. No, the distinction here seems to be a fairly innocent one, paralleled in John 3:6, between the ordinary process of human birth with all its fleshy dimensions, and something that happens when a new relationship to God is established.[15]

Another reason for reading the reference to the "flesh" here through a dark-colored lens may be an association of the dichotomy of flesh and spirit, implicit in this verse, with the other antitheses that structure the Prologue. In particular, the contrast between light and darkness, which dominates the Prologue's stately cadences, suggests at least two ways that its referents should be construed, both of which are in evidence in the Scrolls. At one level, the dichotomy seems to be a fundamental cosmic or ontological distinction. When "the light shines in the darkness, and the darkness did not grasp it" (John 1:5), two distinct cosmic realms are juxtaposed, in much the way that the two spirits of 1QS mark distinct spheres, though in both cases the ultimate creative power of God is assumed.[16] Exactly where the boundary between light and darkness is to be drawn remains problematic. The "cosmos," created by the action of the Word, remains ignorant of him and so apparently falls into the realm of darkness, but the Word illumines everyone as he (or it) comes into the world (John 1:9).[17] Hence, illumination takes place within the world, within the realm of darkness. But how does that happen?

Alongside the cosmic realm, the antithesis of light and darkness marks a social division, between those who accept the Word and those who do not. The boundaries between those groups stand in ironic ten-

---

15. For similar assessments, see Moloney, *John*, 231, following Werner Stenger, "'Der Geist ist es, der lebendig macht, das Fleisch nützt nichts,'" *TTZ* 85 (1976): 116–22; and Udo Schnelle, *Antidocetic Christology in the Gospel of John* (trans. L. M. Maloney; Minneapolis: Fortress, 1992), 194–95.

16. On the complexities of "dualism" in the Scrolls, with reference to earlier literature, see Mladen Popović, "Light and Darkness in the Treatise on the Two Spirits (1QS III 13–IV 26) and in 4Q 186," in *Dualism in Qumran* (ed. G. G. Xeravits; Library of Second Temple Studies 76; London: T & T Clark, 2010), 148–65, relying on his *Reading the Human Body: Physiognomics and Astrology in the Dead Sea Scrolls and Hellenistic-Early Roman Period Judaism* (STDJ 67; Leiden: Brill, 2007).

17. And, of course, God loves "the world" (John 3:16), and it is the object of the divine mission (17:18), despite its hatred (15:18).

sion with conventional boundary markers. "His own," who presumably should know better, fail to recognize him (John 1:11), so the boundaries between the enlightened and those who remain in darkness are somewhat fluid, but they do seem to exist as social limits.

The play on the antithesis of light and darkness with both cosmic and social dimensions recurs at prominent points in the first half of the Gospel.[18] While there may be surprises in store for someone who has encountered such metaphors in other Jewish writings, the general functions of the antithesis are familiar. Hence, it is understandable that those who have seen connections between the dualisms of the Gospel and the Scrolls often begin with the analogous treatments of light and darkness. It is not necessary to test whether the perceptions of such scholars are correct; they are quite understandable.

Our interest, however, is in the dichotomy of flesh and spirit. Attention to the antithesis of light and darkness in the Prologue is important because that more conventional antithesis sets up an expectation for the reader who hears the language of "flesh," which seems to be juxtaposed to something else, not yet clearly defined as "spirit." The clear antitheses establish a pattern of opposition that one expects will be carried out in other antitheses. On the positive side of the ledger stand God, life, and light; on the negative side, the world, (death), and darkness. If one extends the dichotomy into the Gospel, "above" might be added to the positive side, and "below" to the negative side. Would the set of dichotomies be extended to "spirit" on the positive side, and "flesh" on the negative side? The temptation to do so persists through John 1:13, but then comes the utterly unexpected affirmation of John 1:14 that the Word became flesh and thereby dwelt among us.

The use of "flesh" at the crucial juncture of the Prologue is thus counterintuitive for anyone steeped in the traditions of the dichotomous divisions of flesh and spirit found at Qumran and, for that matter, in Paul.[19] The rhetoric of the Prologue suggests that there are divisions — ontological, epistemological, and social — that must be taken seriously,

---

18. See esp. John 8:12; 9:5; 12:35–36; 13:30b.

19. Some of those expectations undergird the famous controversy between Rudolf Bultmann, who insisted that the "glory" of the Word could *only* be seen in and through

but the power of God's creative Word overcomes them. To use a modern analogy, the creative Word of God can engage in an act of "fusion" that totally transforms the ways in which humanity operates. Word becomes flesh and, in an explosive moment, all is changed.

It might seem too wild a conjecture to read this trope into the Prologue, if something similar were not affirmed in the later chapter (John 3), which picks up the "begetting" imagery of the Prologue. On the basis of the Prologue and John 3, therefore, there is strong evidence, not for a parallel with the kinds of expression of the relationship between "spirit" and "flesh" familiar from Qumran and Paul, but almost its mirror opposite. Is the contrast intentional?

FLESH IN THE BREAD OF LIFE DISCOURSE

Before attempting to answer that question, it would be worthwhile to explore one last set of statements about the "flesh," the concluding portion of the Bread of Life discourse in chapter 6. As already noted, the final portion of this discourse contains an extreme concentration of statements about the "flesh" of Jesus as something necessary for the eternal well-being of his disciples. The unity of this whole block of material has long been challenged and, since Bultmann, many have thought of the bulk of it, 6:52–58, as the work of an "ecclesial redactor" intent on incorporating a realistic sacramental theology into the Gospel.[20] Others have argued for the integrity of the whole discourse on form-critical grounds.[21]

---

the flesh of Christ, and his student Ernst Käsemann, who deemed the flesh of Jesus irrelevant to the point of the Gospel. For an account of the controversy and its aftermath, see Nicole Chivbici-Revneanu, *Die Herrlichkeit des Verherrlichten: Das Verständnis der δόξα im Johannesevangelium* (WUNT 2.231; Tübingen: Mohr Siebeck, 2006), 9–12.

20. For literature on the topic, see Paul Anderson, *The Christology of the Fourth Gospel: Its Unity and Disunity in the Light of John 6* (WUNT 2.77; Tübingen: Mohr Siebeck, 1995).

21. See, e.g., Peder Borgen, *Bread from Heaven: An Exegetical Study of the Concept of Manna in the Gospel of John and the Writings of Philo* (NovTSup 10; Leiden: Brill, 1965).

However the issue of the integrity of John 6 is to be decided, "flesh" is a theme that brings the discourse to its climactic conclusion. If the more explicitly "sacramental" verses are a redactional addition to the Gospel, John 6:51 at the very least provides a plausible and dramatic conclusion to the discourse. If the original discourse did end there,[22] the "flesh" that is the true bread from heaven, which Jesus gives for the life of the world, is no doubt the flesh that hangs in anguished glory on the cross, the flesh into which the Word was initially poured and from which the vivifying and enlightening Spirit will come (John 19:30; 20:22). "Eating" that "flesh" refers to the same kind of comprehension of the truth to which "drinking" the "living water" points (John 4), the recognition that in encountering an act of self-giving love in Jesus' death on the cross, one encounters the Divine.

The next verses (John 6:52–58), with their insistence on the physical eating (*trōgō*), extend the imagery to the realm of the Christian ritual meal, construed in a way that the elements of the celebration recall the death of Christ, as is the case in several of the other New Testament "eucharistic" passages.[23] If this is indeed a secondary rewriting of the discourse, it adds a new layer of meaning to the notion of "bread from heaven," one which would have a long afterlife in the Christian world. Nonetheless, it does not change the valuation of "flesh" inherent in the climactic verse 51. The flesh, at least of Christ, is not a vehicle that generates sin and produces alienation from God, but rather the instrument by which the Son of Man does what he came to do: provide life to the world. The subsequent verses simply affirm that the saving flesh of the incarnate Word is indeed available to disciples now.

---

22. So, e.g., Raymond E. Brown, *The Gospel according to John I—XII* (AB 29; New York: Doubleday, 1966), 291.

23. See 1 Cor 11:23–26; Matt 26:26–30; Mark 14:22–26; Luke 22:15–20, though throughout these passages *sōma*, not *sarx*, is consumed. Of course, not all early followers of Jesus attributed this significance to their thanksgiving meals (see *Didache* 9 and 10). On the variety in early "eucharistic theology," see Paul Bradshaw, *Early Christian Worship: An Introduction to Ideas and Practice* (London: SPCK, 1996); and Andrew McGowan, *Ascetic Eucharists: Food and Drink in Early Christian Ritual Meals* (Oxford: Clarendon, 1999).

The aftermath of the Bread of Life discourse in the Johannine narrative, John 6:60–65, is the alienation of some of Jesus' disciples. This is possibly one of those places where John's narrative world echoes something that took place in the historical world of the Johannine community,[24] a schism among the followers of the Beloved Disciple over some doctrinal matter. The point of contention may have been the interpretation of the Eucharist, with the schismatics rejecting the realistic interpretation of the elements. Yet that interpretation of the schism could be an anachronistic reading into John of the polemics of the Reformation. The real point of contention could also have been the understanding of the character of the "flesh" of Christ. The position of those who withdrew from fellowship with those who transmitted the canonical form of the Gospel could have been that the "flesh" of Christ was irrelevant to the salvific work that he came to do. Such a position was represented among Johannine Christians in the second century by those who composed the *Acts of John*, whose decidedly docetic Christology is firmly rooted in theological principles enshrined in the Gospel.[25] The position of such Johannine Christians may be the occasion for the insistence in 1 John that it is essential to confess that "Jesus Christ came in the flesh" (4:2).

The reality and saving value of the flesh of Christ was clearly an object of debate in early Johannine circles. The side that won the debate, insisting on the reality and importance of Christ's flesh, shaped the final stage of the Gospel, whatever the process was by which it came to be. That side also defended its position in the first

---

24. That much of the Gospel in fact works in that fashion is the well-known theory of J. Louis Martyn, *History and Theology in the Fourth Gospel* (rev. ed.; Nashville: Abingdon, 1979).

25. The relationship of the *Acts of John* to the Johannine tradition is disputed. See Harold W. Attridge, "The Acts of John and the Fourth Gospel," in *From Judaism to Christianity: Tradition and Transition: A Festschrift for Thomas Tobin, S.J., on the Occasion of His Sixty-Fifth Birthday* (ed. P. Walters; NovTSup 136; Leiden: Brill, 2010), 255–65; and idem, "Invention, Rewriting, Usurpation: The Case of the Johannine Gospel in the Second Century," in *Invention, Rewriting, Usurpation: Discursive Fights over Religious Traditions in Antiquity* (ed. J. Ulrich, A.-C. Jacobsen, and D. Brakke; Frankfurt: Lang, 2012), 1–8.

Johannine epistle, whatever its precise relationship with Gospel,[26] but in doing so the "pro-flesh" theologians also added something foreign to the Gospel, the hint that there is a downside to flesh. It is a vehicle for or instrument of sin, a position that is at least reminiscent of the position of 1Q/4Q Instruction and its heirs.

SUMMARY

The ever-so-brief reading of the evidence outlined in this paper suggests a trajectory of the ways in which discourse about flesh and spirit operated in the generation of the Johannine literature. Before the advent of Jesus and his radical preaching about God's reign, a discourse developed about the relationship between sin, which appears to be activity that alienates from or is incompatible with relationship to God, and "flesh," a metonym for the human condition. Paul and Pauline Christianity followed the path sketched by their Jewish sapiential predecessors and affirmed the connection between sin and flesh. They also celebrated the liberation from the bonds of both that the death and resurrection of Christ and the presence of the Spirit made possible.

Johannine theologians took another path, perhaps in conscious dialogue with the kind of thinking associated with the Scrolls and Paul. Whoever was responsible for the Prologue of the Fourth Gospel,

---

26. For the position that 1 John is later and probably dependent on the Gospel, perhaps contemporaneous with a redactional layer, see Raymond E. Brown, *The Epistles of John* (AB 30; Garden City, NY: Doubleday, 1982), 86–115; Hans-Josef Klauck, *Der erste Johanhnesbrief* (EKKNT 23/1; Zürich: Benzinger, 1991), 42–47; and Theo K. Heckel, "Die Historisierung der johanneischen Theologie im Ersten Johannesbrief," *NTS* 50 (2004): 425–43. For the position that there is no literary relationship, but reliance on common tradition, see John Painter, *1, 2, and 3 John* (SP 18; Collegeville, MN: Liturgical Press, 2002), 58–73; Judith M. Lieu, *I, II & III John: A Commentary* (Louisville: Westminster John Knox, 2008), 17–18; and Raimo Hakola, "The Reception and Development of the Johannine Tradition in 1, 2, and 3 John," in *The Legacy of John: Second-Century Reception of the Fourth Gospel* (ed. T. Rasimus; NovTSup 132; Leiden: Brill, 2010), 17–47. For the position that the epistles are prior to the Gospel, representing an earlier stage of development of Johannine theology, see Udo Schnelle, "Die Reihenfolge der Johanneische Schriften," *NTS* 57 (2011): 91–113, with earlier literature.

the evangelist for short, knew the seductive power of binary oppositions, which were a feature of some Pauline discourse, as they were of
the conceptual world of at least some of the Scrolls and perhaps their
presectarian forebears. Attuned to the peculiarities of Palestinian
Jewish dualistic discourse, the evangelist appropriated some of its
strategies. That appropriation enabled him or her to make a distinction between those inside and outside the community of the saved.
How that situation came to be and how God's sovereign will and
human responsibility were related in its creation required further
thought.[27] Yet within this "dualistic" framework, which our author
apparently viewed as rhetorical strategy rather than metaphysical
truth, another antithesis loomed large that he found problematic. He
knew of a sharp distinction between flesh and spirit, and gives evidence of that in 3:5 and 6:63. He may have known of the close association of flesh and sin that emerged in Jewish circles and was
appropriated by Paul. Yet our evangelist refuses to follow that path.

The structure of the Prologue, and the conformity of its perspective with the data of the Gospel, suggests that the evangelist
wanted to score a point about the "fleshiness" of Jesus. It was, he
believed, quite central to what it was that Jesus was supposed to do as
his "work." The point so scored was perhaps directed against those
who, like Paul, drew even more of a distinction between flesh and
spirit than he did. Our evangelist may have thought that too sharp a
dichotomy of this sort would lead to too sharp a distinction between
Jesus and the people he was sent to save. If "flesh" was the object of
the salvific process, it could not be disparaged in the ways that Paul did
in Galatians and Romans.

On the issue of flesh and spirit, therefore, the Fourth Gospel
stands in opposition to the position found in the Scrolls and in Paul
that intimately links flesh and sin. Such a notion was not, however,
unknown to the Johannine community, and in the struggle over
Johannine teaching that is reflected in the first epistle, the notion

---

27. That issue is explored in Harold W. Attridge, "Divine Sovereignty and Human
Responsibility in the Fourth Gospel" (Festschrift for Christopher Rowland, forth-
coming).

creeps in at 1 John 2:16, where "desire of the flesh" is something to be avoided, as part of the "cosmos" that is not to be loved. The introduction of this negative note about flesh is of a piece with the insistence in 1 John on the reality of sin (1 John 1:8, 10), which should be confessed in order to be forgiven (1 John 1:9). But this position in 1 John does not represent the dominant position of the Beloved Disciple's tradition, according to which "flesh" was the object to be transformed by the infusion of the Spirit and the vehicle through which that transformative Spirit comes to humankind.

15

Moses in the Gospel of John

Pheme Perkins
(BOSTON COLLEGE)

Whether through his work on Jewish texts from the Second Temple period, his commentary on Matthew, or his suggestions for treating "the Jews" in preaching the lectionary, Fr. Harrington has kept us all engaged with the Jewish family tree of the New Testament.[1] When we were graduate students studying Jewish pseudepigrapha and Dead Sea Scrolls with Professor Strugnell at Harvard, we might not have imagined the extent to which recovery of the diverse forms of Judaism would transform our research and teaching. At that time, the first volume of Raymond Brown's magisterial commentary on John had just been published.[2] His emphasis on interpreting the Gospel as engaged with Jewish religious symbols and the developments of the post-70 CE period was an initial push back against prioritizing Hellenistic sources in popular philosophy or gnostic mythology.[3] Today, contextualizing the Fourth Gospel within first-century Jewish traditions is the default position.[4]

---

1. For example, Daniel J. Harrington, "Pseudo-Philo," *OTP* 2:297–377; idem, *Wisdom Texts from Qumran* (London: Routledge, 1996); idem, *The Gospel of Matthew* (SP 1; Collegeville, MN: Liturgical Press, 1991); and idem, *The Synoptic Gospels Set Free: Preaching without Anti-Judaism* (Mahwah, NJ; Paulist, 2009).

2. Raymond E. Brown, *The Gospel according to John I—XII* (AB 29; New York: Doubleday, 1966).

3. Ibid., lii–lxiv.

4. This is so, even though most commentators do survey the alternative hypotheses linked to Hellenistic philosophical speculation, Gnosticism, and even Buddhism. See

Brown incorporated early work on Moses and exodus typology as well as suggested parallels between Deuteronomy and Johannine discourses.[5] At the same time, he cautioned against the excesses in detecting structural and thematic parallels between the Fourth Gospel and the Old Testament. The evangelist provides explicit statements about Moses that distinguish the Christian view of his significance from that of a Jewish counterstory in John 1:17–18[6] and 5:46.[7] Explicit examples of Moses typology in the service of Johannine Christology involve the lifting up of the bronze serpent in John 3:14–15 (see Num 21:8–9), and manna in the wilderness anticipating Jesus' gift of "bread from heaven" in John 6:25–51 (see Exod 16:4, 15). A third, indirect allusion to the exodus narrative of the water from the rock (see Exod 17:6; Ps 78:16) might lie behind the saying in John 7:38.[8] In addition to these narrative elements, the distinctive Johannine terminology for Jesus' miracles, "signs" (*sēmeia*), as well as the more general term "works" (*erga*) are rooted in the exodus traditions.[9]

Craig S. Keener, *The Gospel of John: A Commentary* (2 vols.; Peabody, MA: Hendrickson, 2003), 1:140–232.

5. Brown, *John I—XII*, lx, citing Howard M. Teeple, *The Mosaic Eschatological Prophet* (SBLMS 10; Philadelphia: Society of Biblical Literature, 1957); and Thomas F. Glasson, *Moses in the Fourth Gospel* (SBT 40; London: SCM, 1963). Subsequent studies of Moses and exodus traditions in the Fourth Gospel include Peder Borgen, *Bread from Heaven: An Exegetical Study of the Conception of Manna in the Gospel of John and the Writings of Philo* (NovTSup 10; Leiden: Brill, 1965); Wayne A. Meeks, *The Prophet-King: Moses Traditions and the Johannine Christology* (NovTSup 14; Leiden: Brill, 1967); Severino Pancaro, *The Law in the Fourth Gospel: The Torah and Gospel, Moses and Jesus, Judaism and Christianity according to John* (NovTSup 62; Leiden: Brill, 1975); and Aelred Lacomara, "Deuteronomy and the Farewell Discourse (Jn 13:31 — 16:33)," *CBQ* 36 (1974): 67–74.

6. Brown (*John I—XII*, 35–36) focuses on covenant theology in presenting the conclusion to the Prologue as announcing a new covenant replacing that of Sinai. Drawing attention to Moses' failure to see God (Exod 33:18) in John 1:18 enables the reader to discern the inferiority of Moses to the "Son who has not only seen the Father but is ever at His side." Since this motif is repeated in John 5:37 and 6:46, Brown concludes that it was likely part of the evangelist's polemic against the synagogue (36).

7. Brown (ibid., 229) reads John 5:45–47 as an attack on the Jews for their refusal to believe in Jesus out of loyalty to Moses (John 9:29) by turning Moses, their intercessor before God, into the one who will accuse or condemn their disbelief.

8. Ibid., 322–23.

9. "Works" is a more general term than "signs," since it sums up the whole ministry of

238

At strategic points in the narrative, Jesus is acknowledged to be "the prophet" like Moses foretold in Deut 18:15–18 (John 4:19; 6:14; 7:40; 9:17). Examples of the anticipation of a "prophet" associated with messianic figures in the Dead Sea Scrolls highlight the significance of this designation in the Fourth Gospel.[10] It always remains an insufficient confession of Jesus' identity in the narrative contexts in which it is used and, with the exception of John 4:19, is embedded in scenes of controversy with Jewish authorities. Deuteronomy 13:1–5 warned against false prophets, using signs or visions, who might lead the people astray from Moses' commandments. That charge animates the accusation against Jesus in John 7:47.

Brown's commentary, which employed the hypotheses of sources that had undergone several stages of editing, remained firmly committed to understanding the relationship between the Fourth Gospel and the Jesus traditions found in the Synoptic Gospels. At the same time, his detailed observations of differences between major blocks of material within the Gospel, particularly what he called the "Book of Signs" (chs. 1 – 12) and the "Book of Glory" (chs. 13 – 21),[11] provided the framework for subsequent treatments of the Gospel from a literary perspective.[12] The Moses references are confined to the first section of the Gospel, which details Jesus' public ministry. Concomitantly, the virulent hostility of opponents designated "the

---

Jesus (John 14:10; 17:4). Acts 7:22 refers to Moses as one "mighty in words and works." John characteristically uses "sign" as a designation for miracles leading to faith in Jesus (John 2:11; 4:54; 20:30). Philo uses comparable terminology (Philo, *Moses* 1.95), as does the LXX, where God multiplies signs through Moses (Exod 10:1; Num 14:22; Deut 7:19), though the people persist in disbelief (Num 14:11) in a fashion comparable to the limited success of Jesus' signs (John 12:37; Brown, *John I–XII*, 528–29).

10. Brown, *John I–XII*, 49–50. Again Brown raises a cautionary note against the early attempts to take the phrase "until the coming of the prophet and the messiahs of Aaron and Israel" from 1 QS ix 11 as a mold into which the Baptist's testimony that he is not the [Davidic] messiah, Elijah, or "the prophet" can be fitted by asserting that Elijah is the priestly messianic figure.

11. Ibid., cxxxviii–cxlvi.

12. E.g., R. Alan Culpepper, *Anatomy of the Fourth Gospel: A Study in Literary Design* (Philadelphia: Fortress, 1983). Even scholars whose methodologies attempt to shake off that framework are influenced by it.

Jews" gives way in the Farewell Discourses to a broader danger posed by "the world" and its ruler (John 14:30; 15:18—16:4), as Jesus turns from addressing "the Jews" to his own disciples.

This survey of the treatment of Moses in Brown's seminal commentary on the Fourth Gospel suggests three lines of investigation: (1) assessment of the Jewish evidence, particularly in view of more recent study of the Qumran evidence (treated in the first two sections below), (2) exploration of the literary functions of Moses motifs in the Gospel, and (3) examination of the apparent anti-Judaism of the polemic within the narrative. Concerns over the latter issue and its ecumenical significance were not on the academic radar screen half a century ago. Brown acknowledges the violence of the exchange in John 8. He concludes that the Johannine community now resided in the Diaspora (ironically indicated in John 7:35) with no interest in winning over Jews: "John's attitude toward 'the Jews' is not missionary but apologetic and polemic."[13]

MOSES AND THE PROPHET

The Fourth Gospel introduces Moses as the one who gave the Law but not its associated "grace (loving kindness) and truth" (John 1:17). Jesus' superiority to Moses is a consequence of his special relationship with God: "No one has ever seen God" (1:18). While Moses' special relationship to God is evident in the Old Testament (Exod 3:2–6; 19:20; 33:9, 22–23), Jewish sources are hesitant to include his "seeing God" in the encounter on Sinai or in his entry into God's presence in the tabernacle. Philo of Alexandria introduces appropriate philosophical caveats against Moses grasping the essence of God.[14] But unlike other human beings, Moses is able to "display" the divine

---

13. Brown, *John I—XII*, lxxii. For a contemporary Jewish perspective on the Fourth Gospel, see Adele Reinhartz, "A Nice Jewish Girl Reads the Gospel of John," *Semeia* 77 (1997): 177–93; and eadem, *Befriending the Beloved Disciple: A Jewish Reading of the Gospel of John* (New York: Continuum, 2001).

14. At the burning bush, Moses saw an angel, not the essence of the "one who is" (*Moses* 1.66).

life in his own for others to imitate (Philo, *Moses* 1.158).[15] John 1:18 lacks the philosophical precision employed in Philo. However the Son will make the Father known by his incarnation (1:14), it does not involve the philosophical conversion of the soul in imitation of the divine form it is able to see. Philo's accounts of the ascent of the soul toward the divine and its divinization typically have the soul identifying with the Logos but being overwhelmed before it actually sees God.[16]

Jewish sources generally agree that Moses did not "see God" but heard God's voice as did the prophet Elijah.[17] Thus the Jewish authorities in John 9:29 affirm, "We know that God spoke to Moses." Other figures such as Ezekiel and Enoch are said to have seen at least God's glory, a human-like form or garment, though not necessarily God's self.[18] *Testament of Levi* 5.1–5 has Levi receive his priesthood from the Most High enthroned in heaven. The unnamed angelic figure who accompanies Levi on the visionary journey into heaven and his return identifies himself as "the angel who makes intercession for the nation Israel, that they might not be beaten."[19] These observations have two important consequences for interpreting the Gospel of John. First, since "no one has ever seen God" is the default position among first-century Jews, the phrase is not a polemical attack on Moses or other Jewish figures. Second, since first-century Jews know of angelic intercessor figures, the appearance of a Paraclete, a Spirit of Truth, with those attributes set forth in the Farewell Discourses (e.g., John 16:7–11) need not serve as a veiled allusion to Moses.

The authorities employ a list of three messianic figures in interrogating John the Baptist: "messiah, Elijah, the prophet" (John 1:21, 25).

---

15. "And like a well-crafted painting he [i.e., Moses] set himself and his life as a very beautiful and divine work, a model (*paradeigma*) for those wishing to imitate (it)" (my translation).

16. Peter Schäfer, *The Origins of Jewish Mysticism* (Tübingen: Mohr Siebeck, 2009), 165–73.

17. Ibid., 45–46.

18. Ibid., 48–67.

19. *OTP* 1:789–90. The angel Michael functions as intercessor in Dan 10:13, 21; 12:1; an unnamed angel in *1 En.* 89.76; 90.14.

Since Elijah is listed separately, he cannot be identified as "the prophet" in question. Therefore "the prophet like Moses" of Deut 18:15–18 appears to be the most plausible candidate. That identification permits the preliminary use of the designation by a Samaritan woman (John 4:19), as well as by a Jewish crowd (6:14). To what extent should the "like Moses" tagged onto the term "the prophet" be emphasized? The list appears to be in descending order of importance. The examples from Qumran also suggest that "the prophet" is preliminary or subordinate to the messiahs of Aaron and Israel: "[They] shall be ruled by the first directives which the men of the Community began to be taught until the prophet comes, and the Messiahs of Aaron and Israel" (1QS IX, 10–11).[20] A similar ordering may be responsible for the first three quotations in 4QTestimonia (4Q175): (1) a combination of Deut 5:28b–29 and 18:18–19 found in the Samaritan version of Exod 20:21; (2) Num 24:15–17, a prophecy of a royal figure; and (3) Deut 33:8–11, Moses' blessing of Levi, which includes teaching of the Law among Levi's duties, all of which point to the priestly messiah figure.[21]

The slim examples of an eschatological prophet in the Dead Sea Scrolls and other Jewish texts surveyed by John Collins raise questions about scholars who stress the "Mosaic connection."[22] The dominant figure associated with the end of days is the prophet Elijah. Expectation for the return of Elijah, perhaps prior to the coming of a Davidic messiah, appears in 4Q558, citing Mal 4:5 (3:22).[23] Elijah also

---

20. Quoted from Florentino García Martínez and Eibert J. C. Tigchelaar, eds., *The Dead Sea Scrolls Study Edition. Vol. 1:1Q1–4Q273* (Leiden: Brill, 1999), 93.

21. Michael A. Knibb, "Apocalypticism and Messianism," in *The Oxford Handbook of the Dead Sea Scrolls* (ed. T. H. Lim and J. J. Collins; Oxford: Oxford University Press, 2010), 421.

22. John J. Collins, *The Scepter and the Star: Messianism in Light of the Dead Sea Scrolls* (2nd ed.; Grand Rapids: Eerdmans, 2010), 128–41. Collins describes the eschatological prophet as a shadowy figure whose biblical links are to the prophet like Moses and to the identification of the "messenger" of Mal 3:1 with Elijah coming before the Day of the Lord in Mal 4:5 (128). The future prophet referred to in 1 Macc 14:41 is not necessarily one "like Moses," though some scholars have made that assumption (129).

23. Knibb, "Apocalypticism and Messianism," 424.

appears to be the most plausible identification for the figure identified as "his anointed one" in 4Q521 (4QMessianic Apocalypse) 2 II, and 4.[24] Collins concludes that though a "prophet like Moses" could be assimilated to the sect's priestly messiah in that both are messianic teachers of righteousness, equating an eschatological prophet with the messiah would be quite anomalous in the Dead Sea Scrolls.[25]

Approaching the Fourth Gospel from the more complex and differentiated picture of first-century CE messianic expectations that has emerged from analysis of the Dead Sea Scrolls upends many assumptions of Johannine scholarship. Rather than adopt Philo's portrayal of Moses as the ideal philosopher-king who combines the offices of prophet, priest, and king as the basis for understanding Johannine Christology,[26] one should read the Gospel as engaging elements of diverse, free-floating messianic speculation. This adaptation shifts the tenor of statements that identify Jesus as "the prophet." Certainly the evangelist has Deut 18:15–18 in his sights when Philip asserts that "we have found the one about whom Moses in the Law and also the prophets wrote" (John 1:45), since John 1:19–51 assembles a catalogue of messianic titles that express correct though partial insights into Jesus' identity. Characters who identify Jesus as "prophet" during the narrative can be understood as advancing a preliminary, ill-defined association between Jesus and the end-time. The benign skepticism associated with Jesus' origins in 1:46 reappears with a harsher tone in the polemic of 7:41–42 ("the messiah") and 7:52 ("prophet"). John repeats the affirmation that both Moses (5:46) and the prophets (12:39–41, referring to Isaiah) wrote about Jesus.

---

24. Ibid.; and Collins, *Scepter and the Star*, 130–37. Collins suggests the possibility that 4Q521 is one of the nonsectarian documents preserved at Qumran, since it refers to resurrection of the dead (fr. 7 I, 6), a motif not typical of the sect's theology (139).

25. Collins, *Scepter and the Star*, 141.

26. A tactic that Meeks (*Prophet-King*, 17–29) employs to inject a more prominent element of Davidic messianism into the Gospel than scholars had previously identified.

MOSES, THE WITNESS OF JESUS

Daniel K. Falk cautions against assuming that the figure of Moses was of equal significance to all expressions of Judaism. The Hellenistic Jewish apologetic common to Aristobulus, Artipanus, Philo, and Josephus recasts the figure of Moses to express Greek ideals of the culture hero, ideal king, legislator, and philosopher. An alternative Palestinian line of development amplifies biblical roles to depict Moses as the one predestined to be Israel's mediator or intercessor and the one to whom God revealed all things up to the end of days.[27] Composed in the first half of the second century BCE, the rewritten account of Gen 1 to Exod 19 in the book of *Jubilees*, which had only been known from its Ethiopic and Latin versions, survives in fifteen fragmentary manuscripts among the Dead Sea Scrolls.[28] Confronted with a minihistory of Israel's apostasy, murder of the prophets ("the witnesses"), persecution of the righteous ("those who search out the Law"), exile, captivity, and restoration, Moses prays for the people in *Jub.* 1.19–21. God instructs Moses, or the angel of the presence, to write down everything from the beginning until the end-time when God will dwell with his people on Zion forever (*Jub.* 1.26–28). These words will serve as testimony to God's justice and fidelity to Israel despite its sinfulness.[29]

The figure of Moses in *Jubilees* points to additional features of the Johannine picture that can be reread within a more differentiated first-century CE context. Not only has Moses written about Jesus because he has been shown the entire history of God's people up to the end-time, but the function of that book is to serve as a witness or testimony. Indeed, the terminology of testimony dominates the Johannine narrative from the initial messianic disclaimers of the Baptist (John 1:19) to

---

27. Daniel K. Falk, "Moses", *EDEJ* 967–70.

28. James C. VanderKam and J. T. Milik, eds., "Jubilees," in *Qumran Cave 4, VIII: Parabiblical Texts, Part 1* (ed. H. W. Attridge; DJD 13; Oxford: Oxford University Press, 1994), 1–140; Michael Segal, *The Book of Jubilees: Rewritten Bible, Redaction, Ideology and Theology* (Leiden: Brill, 2007); and idem, "Jubilees," *EDEJ* 843–46.

29. Cf. 4Q216 I, 11–17.

the highly charged debates over Jesus' testimony about his relationship with the Father (5:31–39; 8:13–18). Against the backdrop of a book recorded at the dictation of the "angel of the presence," the insistence that the Father or Scripture have testified to Jesus (5:32, 37–39; 8:18) serves as shorthand for knowledge of the truth revealed on Sinai.

The culmination of the dispute in John 5:45–47 picks up the idea that the book that Moses wrote would function as testimony to future generations. Israel's apostasy, murder of God's witnesses (i.e., the prophets), and hostility to those engaged in searching out the true meaning of the Scriptures are all recorded in the book. Yet, despite the evils that the people had done and the just judgments of God, the testimony as *Jubilees* presents it is positive, "so that their generations may know that I have not forsaken them" (4Q216 1 3). However, it is a very small step to read the same litany of a people turning away from God as evidence for the prosecution of those opposed to the one who has been sent from the Father.[30] John 5:45–47 makes that shift from Moses as intercessor, who prayed on behalf of a sinful people (*Jub.* 1.19–21), to one who will testify for the prosecution against the present generation.[31]

Has Moses switched sides? Not at all, if one treats the Johannine passage as representative of intra-Jewish debates in the first century CE.[32] In fact, his role as intercessor for Israel in the past makes this appearance on Jesus' behalf even more striking. The rumbling that broke out in John 5 returns in a section that the present narrative order includes with Jesus' testimony at a later point, at the Feast of Tabernacles

---

30. Andrew Lincoln suggests a parallel with the use of the lawsuit in Second Isaiah, where the Lord defends his actions by turning accusations against him back on the people Israel. See his *Truth on Trial: The Lawsuit Motif in the Fourth Gospel* (Peabody, MA: Hendrickson, 2000), 80–81.

31. Although the verb *kategoreō* can be read to imply that Moses is stepping into the shoes of a heavenly prosecuting attorney, the forensic image only requires that Moses take the stand as witness to the true interpretation of his writings. Keener (*Gospel of John*, 1:661) points out that the expression is employed for the witness against someone, not the prosecutor in a Palestinian context.

32. J. D. Atkins constructs an elaborate set of patches to 5:30–47 in arguing that a full-fledged "trial" of Jesus as false prophet lies behind this section. See his "The Trial of the People and the Prophet: John 5:30–47 and the True and False Prophet Traditions," *CBQ* 75 (2013): 279–96.

(7:14–35). Rudolf Schnackenburg defends the older source- and redaction-critical approach to resolving the Gospel's discontinuities by reconstructing narrative sequences that were dislocated by subsequent editing.[33] He suggests that 7:15–24 was initially the conclusion to chapter 5.[34] The allegation that Jesus claims a knowledge of the Scriptures that an uneducated person could not possess in 7:15 thus picks up the reference to "the writings of Moses" in 5:47. Jesus' claim to have been "taught by the one who sent me [i.e., God]" evokes the revelation of the Law to Moses on Sinai, which in *Jubilees* involved mediation of what was written by the "angel of the presence."[35] Jesus' claim is comparable to that advanced for Moses.

Though the crowd is incredulous when Jesus charges those who seek to kill him with violating the Mosaic Law (John 7:19–20), *Jubilees* suggests that death is the appropriate penalty for Sabbath violators.[36] The legal argument that Jesus offers in defense of healing the paralytic on the Sabbath—namely, circumcising on the Sabbath—is less radical than the assertion of a unique relationship with the Father in John 5:19–23. The vignette concludes with an injunction to judge justly, not by appearances (7:24). To whom are those words addressed? To the opposition designated here as "the Jews" (7:15)? Or to the "crowd" (7:20) that is often partially aware of Jesus' identity? Although this pericope reaches back to the earlier debate, 7:24 provides a transition to the divided opinions of 7:25–31, concluding with many in the crowd asking, "the messiah when he comes, will he do more signs than this man has done?" (7:31).[37]

The evangelist or final redactor patched the awkwardness of not appearing to have a capital charge against Jesus by inserting the com-

---

33. Rudolf Schnackenburg, *The Gospel according to St. John* (3 vols.; trans. K. Smyth; New York: Seabury, 1979–82), 2:1–4.

34. Ibid., 2:131.

35. Some scholars treat the angelic mediator as a demotion of Moses from direct contact with the deity (e.g., Falk, "Moses," 968; and Segal, "Jubilees," 845).

36. Cf. 4Q218 fr. 1.

37. Even though the evangelist has only narrated one "sign," the healing of the paralytic in Jerusalem, John 2:23 reveals that Jesus has worked other miracles there during a previous Passover, which is confirmed by Nicodemus's words in his private visit to Jesus: "No one can do the signs which you do if God is not with him" (John 3:2).

ment at John 7:1, "after these things Jesus went about in Galilee because he did not wish to go about in Judea since the Jews [or Judeans?][38] were seeking to kill him." Solving one problem created another. John 6 presents a long account of Jesus' activities in Galilee and is not an appropriate referent for "these events." Schnackenburg concurs with the view that chapter 6 is also out of its original sequence, which originally had it after chapter 4.[39] On either ordering, 7:1 is more of a narrative placeholder that presumes an audience will fill in the temporal gap between the "near Passover" of 6:4 and "near Tabernacles" of 7:2 with more of the same.

Another set of awkward "joins" between episodes marks the second half of chapter 7. Authorities, here designated as "Pharisees" and "chief priests and Pharisees" (7:32), send servants to nip in the bud the growing belief among the crowd. Jesus speaks cryptic words about his departure, which "the Jews"—the phrase is apparently being used here as a neutral term for those in the crowd—interpret as a departure to the "Greeks" (i.e., to the Diaspora).[40] Then a temporal notice marks another speech by Jesus as "on the last great day of the feast."[41] The crowd resumes debate over whether Jesus is "the prophet" or "the Davidic messiah" (7:40–44), and the servants return sufficiently convinced of Jesus' special status so that they do not arrest him (7:45–46).

Thus the narrative sequence marking Jesus' appearance at the Feast of Tabernacles concludes by pitting the religious authorities designated as "high priests" and "Pharisees," who will not believe in any prophet from Galilee, against the emerging faith of "this crowd which does not know the Law" (John 7:49). A similar dynamic will play out in chapter 9 when local authorities identified as "Pharisees" (9:13, 15, 16) or "the Jews" (9:18, 22) interrogate a blind man whom Jesus

---

38. Since the violence is associated with a geographical region, it is more appropriate to translate *Ioudaioi* as the designation of those who live there rather than as an ethnic or religious term (Keener, *Gospel of John*, 1:704).

39. Schnackenburg, *Gospel according to St. John*, 2:4–9.

40. When "the Greeks" come seeking Jesus in John 12:20–22, Jesus announces that the hour of his glorification/death has come (12:23–24).

41. Apparently the added "eighth day." See *Jub.* 32.27–29.

healed on the Sabbath. This exchange contains elements that echo experiences of the implied audience: fear of authorities who can expel believers from the synagogue (9:22; repeated in 12:42–43; 16:1–4a); and being labeled as "sinners" by those who proudly call themselves "disciples of Moses" (9:28–29). Yet the reader knows that Moses will testify against these leaders (5:45). Nicodemus breaks up the united front of the "leaders" and "Pharisees" by suggesting that they are in violation of the Law by judging someone without hearing from him (7:51).[42] Thus the reader knows that the Law of Moses cannot be blamed for Jesus' death. Despite the claim of "the Jews" before Pilate—"we have a law and according to the law he ought to die because he made himself Son of God" (19:7)—the authorities never properly investigated the charge. The decision to execute was made by a council of "high priests and Pharisees" acting outside the Law (11:45–53).

Attending to the figure of Moses in John 5, 7, and 9 raises a complex set of relationships between opposition to Jesus by "disciples of Moses"—variously described as "Jews," "Pharisees," or "high priests"— and the Law. God has indeed spoken to Moses as these authorities allege (9:29). But their efforts to interpret Moses' writings ("searching the Scriptures," 5:39) fail to discern the truth that had been revealed to Moses on Sinai. Jesus as the one sent from the Father has both heard *and seen* God (5:36–37). The evangelist is able to enlist Moses as a witness on Jesus' behalf by appealing to a Moses tradition that focuses on the eschatological terminus of the story. God presented the entire story up to the end-time. Consequently, both Moses and the Law are witnesses for Jesus and against those who do not believe in him. Even if local authorities expel "disciples of that man [Jesus]" from the synagogue, Moses along with the patriarchs and prophets remain with them.

---

42. In case the reader has forgotten, the narrator points out that Nicodemus had come to Jesus (John 7:50).

MOSES TYPOLOGY AND SIGNS

Our final examples of Moses in the Fourth Gospel consider narratives that cast Moses as pointing forward to Christ. As noted above, there are at least two and possibly three such examples in the Book of Signs. Although Jewish sources do not indicate that any particular list of signs was required of a messianic claimant,[43] the positive link between the miracles understood as "signs" and faith is presumed in the narrative (John 2:11, 23; 3:2; 4:54; 6:2, 14; 7:31; 9:16; 12:18; 20:30–31). Not everyone is convinced by "signs." Demands to produce a "sign" indicate a lack of faith (2:18; 4:48; 6:26, 30; 12:37). Authorities' concern about the belief evoked by Jesus' signs motivates the plot to kill him (11:47). This complex picture may reflect a corrective to the Christology of a miracle source employed by the evangelist.[44] Only one of Jesus' miracles in the Gospel is associated with Moses, the multiplication of the loaves, which provokes the crowd to identify Jesus as "the prophet" (6:14). In the ensuing discourse between Jesus and the crowd, the analogy between the manna in the wilderness and Jesus' gift of "bread from heaven" points to the distinction between a literal expectation of food and the symbolic representation of the life-giving word or bread from Jesus (6:30–51). Jesus' self-identification as bread and water that ends hunger and thirst (6:35) could be associated with the Law[45] or with Wisdom (see Sir 24:21). In any case, Jesus charges those who continue to press for some additional sign: "You have seen and yet do not believe" (6:36). Signs only awaken faith in those given to Jesus by God (6:39–40).

The evangelist employs a simpler Mosaic typology to illustrate the saving significance of Jesus' death on the cross in John 3:14–15. The continuation by the narrator in 3:16 clarifies the reference to the

---

43. Keener, *Gospel of John*, 1:278.

44. Robert T. Fortna, "From Christology to Soteriology: A Redaction-Critical Study of Salvation in the Fourth Gospel," *Int* 27 (1973): 31–47; and idem, *The Fourth Gospel and Its Predecessor: From Narrative Source to Present Gospel* (Philadelphia: Fortress, 1988).

45. Borgen, *Bread from Heaven*, 69–80.

death of Jesus in 3:14, namely, "the Son of Man must be lifted up."[46] Neither the MT nor the LXX of Num 21:9 associates elevation or lifting up with the bronze serpent. However, the LXX uses the Greek word *sēmeion* ("sign") to translate the Hebrew "flag" or "standard" (*nēs*).[47] What follows in 3:16–21 provides an application of the image for the Johannine believer. What precedes suggests that Nicodemus's failure to comprehend Jesus' discourse on rebirth through the Spirit shows that he (and anyone who has similar difficulty with elementary topics) will not grasp what Jesus has come down from heaven to reveal (3:10–13).

Both of these Mosaic typologies associate faith in Jesus as the one who has come down from heaven with salvation as the gift of eternal life (John 3:15; 6:27, 33, 40, 51). Brown proposes a third, less direct, allusion to the "water from the rock" episode in Exod 17:6, as reflected in the Psalms (Pss 78:15–16; 105:40–41), for Jesus' declaration on the final day of the Feast of Tabernacles (John 7:37–38).[48] The narrator's explanation in 7:39 recaptures the symbolic equation of water with the Spirit from 3:5–8 and anticipates the gift of the Spirit after Jesus' return to the Father as promised in the Farewell Discourses (14:16–17, 26; 16:13).

Brown hypothesized that a final editing of the Gospel was carried out after the evangelist's death to preserve Johannine material that had not been incorporated into the earlier edition(s) of the work. Rather than rewrite the whole, these additions were attached to the conclusion of appropriate units.[49] The most expansive of the three Moses typologies, the bread of life material in John 6, represents all stages of

---

46. Brown, *John I–XII*, 134.

47. Brown (ibid., 133) appeals to later Targums for the idea of suspending the serpent or placing it on an elevated spot.

48. Ibid., 322.

49. E.g., John 3:31–36; 6:51b–59; and chs. 15–17 (ibid., xxxvi–xxxvii). While much recent English language scholarship has moved away from such analyses on grounds that one can discern a literary unity in the text as we have received it, textual difficulties still persist. For a spirited defense of source- and redaction-critical analysis as the only solution to the difficulties presented by the text of the Gospel as we have it, see John Ashton, *Understanding the Fourth Gospel* (rev. ed.; Oxford: Oxford University Press, 2007), 26–48.

the Johannine tradition, from the Synoptic-type miracle sequence of miraculous feeding (John 6:1–13) and walking on water (6:16–21), to the final editor's incorporation of the eucharistic formulae (6:51b–58). At what point does the Moses typology enter the picture? Most exegetes who adopt this working hypothesis see the bulk of the discourse material in chapter 6 as the evangelist's reworking and expansion of his earlier Gospel.[50] While the manna interpretation of the feeding miracle demonstrates that Jesus is the one about whom Moses wrote (5:46–47), the expanded discourse focuses on the christological confession that Jesus is uniquely the one who has come down from heaven. It reprises the earlier contrast between Jesus and other revealers like Moses with the claim that no one "has seen the Father except the one who is from God" (6:46).[51]

This analysis of the discourse material in John 6 suggests an answer to our question about the Moses typology. It is to be distinguished from the other elements of Moses tradition that engage in intra-Jewish debates over the roles of various figures in the end of days. The evangelist has adapted the Moses exemplar to express a christological perspective that was not shared by all followers of Jesus (so 6:60–69). Peder Borgen's proposal that John 6:30–58 forms an extended midrash on the Scripture citation in 6:31, "bread from heaven he gave them to eat," taking each word in order,[52] indicates that the evangelist follows a homiletic pattern in composing this section of the Gospel. The other two cases are less developed. However, the distinction between preliminary or elementary ("earthly") teaching and the "heavenly" teaching of Jesus as Son of Man in 3:12–15 suggests that the bronze serpent typology can only be grasped by fully initiated Christians. John 3:10–11 sets up the contrast between the two communities of discourse: Nicodemus, a "teacher of Israel" who fails

---

50. For example, see Barnabas Lindars, *The Gospel of John* (London: Oliphants, 1972); Ashton, *Understanding the Fourth Gospel*, 47; and James F. McGrath, *John's Apologetic Christology: Legitimation and Development in Johannine Christology* (SNTSMS 111; Cambridge, UK: Cambridge University, 2001), 173–79.

51. Cf. John 1:18; 3:13; 5:37–38. See McGrath, *John's Apologetic Christology*, 174.

52. Borgen, *Bread from Heaven*, 28–57.

the preliminaries, over against the "we" who know, have seen, and tes- tify. As suggested above, the third example (7:37–39) is little more than notes for future development of the theme, perhaps incorporated by the final editor of the Gospel.

MOSES, THE JEWS, AND THE AUDIENCE

To conclude this overview of Moses in the Fourth Gospel, we turn to its implications for the problems associated with depiction of the Jews. Acerbic polemic in which Jesus denies the Abrahamic descent of his opponents and calls them "children of the devil" because of their disbelief (John 8:39–47), as well as consistently dual- istic rhetoric that distinguishes believers from unbelievers, open the Gospel to charges of being anti-Jewish and a source of deadly anti- Semitism.[53] This perception is heightened when translators, scholars, and preachers fail to represent the differentiations present in the Gospel between determined opponents of Jesus—always religious authorities and referred to as "Pharisees," "Pharisees and high priests," or "the Jews"—and the use of a neutral or regional designation, "the Jews," as well as references to individuals, people, or crowds who respond to Jesus with some degree of anticipation that he might be the anticipated messiah.[54] At the narrative level, such neutral identifying phrases as "Jews from Jerusalem" (1:19), "purification rite of the Jews" (2:6), or "Passover, the feast of the Jews" (6:4) suggest an implied audi- ence at some distance from actual Jews or their concerns.[55]

---

53. See the collection of essays in Reimund Rieringer, Didier Pollefeyt, and Frederique Vandecasteele-Vanneuville, eds., *Anti-Judaism and the Fourth Gospel* (Assen: Van Gorcum, 2001); and Ashton, *Understanding the Fourth Gospel*, 68–95.

54. For surveys of the Johannine usage of "the Jews" and related terminology, see Schnackenburg, *Gospel according to St. John*, 1:287; U. C. von Wahlde, "The Johannine 'Jews': A Critical Survey," *NTS* 28 (1982): 33–60; and Robert Kysar, "Anti-Semitism and the Gospel of John," in *Anti-Semitism and Early Christianity* (ed. C. A. Evans and D. A. Hagner; Minneapolis: Fortress, 1993), 113–27.

55. Kysar, "Anti-Semitism and the Gospel of John," 114.

Such a distancing might suggest that the evangelist, responding to the literary need for a "good villain" in the piece, has simply crafted "the Jews" as diabolic opponents for the conflict-driven central section in John 5—12. After all, the opposition shifts to "the world" and its ruler, the Devil, in chapters 13—17. An analysis of the audience of the Fourth Gospel inspired by performance theory confirms the suggested divisions but challenges the simple equation: implied audience = believers = non-Jews.[56] Viewed from an actor's or storyteller's perspective, Jesus rarely speaks with a non-Jew. In the significant scenes where he does so, the fact is strongly marked by the evangelist. The Samaritan woman distinguishes herself from Jesus in terms of both gender and ethnicity (4:9); Pilate does so in terms of ethnicity (18:35) and authority (19:10). Therefore the narrative actually requires a wider range of Jewish responses to and interactions with Jesus than any of the other Gospels.[57]

Over against the shifting groups of Jews with which he is confronted, the character of Jesus plays out as one who "both fulfills long held hopes and confounds them by his freedom."[58] This approach complements our historical-critical analysis of "the prophet like Moses" and Moses as witness for Jesus in the Fourth Gospel. As we have seen, the evangelist is not at all distant from first-century Jewish debates. His depiction of Jesus in relationship to Moses draws upon established traditions about God's revelation on Sinai. Even the possibility of Moses being called into the heavenly courtroom for the prosecution of those who refused to believe the "one sent by God" and who persecuted Jesus' followers is not anti-Jewish. It reflects the kind of debate over fidelity to the Mosaic revelation at the end of days that divided Jewish groups from each other.

Finally, the Johannine audience can hardly be as detached from its Jewish origins as the polemics in the narrative have suggested. A

---

56. Thomas E. Boomershine, "The Medium and the Message of John: Audience Address and Audience Identity in the Fourth Gospel," in *The Fourth Gospel in First-Century Media Culture* (ed. A. Le Donne and T. Thatcher; London: T & T Clark, 2011), 92–120.

57. Ibid., 107–10.

58. Ibid., 117.

certain separation from the calendar of Jewish feasts would be inevitable a quarter century after the destruction of Jerusalem by the Romans—a tragedy that the high priest ironically hopes to avert with the death of Jesus (John 11:49–52). Our third strand of Moses traditions, the typologies associated with Moses' signs in the wilderness (bronze serpent, manna, water from the rock), provides an additional glimpse of the evangelist at work. These examples point to a homiletic use of the Moses figure to present to believers the deepest truths of their faith: "God so loved the world that he gave his only Son so that everyone who believes in him may not perish but have eternal life" (3:16).

16

Prophecy Revived

The Use of Older Scripture in the Book of Revelation

Adela Yarbro Collins
(YALE DIVINITY SCHOOL)

PRELIMINARY REMARKS

I am happy to dedicate this essay to Dan Harrington and Dick Clifford, two friends of long duration and valued colleagues. Although my focus here is limited, I would like to emphasize that the author of the Book of Revelation drew upon a variety of traditions and practices known to him in his diverse cultural milieu. Although the Scriptures of Israel play a major role in the book, he also drew upon postbiblical Jewish, Greek, and Roman traditions.[1] The second point to note is that John drew upon a wide variety of books from the Jewish Scriptures (or their reoralized traditions). For example, he uses "the tree of life" from the depiction of paradise in Genesis to describe the new Jerusalem (Rev 22:2; cf. Gen 2:9; 3:22–24). He adapts the ten plagues from the

---

1. Adela Yarbro Collins, "Portraits of Rulers in the Book of Revelation," in *Neues Testament und hellenistisch-jüdische Alltagskultur. Wechselseitige Wahrnehmungen. III. Internationales Symposium zum Corpus Judaeo-Hellenisticum Novi Testamenti* (ed. R. Deines, J. Herzer, and K.-W. Niebuhr; WUNT 274; Tübingen: Mohr Siebeck, 2011), 275–99; and eadem, *The Combat Myth in the Book of Revelation* (HDR 9; Missoula, MT: Scholars Press, 1976; repr. Eugene, OR: Wipf and Stock, 2001).

Book of Exodus to present seven eschatological plagues (Rev 9:20; 15:1—16:21; cf. Exod 7:14—12:32). In this essay, however, I will focus on a selection of allusions to the prophets. Among them I include Daniel because of its importance in Revelation.

ALLUSIONS TO DANIEL

The first verse of the Book of Revelation already echoes lines in Dan 2. John's noun "revelation" may have been inspired by Daniel's statement that there is a God in heaven who "reveals mysteries" (Dan 2:28). John's phrase "what must happen soon" affirms the speedy fulfillment of Daniel's "what must happen at the end of days" (2:28). Finally, Daniel declares, "the great God has made known to the king the things that will be in the last days" (2:45). John uses the same verb with Christ as the subject: "and he made (it) known through his angel to his servant John."[2]

John again alludes to Daniel in the prophetic saying that occurs near the beginning of the work, "Look, he is coming with the clouds" (Rev 1:7a; cf. Dan 7:13). John uses the present tense for a future event in order to express a vivid, realistic confidence in the speedy fulfillment of the oracle. The most striking thing about this allusion is its lack of an explicit subject for the verb. That lack is filled later in the first chapter.

In the text of Revelation, this initial allusion to Dan 7:13 is combined with an evocation of Zech 12, "and every eye will see him, including those who pierced him, and all the tribes of the earth will mourn over him" (Zech 12:10–14). In Revelation, the subject of the "seeing" is broadened from the house of David and the inhabitants of Jerusalem to "every eye." Similarly, the subject of the mourning has been expanded to "all the tribes of the earth." In Zechariah, the inhabitants of Jerusalem mourn in a spirit of compassion and supplication. John's interpretation lacks any reference to compassion. A spirit of

---

2. The subject is probably Christ but could be God. Revelation 22:16 supports the inference that Christ is the subject here.

supplication may be implied. Those who do not adhere to the God of Israel and to Christ will mourn when they see his exaltation. They probably mourn because they perceive that he is about to condemn and punish them.

The first section of the main part of Revelation consists of an epiphany of Christ (Rev 1:9—3:22). John sees "seven golden lampstands," and in their midst "one like a son of man" (1:12–13). It is noteworthy that the author of Revelation does not use the quasititular phrase found in all four Gospels, "the Son of Man." Rather, he translates the Aramaic of Daniel with an equivalent phrase in Greek. The conclusion that John alludes to Dan 7:13 here is supported by the attribution, in the next verse, of characteristics of the Ancient of Days to this figure, indicating a link with another part of Dan 7.[3]

It is striking that the risen Christ in the first chapter of Revelation is portrayed as similar to both the Ancient of Days and the one like a son of man. The interpretation of the figure who appears to John in Rev 1 is a challenging and delicate task because it involves the interpretation of images. The similarity between the one like a son of man and the Ancient of Days may be interpreted in a wide variety of ways. One way involves harmonizing this passage with the later Christian creeds. Another way, which I favor, is to interpret this fusion of images in light of comparable texts from the milieu in which John wrote.

The work known as the Parables of Enoch (*1 En.* 37–71) alludes to Daniel's Ancient of Days but transforms the name to the Head of Days (*1 En.* 46.1).[4] This figure is apparently identical to the Lord of the Spirits mentioned in the same context (*1 En.* 46.3). The two epithets are typically used in the Parables to designate the God of Israel.[5] The Head of Days is clearly distinguished from "another, whose face

---

3. In Rev 1:14 the hair of the head of the one like a son of man is white, like white wool, like snow. This verse alludes to Dan 7:9 and transfers the "white as snow" from the raiment of the Ancient of Days to his hair.

4. See George W. E. Nickelsburg and James C. VanderKam, *1 Enoch: A New Translation Based on the Hermeneia Commentary* (Minneapolis: Fortress, 2004), 59 and note c. Quotations from *1 Enoch* are taken from this volume.

5. George W. E. Nickelsburg, *1 Enoch 1: A Commentary on the Book of 1 Enoch, Chapters 1–36; 81–108* (Hermeneia; Minneapolis: Fortress, 2001), 43.

was like the appearance of a man," who is also called "that son of man" (*1 En.* 46.1–2). Here we have a second allusion, this time to Daniel's "one like a son of man." This second figure is similar to the angels: "His face was full of graciousness like one of the holy angels" (*1 En.* 46.1). Yet he has a higher status than they insofar as he is the one whom the Lord of Spirits has chosen to execute judgment on sinners, presumably as God's delegate or agent (*1 En.* 46.3–8).

In the *Apocalypse of Abraham*, an angel by the name of Iaoel guides Abraham on his heavenly journey (*Apoc. Ab.* 10.1–17; 15.1—29.21).[6] In this work, Iaoel is both the name of this angel and a name of God (*Apoc. Ab.* 10.3, 8; 17.13). Abraham hears the voice of God saying, "Go, Iaoel of the same name, through the mediation of my ineffable name, consecrate this man for me and strengthen him against his trembling" (*Apoc. Ab.* 10.3). Abraham then remarks, "The angel he sent to me in the likeness of a man came" (*Apoc. Ab.* 10.4). A little later, Abraham describes the angel as follows,

> "The appearance of his body was like sapphire, and the aspect of his face was like chrysolite, and the hair of his head like snow. And a [headdress] (was) on his head, its look that of a rainbow, and the clothing of his garments (was) purple; and a golden [scepter] (was) in his right hand." (*Apoc. Ab.* 11.2–3)[7]

The sapphire and rainbow evoke the one seated on the chariot throne in Ezekiel (1:26–28). The scepter suggests governing power. The name of this angel, as well as his appearance, leads to the conclusion that he is the highest angel, God's deputy, appointed to exercise God's power and authority in his place.

---

6. See Ryszard Rubinkiewicz, "Apocalypse of Abraham," in *OTP* 1:681–705, esp. 693–94, 696–704; A. Pennington, "The Apocalypse of Abraham," in *The Apocryphal Old Testament* (ed. H. F. D. Sparks; Oxford: Clarendon, 1984), 363–91, esp. 376–77, 379–90; and Steven L. McKenzie, "Jaoel," in *ABD* 3:641. Rubinkiewicz ("Apocalypse of Abraham," 683) and McKenzie date the work to the late first or early second century CE; Pennington ("Apocalypse of Abraham," 366–67) to some point between 70 and 350 CE. Quotations from *Apocalypse of Abraham* are taken from Rubinkiewicz's translation.

7. See Rubinkiewicz, "Apocalypse of Abraham," notes b and c to ch. 11.

The figure of Iaoel is a very interesting analogy to the risen Christ in the first chapter of Revelation. Both figures have features characteristic of the Ancient of Days, yet they are not identical with the God of Israel. The Parables of Enoch do not apply attributes of the Ancient of Days to the humanlike figure of Dan 7. The Parables explicitly state, however, that the Son of Man will exercise judgment, an activity that is typically ascribed to God in the Hebrew Bible. Similarly, in Revelation the execution of judgment is an activity ascribed to the figure in human form identified with the risen Christ (see esp. Rev 19:11–16). These roughly contemporary texts suggest that the fusing of images in the description of the one like a son of man in Revelation expresses the idea that Christ is God's deputy, the one to whom God delegates activities such as judging sinners.

PROPHETIC ALLUSIONS TO PERSONIFIED BABYLON

As is well known, John depicts the singularity of the Roman Empire by rewriting Daniel's vision of four beasts coming up out of the sea (Dan 7:2–8). Instead of depicting four beasts representing four kingdoms, John combines their features to describe one horrific beast that represents an empire greater and more fearsome than any of Daniel's four. John also refers to this empire with the code name "Babylon," thus invoking prophetic texts concerning the earlier imperial city. This code name was selected because agents of the Roman emperor destroyed Jerusalem in John's time, just as agents of the ruler of Babylon did at an earlier time.[8]

The first use of the code name occurs in Rev 14, where John sees three angels flying in midheaven, each making a proclamation in turn. The second angel declares, "Fallen, fallen is Babylon the great, who has caused all the nations to drink of the wine of her passionate

---

8. Adela Yarbro Collins, *Crisis and Catharsis: The Power of the Apocalypse* (Philadelphia: Westminster, 1984), 57–58.

whoring" (Rev 14:8).[9] John's phrase "Fallen, fallen is Babylon the great" echoes the Hebrew of Isa 21:9 in its repetition of the verb. The claim that the new Babylon had caused all the nations to drink wine associated with fornication may have been inspired by Jeremiah's remark, "Babylon was a golden cup in the LORD's hand, / making all the earth drunken; / the nations drank of her wine, / and so the nations went mad," since the following verse announces, "Suddenly Babylon has fallen and is shattered" (Jer 51:7–8 MT; LXX 28:7–8).

The fall of the new Babylon is predicted in more detail in the account of the seventh bowl: "And the great city split into three parts, and the cities of the nations fell. And Babylon the great was remembered in the presence of God, and she was given the cup of the wine of the wrathful anger of God" (Rev 16:19).[10] This oracle picks up the angel's announcement in chapter 14 and prepares for the detailed treatment of the judgment of Babylon in the following chapters.

At the beginning of Rev 17, one of the seven angels who had the seven bowls comes to John and offers to show him "the judgment of the great whore who is seated by many waters." This phrase echoes Jer 51:13 (LXX 28:13):

> You who live by mighty waters,
> rich in treasures,
> your end has come.

Since Jeremiah's oracle is spoken against "the inhabitants of Babylon" (51:12 MT; LXX 28:13), this allusion identifies the whore of Revelation as the new Babylon. This inference is confirmed by Rev 17:5, which declares: "And upon her forehead, a name (is) written, a mystery, Babylon the great, the mother of whores and of the abominations of the earth."

In the Hebrew Bible and the LXX, the term *whore* (and the

---

9. Translations from the Greek New Testament and LXX are mine; those from the Hebrew are from the NRSV.

10. The breaking of the city into three parts may be understood as a result of the great earthquake mentioned in the previous verse; so David E. Aune, *Revelation 6–16* (WBC 52B; Nashville: Nelson, 1998), 862, 900.

related verb) is most often used of Israel, Samaria, Judah, and Jerusalem.[11] On two occasions, it is used of foreign cities: Nineveh in the Book of Nahum and Tyre in Isa 23. In both Nahum and Isa 23, the literary context suggests a variety of reasons for the use of language about whoring. At the beginning of the relevant oracle against Nineveh in Nahum, bloodshed, deceit, and plunder are mentioned (Nah 3:1). The immediate context has a different nuance:

> Because of the countless fornications of the whore,
>   beautiful and pleasing, mistress of sorcery,
> who sells nations through her fornication
>   and peoples through her sorcery,
> I am against you,
>   says the LORD of hosts,
>   and will lift up your skirts over your face;
> and I will let the nations look on your nakedness
>   and kingdoms on your shame.
> I will throw filth at you
>   and treat you with contempt,
>   and make you a spectacle.
> Then all who see you will shrink from you and say,
> "Nineveh is devastated; who will bemoan her?"
>   Where shall I seek comforters for you? (Nah 3:4–7)[12]

The language here is open to a number of interpretations. The previous references to bloodshed and plunder link the oracle to the violent military conquests of the Assyrians.[13] In this light, the beauty and pleasing allure of the personified city may express the attraction exercised by power and dominance. In the immediate context of the whor-

---

11. See Hos 4:10–19 (Israel); Isa 1:21 (Jerusalem); Isa 57:3 (the postexilic community in Judah); Jer 3:3 (Israel and Judah); Ezek 16:30, 31, 35 (Jerusalem); and Ezek 23:43, 44 (Samaria and Jerusalem).

12. I have revised the NRSV translation of the Hebrew in light of some features of the Greek version.

13. On the date of Nahum, see Kevin J. Cathcart, "Nahum, Book of," *ABD* 4:998–1000, esp. 998–99.

ing imagery, however, the language of "selling nations" suggests that it has to do with trade or some other kind of commercial interaction.

Isaiah 23:1–14 is "an ironic injunction to others to lament."[14] This passage may have been a model for Rev 18, which is also an ironic lament.[15] The poem of Isa 23:1–14, however, does not use imagery of whoring. Such imagery occurs in the later addition in verses 15–18. These verses envision an improvement in the condition of Tyre, seventy years after the destruction described in the preceding poem:

> At the end of seventy years, it will happen to Tyre as in the song about the whore:
> Take a harp,
>   go about the city,
>   you forgotten whore!
> Make sweet melody,
>   sing many songs,
>   that you may be remembered.

> At the end of seventy years, the LORD will visit Tyre, and she will return to her trade, and will whore with all the kingdoms of the world on the face of the earth. Her merchandise and her wages will be dedicated to the LORD; her profits will not be stored or hoarded, but her merchandise will supply abundant food and fine clothing for those who live in the presence of the LORD.[16]

It is somewhat paradoxical that the trade and merchandise of Tyre is associated with whoring, yet nevertheless will be dedicated to the Lord and used by the people of the Lord. A reason for the use of imagery of whoring may be found in the preceding poem (Isa 23:8–9):

---

14. Joseph Blenkinsopp, *Isaiah 1–39* (AB 19; New York: Doubleday, 2000), 344.

15. The two texts also share references to merchants, trade upon the sea, and princes, rulers, or kings—merchants: Isa 23:8; Rev 18:3, 11; trade upon the sea: Isa 23:2–3; Rev 18:17, 19; rulers: Isa 23:8 (MT: whose merchants were princes; LXX: whose merchants were glorious rulers of the earth); and kings of the earth: Rev 18:3, 9.

16. See also Ezek 28:16–18, part of a lament over Tyre, which attributes its downfall to violence, pride, and injustice in trade.

Who has planned this
    against Tyre, the bestower of crowns,
whose merchants were princes,
    whose traders were the honored ones of the earth?
The LORD of hosts has planned it—
    to defile the pride of all glory,
    to shame all the honored of the earth.

From this point of view, it is not trade and merchandise themselves that are problematic. Rather, it is the pride of the people of the city that is offensive. This interpretation explains the reversal by which it is the people of the Lord who will enjoy the profits of Tyre's trade.

The additional verses (Isa 23:15–18), however, speak about Tyre returning to her trade and whoring with all the kingdoms of the world on the face of the earth. Such language implies that there is something wanton or immoral about trade. This implication may be due to the assumption that dishonesty and exploitation are inevitably involved in intercity or international trade. Another possibility is that the whoring metaphor expresses a conservative social perspective that values wealth resulting from land more highly than wealth deriving from commerce.[17] Finally, economic changes may be viewed in moral terms.[18]

---

17. Cf. Robert M. Royalty Jr., *The Streets of Heaven: The Ideology of Wealth in the Apocalypse of John* (Macon, GA: Mercer University Press, 1998), 102–11, 209–10.

18. Marvin L. Chaney has argued that in the eighth century BCE the kings of Israel and Judah (Jeroboam II and Uzziah) reorganized their economies to facilitate participation in international trade. The creation of more efficient, large farms destroyed the old system of subsistence farming by the peasants and made their lives less stable and secure. See his "Bitter Bounty: The Dynamics of Political Economy Critiqued by the Eighth-Century Prophets," in *The Bible and Liberation: Political and Social Hermeneutics* (rev. ed.; ed. N. K. Gottwald and R. A. Horsley; Maryknoll, NY: Orbis; 1993), 250–63; and idem, "Micah—Models Matter: Political Economy and Micah 6:9–15," in *Ancient Israel: The Old Testament in Its Social Context* (ed. P. F. Esler; London: SCM, 2005), 145–60, esp. 146–49. For an analysis of similar changes in the economy of Judea in the first century CE, see Martin Goodman, *The Ruling Class of Judea: The Origins of the Jewish Revolt against Rome A.D. 66–70* (Cambridge, UK: Cambridge University Press, 1987), 51–75. See also Keith Hopkins, "Taxes and Trade in the Roman Empire (200 B.C.–A.D. 400)," *JRS* 70 (1980): 101–25. Hopkins describes the hardship imposed on simple cultivators by the Roman imposition of money taxes and their expenditure outside the region where they were levied (101). For a defense of the market economies of ancient Israel and Judah and criticism of the

The significance of the "whore" metaphor in Rev 17 may be found in verse 2: "The kings of the earth went whoring [with her] and the inhabitants of the earth became drunk with the wine of her whoring." This imagery could signify the great attractiveness of Rome's power and wealth. The language of whoring and drunkenness implies that all who dwell on the earth, including kings, took leave of their senses and acted irrationally in seeking to fulfill their desires, desires that the woman was able to satisfy.

In the portrayal of the great whore's downfall in Rev 18, one of the reasons for the judgment against her is that "all the nations have collapsed because of the wine of her passionate whoring" (18:3).[19] Another reason is that "all the nations have been deceived by" her sorcery (18:23). The reference to "Babylon's" sorcery may be an allusion to Isa 47:9.[20] The context in Isaiah suggests that the sorceries and enchantments of personified Babylon were insufficient to guarantee her safety and security. The statement in Rev 18:23, however, picks up and rounds off the remark about all the nations falling down drunk because of the wine of her passionate whoring in 18:3. This intratextual relationship suggests that her "sorcery" in 18:23 alludes to a specific kind of magic, love spells of attraction or spells for binding a lover.[21] In this case, the term "sorcery" has a metaphorical sense, like the woman's whoring.

---

prophets' economic and social views, see Morris Silver, *Prophets and Markets: The Political Economy of Ancient Israel* (Social Dimensions of Economics; Boston: Kluwer-Nijhoff, 1983), 247–51. I am grateful to Peter Machinist for calling the studies of Chaney and Silver to my attention.

19. For an argument in favor of the variant "collapse" over "drink," see David E. Aune *Revelation 17—22* (WBC 52C; Nashville: Nelson, 1998), 966n3c. In 18:3 and 14:8 the Greek noun *thymos* means "intense passion" (contra the NRSV and with Aune), whereas in 14:10 it means "fury, intense anger." In the former two passages, the word refers to the desire experienced and awakened by the whore; in the latter it refers to the wrath of God.

20. Aune, *Revelation 17—22*, 1010.

21. See, e.g., Hans Dieter Betz, ed., *The Greek Magical Papyri in Translation* (2nd ed.; Chicago: University of Chicago Press, 1992), 39–40 (a love spell of attraction); 44-47 (spells binding a lover).

PROPHETIC ALLUSIONS IN THE DESCRIPTION OF THE FATE OF THE WHORE

Although there are other interesting allusions to prophetic passages, I shall conclude with a discussion of the fate of the whore as portrayed in Rev 17. The last verse of the chapter identifies her explicitly with "the great city that rules over the kings of the earth" (Rev 17:18). Interpretation of the brief description of her destruction in 17:16 has been controversial. Marla Selvidge and Tina Pippin have approached it with feminist critiques, speaking of rape, misogyny, and sexual murder.[22] Barbara Rossing has argued against them that the emphasis here is not on a woman's body but on the destruction of a city and the collateral ecological damage.[23]

The hermeneutical key to the account of Rome's destruction is given in the following verse: "For God put it into [the] hearts [of the ten kings] to do his purpose and to carry out a single purpose and to give their kingly power to the beast until the words of God are accomplished" (Rev 17:17). In light of this statement, the preceding description of the devastation of Rome appears to be a concise fusion of several prophetic passages, interpreted as predictions of events of the last days. Thus, the original application of the imagery need not control the eschatological prophetic interpretation. The idea that the kings and the beast "will hate the whore" (Rev 17:16) may allude to Ezek 23:28–29:

> For thus says the Lord GOD: I will deliver you into the hands of those whom you hate, into the hands of those from whom you turned in disgust; and they shall deal with

---

22. Marla J. Selvidge, "Powerful and Powerless Women in the Apocalypse," *Neot* 26 (1992): 157–67; Selvidge speaks of "rape, fire, and cannibalism" (164); and Tina Pippin, *Death and Desire: The Rhetoric of Gender in the Apocalypse of John* (Literary Currents in Biblical Interpretation; Louisville: Westminster John Knox, 1992), 58, 60–64, 83.

23. Barbara R. Rossing, *The Choice between Two Cities: Whore, Bride, and Empire in the Apocalypse* (HTS 48; Harrisburg, PA: Trinity Press International, 1999), 87–97.

you in hatred, and take away all the fruit of your labor, and leave you naked and bare.

This speech is addressed to Oholibah (representing Jerusalem), who whored after various lovers. The idea that Rome will be made "bare," "desolate," or "laid waste" may come from an oracle against Tyre that begins with Ezek 26:19:

> For thus says the Lord GOD: When I make you a city laid waste, like cities that are not inhabited, when I bring the deep over you, and the great waters cover you, then I will thrust you down into the Pit,...so that you will not be inhabited or have a place in the land of the living.

Another possible allusion is to the whore of Hosea (Hos 2:3 NRSV; 2:5 in the MT and LXX), who is threatened as follows:

> I will strip her naked
>   and expose her as in the day she was born,
> and make her like a wilderness,
>   and turn her into a parched land,
>   and kill her with thirst.

The prophecy that they will devour her flesh may have been inspired by the indictment of the wicked rulers of Israel in Mic 3:1–3:

> Should you not know justice?—
>   you who hate the good and love the evil,
> who tear the skin off my people,
>   and the flesh off their bones;
> who eat the flesh of my people,
>   flay their skin off them,
> break their bones in pieces,
>   and chop them up like meat in a kettle,
>   like flesh in a caldron.

Destruction of cities by fire was, of course, common practice, and John may have witnessed or heard about the burning of Jerusalem by the troops of Titus. He may thus have taken this feature from experience. Or he may have taken Jer 34:22 as a prophecy against Rome: "I am going to command, says the LORD, and will bring them back to this city; and they will fight against it, and take it, and burn it with fire."

CONCLUSION

The author of Revelation, John the prophet and seer, has adapted language from Daniel, Zechariah, Isaiah, Jeremiah, Nahum, Ezekiel, and Micah to express his understanding of the resurrection and coming of Christ. He also borrows their indictments and imagery to articulate his hope for vindication and justice. Some of this language and imagery is violent and potentially misogynistic. In the traumatic aftermath of the destruction of Jerusalem and the temple, the utilization of passages originally applied to Israel and Judah to the perpetrator of this recent violence, Rome, is understandable. The transformation of such rhetorical and imaginative passages into actual violence is another matter.[24]

---

24. For an ethical discussion of the use of violence in Revelation, see Susan E. Hylen, "Metaphor Matters: Violence and Ethics in Revelation," *CBQ* 73 (2011): 777–96.

IV

EARLY RECEPTION OF
NEW TESTAMENT TEXTS

17

How New Testament Textual Variants Embody and Exhibit Prior Textual Traditions

Eldon Jay Epp
(Emeritus, Case Western Reserve University)

Textual criticism of the New Testament, at its very core, is concerned with prior textual traditions, for it seeks to identify and to track the transmission of multiple levels or layers of text over time. It does this by assessing the quality of the myriad textual variants found among some 5,550 different Greek manuscripts, the perhaps 12,000 versional manuscripts that are extant for the writings now in the New Testament, as well as numerous patristic quotations. Each variation-unit (a small segment of text containing two or more variant readings) is examined to discover, if possible, the reading prior to the others for that unit. Indeed, textual criticism recently was defined as "the analysis of variant readings in order to determine in what sequence they arose."[1] Hence, an overall goal has been to establish the earliest attain-

---

1. David C. Parker, *An Introduction to the New Testament Manuscripts and Their Texts* (Cambridge, UK: Cambridge University Press, 2008), 159. A "reading" is a general term for any segment of text in any witness to the New Testament writings. A "variant" or "textual variant" or "variation" or "variant reading" is a segment of text (a word, phrase, clause, sentence, or more) that differs in some way from a similar portion of

able text for each variation-unit and then cumulatively for the entire New Testament text.[2]

A NEW PHASE WITH A NEW EMPHASIS IN NEW TESTAMENT TEXTUAL CRITICISM

During the past two decades, a fresh emphasis has opened a new phase in New Testament textual criticism. In 2007, J. Eugene Botha, under the startling title "New Testament Textual Criticism Is Dead! Long Live New Testament Textual Criticism!," reported his growing conviction that textual criticism, in its traditional form, increasingly has been ignored by "the vast majority of New Testament scholarship." Botha asserts that the majority "know nothing and frankly, don't care" about the complex, technical aspects of the discipline. Rather, they generally are content to accept the text as provided in the standard hand-editions of the Greek text. Above all—while acknowledging that textual criticism is "a necessary and fundamental New Testament endeavour"—Botha laments the fact that for over hundreds of years its "basic assumptions and presuppositions" have not been questioned. Thus, in spite of new technology, "the ultimate object of textual criticism has not changed at all," namely, "a quest (still elusive) for the

---

text in another textual witness. "Variation-unit" describes a segment of text in which two or more textual variants are found. The portion of text encompassed by a variation-unit is determined by the convenience of showing how variants in that segment compare with one another. At a minimum, a unit will consist of one word in each of two or more witnesses that differ, or it may cover a phrase in which various witnesses have differing words and word order, etc.

2. On the complex process for determining the earliest attainable text, see Eldon J. Epp, "Traditional 'Canons' of New Testament Textual Criticism: Their Value, Validity, and Viability—or Lack Thereof," in *The Textual History of the Greek New Testament: Changing Views in Contemporary Research* (ed. K. Wachtel and M. W. Holmes; SBLTCS 8; Atlanta: Society of Biblical Literature, 2011), 79–127; and idem, "Textual Criticism and New Testament Interpretation," in *Method and Meaning: Essays on New Testament Interpretation in Honor of Harold W. Attridge* (ed. A. B. McGowan and K. H. Richards; Atlanta: Society of Biblical Literature, 2011), 79–105.

original text."[3] It is this long-standing, traditional phase of New Testament textual criticism that he declares to be dead.

But then follows the pronouncement, "Long Live New Testament Textual Criticism!"—recalling that the declaration of the death of a king is followed immediately by the coronation of a new king or queen, for whom the hope is: "May he/she live long." So, for Botha, a new phenomenon or phase of textual criticism has arrived, and he expects that it will enjoy a long life and vibrancy, but most of all he hopes that it will "lead to a re-imagining and re-discovery of the role of textual criticism in New Testament scholarship."[4] What triggered this abrupt turnabout in his views? Botha attributes it to David Parker's *The Living Text of the Gospels,*[5] which speaks of the long-lasting fluidity of the Jesus traditions, asserts that there were multiple originals, and questions the utility of seeking a "single original text" of the New Testament writings—implying the futility of such a task. Botha views Parker's emphases as heralding "the death of textual criticism. It [traditional textual criticism] exists to recover something that never existed!"[6]

I resonate substantially with Botha's views, though the search for the earliest attainable text, variation-unit by variation-unit, remains a useful part of the goal of New Testament textual criticism, not least because it creates an accessible and functional baseline text. This constructed baseline text, however, is not to be identified with a "single original text"; rather, it serves to disclose and to display the available variants but it remains what it is: the earliest attainable text, open, of course, to modification as new evidence emerges and fresh methods are employed. The significance of Botha's pronouncement lies in its assertion that a new era, a new understanding of textual criticism has been inaugurated—one that de-emphasizes

---

3. J. Eugene Botha, "New Testament Textual Criticism Is Dead! Long Live New Testament Textual Criticism!" *HTS* 63 (2007): 561–63.

4. Ibid., 563; see also 571.

5. David C. Parker, *The Living Text of the Gospels* (Cambridge, UK: Cambridge University Press, 1997).

6. Botha, "New Testament Textual Criticism," 567; see 563–67 for Botha's spirited description of Parker's views.

"a quest for an elusive original" and emphasizes a quest "to discover and recover something of the diversity and fluidity and vibrancy of early Christianity."[7] It is this phenomenon that I now wish to discuss and exemplify.

There is, of course, a longer history than Botha has acknowledged of textual critics viewing variant readings as providing "a window into the social history of early Christianity," as Bart Ehrman has phrased it.[8] Already in 1904 Kirsopp Lake called upon his colleagues to examine textual variants because "we need to know what the early church thought [a passage] meant and how it altered its wording in order to emphasize its meaning."[9] Lake's clarion call was followed only by a sprinkling of scholars from his day to our own. One prominent group of proponents, however, could be found, just before and after World War II, among the University of Chicago faculty (Donald W. Riddle and Ernest C. Colwell) and doctoral graduates (Kenneth W. Clark and Merrill M. Parvis). Riddle, for example, with reference to meaningful variants, declared as early as 1936 that "there are no 'spurious readings': the various forms of the text are sources for the study of the history of Christianity."[10]

In more recent times, it was Ehrman, four years prior to Parker's book, who accorded special significance to variant readings in his now classic and highly compelling work, *The Orthodox Corruption of*

---

7. Ibid., 568, 571.

8. Bart D. Ehrman, "The Text as Window: New Testament Manuscripts and the Social History of Early Christianity," in *The Text of the New Testament in Contemporary Research: Essays on the Status Quaestionis* (ed. B. D. Ehrman and M. W. Holmes; 2nd ed.; NTTS 42; Leiden: Brill, 2013), 804.

9. Kirsopp Lake, *The Influence of Textual Criticism on the Exegesis of the New Testament* (Oxford: Parker, 1904), 12. For a brief history of what has been called theological tendencies in textual variants, see Eldon J. Epp, *The Theological Tendency of Codex Bezae Cantabrigiensis in Acts* (SNTSMS 3; Cambridge, UK: Cambridge University Press, 1966), 1–28.

10. Donald W. Riddle, "Textual Criticism as a Historical Discipline," *AthR* 18 (1936): 221, with examples on 221–24. Colwell and Parvis offered contributions in 1952; Clark in 1953; for a summary of the stimulating views of this "Chicago School," see Epp, *Theological Tendency*, 15–19; idem, "The Multivalence of the Term 'Original Text' in New Testament Textual Criticism," *HTR* 92 (1999): 272–74.

Scripture.[11] His well-known thesis is that certain scribes of the second and third centuries, whom he designates "Proto-Orthodox Christians," sought to advance their own christological doctrines against detractors of three types: adoptionists, docetists, and separationists. Their method was to introduce intentionally variant readings that would alter the texts that were to become the New Testament writings (to repeat once again his noteworthy expression) so as to "make them *say* what they were already known to *mean*."[12] Thereby, for theological reasons, came the "correction" (or, from another vantage point, "corruption") of the Greek texts known to them in their day, and in many cases the variants that were overwritten were destined for the apparatus as the later, secondary readings took their places in the printed Greek texts. It may well be, however, that we should think more about our text being "enriched" rather than "corrupted" by such alterations, for the rejected readings that, in reality, were previously the priority readings now enable us to witness some of the controversies and socioethical struggles in the early churches. Hence, in the new phase of textual criticism, meaningful or meaning-changing variants—especially rejected variants—are not viewed as chaff to be whisked away by the wind; rather, they convey alternate interpretations, drawn from the real life of the church, and therefore represent new knowledge and are to be welcomed as enrichments to our understanding of early Christianities.

This new emphasis in New Testament textual criticism has been given a name: narrative textual criticism, which I take to mean, perhaps simplistically, that every meaningful variant has a story to tell. Whether deemed suitable or not, the designation has caught on. Actually, Parker first offered the name, three years prior to his *Living Text of the Gospels*, in a review of Ehrman's book.[13] While referring to Ehrman's volume, he also invoked the present writer's older book on

---

11. Bart D. Ehrman, *The Orthodox Corruption of Scripture: The Effect of Early Christological Controversies on the Text of the New Testament* (2nd ed.; New York: Oxford University Press, 2011). The first edition appeared in 1993.

12. Ibid., xii (italics are found in the first edition).

13. David C. Parker, review of B. D. Ehrman, *Orthodox Corruption*, *JTS* 45 (1994): 704.

The Theological Tendency of Codex Bezae Cantabrigiensis in Acts (1966) as an early participant, and shortly after Parker's own volume would place him centrally in that group, with a cadre of authors since then.

The foregoing discussion might suggest that scribes ran fast and loose in taking liberties with the text that presumably they were to copy accurately. Indeed, on occasion it has been suggested that scholars in this new phase have inappropriately overstated the activity of scribes in altering texts and that, perhaps justly, they have too easily attributed intentionality to the alterations observed. To be sure, the entire issue of scribal activity is highly complex and disputable.[14] For one thing, textual alterations are created not only by scribes, but from readers' notations, or by those who prepare a manuscript for copying, among other causes. Much less is known about scribal behavior than we would like, but surely it is simplistic either to pronounce that scribes merely copied the manuscript before them—period!—or to imply that scribes were rampant in their alteration of texts.

Barbara Aland, for example, emphasizes that "above all, the scribe's task is to copy the text and not to change it arbitrarily," and that this task is performed with full correctness because the job is "to copy and not to theologize." Yet she notes the fine line between mechanical copying and individuals initiating variations, granting, for example, that the scribe of P[72] shows distinct signs of intentional theological alteration, thereby providing us, she asserts, "a new 'source' for understanding Christ in the 3rd/4th centuries."[15] This obviously is a

---

14. See David C. Parker and Hugh A. G. Houghton, eds., *Textual Variation: Theological and Social Tendencies? Papers from the Fifth Birmingham Colloquium on the Textual Criticism of the New Testament* (Piscataway, NJ : Gorgias, 2008). This volume is particularly relevant to scribal behavior, especially the articles by Ulrich Schmid, Richard Goode, Dirk Jongkind, Peter M. Head, Tommy Wasserman, and David C. Parker. See also James R. Royse, *Scribal Habits in Early New Testament Papyri* (NTTSD 36; Leiden: Brill, 2008); idem, "Scribal Tendencies in the Transmission of the Text of the New Testament," in Ehrman and Holmes, *Text of the New Testament in Contemporary Research*, 461–75; and Kim Haines-Eitzen, "The Social History of Early Christian Scribes," in Ehrman and Holmes, *Text of the New Testament in Contemporary Research*, 479–92.

15. Barbara Aland, "Welche Rolle spielen Textkritik und Textgeschichte für das Verständnis des Neuen Testaments? Frühe Leserperspektiven," *NTS* 52 (2006): 305 and n7; 308–10 (author's translation).

balanced though modest view of scribal individuality, a view that is countered on the left of center, for example, by Richard Goode, who describes what we have called "narrative textual criticism" as a "sea change" that will "highlight the deliberate and intentioned engagement with the text by the scribe." He points out that "the earlier notion of scribal neutrality no longer holds the field" and observes, astutely, that "scribality is not passive but hermeneutic in nature."[16] So, a poignant question of Botha becomes relevant: "We know that it was possible for ancient scribes to transmit texts very accurately and precisely. The question we need to ask is why they chose not to do it" in so many instances. Botha offers one answer: "It is perhaps the fact that there has been a long legacy of fluid oral traditions which coexisted with scribal traditions for a long time."[17] In addition, I would suggest that scribes increasingly gained access to other manuscripts with different readings, which prompted them more actively to consider alternative interpretations. Moreover, from the standpoint of narrative textual criticism, a major reason, of course, would be that thinking scribes, immersed in their own doctrinal and liturgical milieu (often monastic), felt obligated to "correct" the manuscript being copied in favor of their own convictions.

Exactly how, then, is the new narrative approach to be described? In view of my failure to appropriate a fresh analogy, I beg to employ one that I have used often. As follows:

Scene: Hollywood, Selznick International Pictures, 1939.

Set: *Gone with the Wind*: Filming, 135 days from January to July 1939.

Producer/Director: "Lights, camera, action!" [Actors perform] "Cut!" [Pause for coaching] "Action!" [resumed] "Cut!" [etc.] Result: Numerous "Takes," totaling 500,000 feet of 35mm film.

---

16. Richard Goode, "Kings or God? Toward an Anthropology of Text," in Parker and Houghton, *Textual Variation*, 30–31.

17. Botha, "New Testament Textual Criticism," 566. The interrelationship of orality and textual transmission deserves more attention within the text-critical discipline.

Postproduction: Film to cutting room for editing, July to November 1939, resulting in retention of 20,000 feet of film.
Event: Premier, Atlanta, December 15, 1939, with running time of nearly four hours.

This describes the traditional way of movie making: the use of actual film that was humanly scanned, with large portions cut and falling to the floor, and the production of the "original" by splicing together all the scenes that were selected to convey the plot. To switch to narrative textual criticism, assuming the construction of some "original" text, textual critics would rush into the cutting room, sweep up the rejected snippets, and examine the meaningful ones to see what story each one had to tell. It is as simple as that: rejected variants are saved, so to speak, from the trash bin to reveal scenes of real life in the early churches—doctrinal issues debated, apologies for the faith formulated, liturgical practices evaluated, moral and social standards discussed, historical matters considered, among other early Christian concerns. In short, meaningful variant readings disclose for us the multiple interpretations rampant in all aspects of early church life, teaching, and worship.[18] But "the proof of the pudding is in the eating," so examples are in order. Those below represent a modest sample of the whole.

EXAMPLES OF NARRATIVES EMERGING FROM VARIANT READINGS

Meaningful and meaning-changing textual variants are replete throughout the New Testament text and always have been, and that they have stories to tell is basic to exegesis and obvious to all. The new emphasis, however, shifts the focus to "rejected" variants in the appa-

---

18. For an overview, see Ehrman, "Text as Window," 803–30. For brief treatments, see, e.g., Epp, "Multivalence," 258–66; and idem, "It's All about Variants: A Variant-Conscious Approach to New Testament Textual Criticism," *HTR* 100 (2007): 287–97.

ratus, especially in situations where textual critics have treated variants in a binary fashion (in or out!) and have chosen largely to ignore those relegated to the apparatus. Regrettably, many scholars of Christian church history, theology, and other disciplines that employ the Greek New Testament tend to avoid the complex material at the foot of the pages, and, as Botha noted, this pattern is followed even by many New Testament scholars. It is understandable, of course, for our colleagues to respect the text-critical decisions that committees of experts have made over the years, and textual critics, I suppose, should be flattered by that characterization. The apparatus is there, however, because reasonable questions exist about which variant in each case belongs where—in the printed text or in the apparatus netherworld. Certainly this is the case with many of the examples below, so frequently it is an open question as to which variant is to be rejected. In either case, a narrative emerges, which is an interpretation, but one that in turn is open to multiple construals, and variants' stories range from the ordinary, even mundane, to significant and occasionally dramatic. The new emphasis views each narrative as an enrichment of our knowledge of the early church, but especially the rejected variants, because the narratives disclosed by readings accredited for the printed text already have been analyzed heavily and discussed by exegetes. The time has come to let the other voices be heard.

Space does not permit elaboration on the examples below, so it must suffice to highlight a number of worthy illustrations, offering only some obvious suggestions as to their significance and motivation. Readers should examine for themselves the primary textual data and secondary sources. In each reference below, the variant mentioned first stands in the printed text of the UBS[4] and Nestle-Aland[28] Greek Testaments,[19] followed by a relevant variant (or variants) in the apparatus. Whether the variants discussed actually belong in the text or in the apparatus will be considered only occasionally. The main point is to see how variants differ from one another and how all of them can enlighten us.

---

19. The Greek texts of UBS[4] and Nestle-Aland[27] and [28] are identical, except in the Catholic Letters of Nestle-Aland[28].

READINGS PORTRAYING SAYINGS OF JESUS

One place to begin is with the two longest and almost universally rejected variants, both of which are enclosed in double square brackets in the printed texts, signifying that they "are known not to be a part of the original text."[20] First, the "longer ending of Mark" (Mark 16:9–20, 171 words), allegedly reporting words of the risen Christ, contains lofty instruction ("Go into all the world, proclaiming the good news" and "The one who believes and is baptized will be saved") that has motivated missions and evangelization. Verses 17–18, obviously intended to enhance the miraculous powers of Christ, fall far short, I would suggest, of enrichment:

> And these signs will accompany those who believe: by using my name they will cast out demons; they will speak in new tongues; they will pick up snakes in their hands, and if they drink any deadly thing, it will not hurt them; they will lay their hands on the sick, and they will recover.

This perilous promise, accepted literally among ultrafundamentalist Christians, has had deadly results when families refuse medical help, often for their children, and when trusting preachers handle venomous snakes or drink deadly poisons in worship services to demonstrate their faith.[21]

The other lengthy and generally rejected variant narrates the episode of a woman caught in adultery (John 7:53–8:11, 169 words—about which I always ask, "What about the man?"). Without this floating piece of tradition, we would not have these poignant words placed in the mouth of Jesus, namely the pronouncement to the accusers about to stone the woman, "Let anyone among you who

---

20. *Novum Testamentum Graece* (28th ed.; ed. H. Strutwolf et al.; Stuttgart: Deutsche Bibelgesellschaft, 2012), 55*. If known not to be part of the earliest text, why are these passages not in the apparatus?

21. For more detail, see Epp, "Textual Criticism and New Testament Interpretation," 103–4.

is without sin be the first to throw a stone at her," which results in their slow departure. Then she is asked, "Has no one condemned you?" Her negative answer evokes compassion: "Neither do I condemn you. Go your way, and from now on do not sin again." A memorable variant, indeed.

Some twenty textual variants reside in the four Gospel passages that portray the sayings of Jesus on marriage and divorce (Matt 5:27–32; 19:3–9; Mark 10:2–12; Luke 16:18). Parker's full chapter analysis of this complex "spaghetti bowl" of variations has become a classic,[22] for his basic and (I think) incontrovertible conclusion is that here "the recovery of a single original saying of Jesus is impossible," nor is any remaining reading "more original than the others." What we do have is "a collection of interpretative rewritings of a tradition," which contraindicates textual criticism's "long accepted…role that has been demanded of it as provider of authoritative text."[23] The marriage/divorce passages, containing multiple variations without resolution about a single original reading or clarity about the sequence of its transmission history, encapsulate an important aspect of narrative textual criticism: in numerous New Testament passages, variants offer an array of interpretations that disclose real life issues of doctrine, worship, and social practice in early Christianity. Such cases go one step further: the lack of resolution not only indicates that multiple options remained open, but also enriches us by preserving many solutions that were considered and an array of actions that were taken as the early churches faced distressing, intractable ethical dilemmas. That means, for Parker, that ever after— up to our own day—"the people of God have to make up their own minds. There is no authoritative text to provide a short-cut."[24] Textual criticism cannot be declared irrelevant or out of date!

A final example is Mark 15:34 (Jesus' last words on the cross): "My God, my God, why have you forsaken me?" However, there exists a variant reading for the question: "Why have you reproached/

---

22. Parker, *Living Text of the Gospels*, 75–94.

23. Ibid., 92–94.

24. Ibid., 212; see also 208–11.

taunted/mocked me?" As Ehrman points out, in the christological controversies the term *enkataleipō* (glossed both as "to forsake" or more simply "to leave behind") was employed by separationists (who claimed that the human Jesus and the divine Christ were separate beings) to refer to the divine nature departing from Jesus before his death: "My God, my God, why have you left me behind?" An orthodox response to neutralize that view could have occasioned the alternative verb *oneidizō* ("to reproach"/"revile"/"mock"), which also fits the preceding narrative where Jesus was mocked repeatedly, and now again by God.[25]

READINGS PORTRAYING ACTIONS OR DESCRIPTIONS OF JESUS

Matthew 27:16–17 (at the trial of Jesus): Another prisoner, offered to the crowds in place of Jesus, was named "[Jesus] Barabbas" (in the printed text, with brackets indicating the reading was preferred, but without full certainty). The full name, as the harder reading, is the earlier reading, because what scribe would add "Jesus" to a criminal's name? Origen agreed, but then asserted that a heretic added it to discredit Jesus by associating his name with an evil person. Thus Origen, who said "Jesus" was absent "in many copies," opted for "Barabbas" alone. A more dramatic story behind "Jesus Barabbas" is surmised by W. D. Davies and Dale Allison, namely that a subtle enhancement of Jesus as Son of God was Matthew's intent by listing the prisoner's full name. How so? Since "Barabbas" in Aramaic is interpreted "son of Abba," that is, "son of the father," there is perhaps a "profound irony" here: "The two prisoners named 'Jesus' are both 'son of the Father,'" and "the crowd must choose between two men named Jesus."[26]

Mark 1:41 (Jesus' encounter with a leper): When approached by a leper, desperate to be healed, Jesus, "moved with compassion," said,

---

25. Ehrman, *Orthodox Corruption*, 168–71. See his full discussion and the reference to *Gos. Phil.* 68.

26. W. D. Davies and Dale C. Allison, *The Gospel according to Saint Matthew* (3 vols.; ICC; Edinburgh: T&T Clark, 1988–97), 3:584–85 and nn23–24; 585–86. On this variation unit, see Epp, "It's All about Variants," 288–89; idem, "Textual Criticism and New Testament Interpretation," 91–96, 98, 102.

"Be clean." The D-Text witnesses portray Jesus as "moved with anger," which, as the harder reading, very likely was the earlier reading, which then was altered—for one reason, at least—to counter criticism from the likes of Celsus that Christian Scriptures portrayed an angry God (as in "the wrath of God") and, therefore, to remove such human, un-Godlike emotions from Jesus.[27]

READINGS CONCERNING DOCTRINAL CONTROVERSY AND IDEOLOGICAL BIAS

Doctrinal Issues

Mark 1:1 is a classic case. Did the Gospel open with "The beginning of the good news of Jesus Christ, the Son of God," or without the phrase "Son of God"? The latter phrase (in brackets in the printed text as preferred but uncertain) is unlikely to have been deleted if it were present. For this and for other reasons, the version lacking "Son of God" is doubtless the earlier text. It lacks emphasis on Jesus' divine sonship, and, in the context of the early christological controversies, someone wary of adoptionism could counter that view by inserting "Son of God." That would make Jesus the Son of God prior to his baptism (Mark 1:11), when (in adoptionism) the adoption to sonship allegedly took place.[28]

Matthew 27:49 (the crucifixion, before Jesus died): "Wait, let us see whether Elijah will come to save him." Here a rejected variant reads: "And another took a spear and pierced his side, and out came water and blood." Then Jesus died. (See John 19:34, where the wounding occurs after his death.) Interpolating this event in Matthew's version would

---

27. Wayne C. Kannaday, *Apologetic Discourse and the Scribal Tradition: Evidence of the Influence of Apologetic Interests on the Text of the Canonical Gospels* (SBLTCS 5; Atlanta: Society of Biblical Literature, 2004), 129–34; and Bart D. Ehrman, "A Leper in the Hands of an Angry Jesus," in *New Testament Greek and Exegesis: Essays in Honor of Gerald F. Hawthorne* (ed. A. M. Donaldson and T. B. Sailors; Grand Rapids: Eerdmans, 2003), 77–98, esp. 95–98; reprinted in idem, *Studies in the Textual Criticism of the New Testament* (NTTS 33; Leiden: Brill, 2006) 120–41, esp. 138–41.

28. Ehrman, *Orthodox Corruption*, 85–88; and Parker, *Living Text of the Gospels*, 145.

oppose docetism—the view that Jesus/Christ was the manifestation of a preexistent divine being, whose humanity was merely "apparent"— because it demonstrated that his body was real flesh and blood.

Luke 22:19b–20 (Jesus' words over the bread and wine): In this "Lord's Supper" account, the D-Text contains the first cup, with Jesus' mention of the bread as "my body" (stopping there), but lacks the second cup and its reference to "my blood, that is shed for you." The point is similar to the preceding instance: the longer text was brought in to counter docetic views: "Christ experienced a real passion in which his body was broken and his blood was shed."[29]

Luke 22:43–44 (Jesus' prayer in the garden) is similar. Prior to the crucifixion, Jesus was at the Mount of Olives, and the printed text reads (v. 42): "Father, if you are willing, remove this cup from me; yet, not my will but yours be done." Verse 44 then reads: "In his anguish, he prayed more earnestly, and his sweat became like great drops of blood falling down on the ground." The latter verse portrays genuine human agony and might well have been interpolated to counter docetic views.[30]

Luke 24:3 (at Jesus' tomb): The printed text reads "But when they [the women] went in, they did not find the body of the Lord Jesus." The D-Text witnesses, however, lack "of the Lord Jesus." That may appear to change little, but the variant becomes a useful example. Ehrman views the shorter reading as earlier because, for example, why would a subsequent scribe or reader omit these words? The longer reading, then, is likely an insertion by "proto-orthodox" advocates to refute docetism by affirming that the body in the tomb was indeed that of Jesus and was the same body that arose from the dead. Parker adds that the shorter reading does not imply that the author of

---

29. Ehrman, *Orthodox Corruption*, 244; see 231–45, with strong support from Parker, *Living Text of the Gospels*, 150–57. See also Eldon J. Epp, "The Disputed Words of the Eucharistic Institution (Luke 22, 19b–20): The Long and Short of the Matter," *Bib* 90 (2009): 407–16.

30. The sentence "In his anguish…" is in double brackets in Nestle-Aland, indicating that editors have judged it as "known not to be part of the original text." See details in Ehrman, *Orthodox Corruption*, 220–27; and Parker, *Living Text of the Gospels*, 157–59.

Luke held a docetic view, which could not have been anticipated at the time the Gospel of Luke was composed.[31]

Anti-Judaic Sentiments

Acts 3:15–17 (Peter speaking to "Israelites"): "You killed the Author of life, whom God raised from the dead" (v. 15). "And now, friends, I know that you acted in ignorance, as did also your rulers" (v. 17). But the D-Text cluster of witnesses reads: "And now, friends, we know that you indeed did *this evil thing* in ignorance, as did also your rulers." Here Peter's point is that the Jews cannot be guiltless because of their ignorance (of God's plan), so the responsibility for Jesus' death rests squarely on them. This accusation in the D-Text at the outset of Acts sets the stage for a plethora of anti-Judaic tendencies in that textual cluster throughout Acts.[32]

Briefly, the omission of Jesus' words on the cross in Luke 23:34— "Father, forgive them, for they do not know what they are doing"—is undoubtedly "a consequence of Christian anti-semitism."[33] And concerning Rom 1:16: Was salvation "to the Jew *first* and also to the Greek," or "to the Jew and also to the Greek"?

Diminution of Women

Acts 1:14 (after listing eleven apostles): "All these were constantly devoting themselves to prayer, together with [certain] women, including Mary the mother of Jesus, as well as his brothers." A variant in Codex Bezae (D) adds "and children" after "women," thus altering

---

31. Ehrman, *Orthodox Corruption*, 256–57, 283; and Parker, *Living Text of the Gospels*, 165–66.

32. See Epp, *Theological Tendency*, passim; idem, "Anti-Judaic Tendencies in the D-Text of Acts: Forty Years of Conversation," in *The Book of Acts as Church History: Text, Textual Traditions and Ancient Interpretations/Apostelgeschichte als Kirchengeschichte: Text, Texttraditionen und antike Auslegungen* (ed. T. Nicklas and M. Tilly; BZNW 120; Berlin: de Gruyter, 2003), 111–46; reprinted in idem, *Perspectives on New Testament Textual Criticism: Collected Essays, 1962–2004* (NovTSup 116; Leiden: Brill, 2005), 699–739.

33. Parker, *Living Text of the Gospels*, 162. See also Epp, *Theological Tendency*, 45.

the text to "their [the apostles'] wives and children," which (quoting Elisabeth Schüssler Fiorenza) "eliminates totally" any ecclesial role the women might have had.[34] Similarly, in Acts 17:4 Paul's preaching in a synagogue in Thessalonica persuaded "a great many of the devout Greeks and not a few of the prominent women." A D-Text variant, however, makes this read "not a few wives of prominent citizens."[35]

In Col 4:15 the name Nympha/Nymphas in a Greek accusative form can be feminine or masculine, depending on the accent. The printed text has "Give my greetings to...Nympha and the church in *her* house," but Pauline D-Text witnesses have "*his* house." If the shift was from "her" to "him," that would deprive a woman of being the leader of a house church. (Nestle-Aland[28] and UBS[4] have "her," while those of Merk, Bover, and Bover-O'Callaghan read "his.")

A similar but more significant situation, involving the same ambiguity in accenting the accusative case, concerns Rom 16:7 and the name Junias/Junia: "Greet Andronicus and Junia, my relatives who were in prison with me; they are prominent among the apostles." The name was understood as feminine (Junia) by all Christian writers of late antiquity up to Aegidius/Giles of Rome in the thirteenth century, in all extant early versions (Old Latin, Vulgate, Coptic, and Syriac), and—with one or two exceptions—was accented as feminine in all Greek New Testaments from Erasmus (1516) to the 1927 Nestle edition. The masculine name, Junias, is found nowhere, for it was invented and perpetrated by late nineteenth-century grammarians, lexicographers, and exegetes who were unable to admit that a woman could be an apostle.[36] Two oft-repeated, clever but poignant remarks remain. Bernadette Brooten comments, "Because a woman could not have been an apostle, the woman who is here called apostle could not have been a woman." And Elizabeth Castelli observes, "The reference

---

34. Elisabeth Schüssler Fiorenza, *In Memory of Her: A Feminist Theological Reconstruction of Christian Origins* (New York: Crossroad, 1983), 52. For a survey of variants involving women, see Kannaday, *Apologetic Discourse*, 176–89.

35. Richard I. Pervo, *Acts: A Commentary* (Hermeneia; Minneapolis: Fortress, 2009), 420.

36. See Eldon J. Epp, *Junia: The First Woman Apostle* (Minneapolis: Fortress, 2005).

to Junia…has inspired remarkable interpretative contortions, resulting ultimately in a sex-change-by-translation."[37] Junia would reappear seventy-one years later in the fifth corrected printing (1998) of Nestle-Aland[27].

CONCLUSION

Assuredly, the question will arise, "What is so new about narrative textual criticism?" To be sure, textual criticism still involves the examination of variants by utilizing the various criteria for the priority of readings, resulting in a decision about the earliest attainable text, which then is placed in the printed text. Though there are numerous difficult cases, the vast majority of decisions can be made with reasonable confidence. Then the remaining variants, as always, reside in the apparatus.

The newness of approach comes with the insistence that, except for obvious scribal errors and nonsense readings, there no longer are "right" and "wrong" variants. Not only is it the case that any "original text" in the simplistic sense is elusive, but most important is the conviction that the remaining variants in each unit—Let's no longer call them rejected variants!—have much to tell us about the life, thought, and practice in the early churches, enhancing our knowledge in significant ways. They should always be in our thoughts when exegesis is underway or history is being written, and their voices should never be silenced.

This change in emphasis and in attitude toward variant readings enriches our knowledge and stretches our minds, opening us to the narratives of forces that constantly were at work as the traditions about Jesus were transmitted, as doctrinal and ethical viewpoints evolved,

---

37. Bernadette J. Brooten, "'Junia…Outstanding among the Apostles' (Romans 16:7)," in *Women Priests: A Catholic Commentary on the Vatican Declaration* (ed. L. S. Swidler and A. Swidler; New York: Paulist, 1977), 142; and Elizabeth A. Castelli, "Romans," in *Searching the Scriptures. Vol. 2: A Feminist Commentary* (ed. E. Schüssler Fiorenza; New York: Crossroad, 1994), 279. My public lecture on Junia at Wellesley College in 2004 carried the title "Junia: Apostle Deposed by Gender Change."

and as worship practices were enhanced. All of these and more are inherent in the array of meaningful variants that our rich manuscript and patristic resources provide for us, and they should not be overlooked. Long live New Testament textual criticism!

The Unitary Goal of New Testament Textual Criticism for the Twenty-First Century

New Testament textual criticism, employing aspects of both science and art, studies the transmission of the New Testament text and the manuscripts that facilitate its transmission, with the unitary goal of establishing the earliest attainable text (which serves as a baseline) and, at the same time, of assessing the textual variants that emerge from the baseline text so as to hear the narratives of early Christian thought and life that inhere in the array of meaningful variants.

18

Christ Suffers in Me

The Martyr's Experience Shaped by the Passion of Christ

Carolyn Osiek, RSCJ
(EMERITA, BRITE DIVINITY SCHOOL)

This collection of essays honors two scholars and teachers who have devoted their adult years to the study of the Scriptures and have in many ways laid down their lives daily, monthly, and yearly in its cause. The focus for the volume is on the ways in which biblical texts employ and adapt earlier traditions. Here, a slight variation is offered, in continuity with the same theme: how early accounts of the deaths of martyrs in the centuries immediately following the time of the New Testament continued the process of employing and adapting one of its most significant themes, participation in the sufferings of Christ. A good number of these examples, though not all, are women, and it was the conviction of early Christians that the triumph of women in extreme suffering was one of the signs of the Spirit at work.

Two passages from the Pauline letters express the apostle's thought on how the life and sufferings of Christ continue in his own life: Gal 2:20 and the puzzling Col 1:24. Two very recent translations of each of these passages show some of the interpretive variants:

It is no longer I who live, but it is Christ who lives in me. And the life I now live in the flesh I live by faith in the Son

289

of God, who loved me and gave himself for me. (Gal 2:20, NRSV)

Yet I live, no longer I, but Christ lives in me; insofar as I now live in the flesh, I live by faith in the Son of God who has loved me and given himself up for me. (Gal 2:20, NABRE)

I am now rejoicing in my sufferings for your sake, and in my flesh I am completing what is lacking in Christ's afflictions for the sake of his body, that is, the church. (Col 1:24, NRSV)

Now I rejoice in my sufferings for your sake, and in my flesh I am filling up what is lacking in the afflictions of Christ on behalf of his body, which is the church. (Col 1:24, NABRE)

Theologians ponder the passage in the letter to the Colossians with desperate attempts to explain how anything could be lacking in the afflictions suffered by Christ. Yet the author of Colossians, whether Paul or a later follower, had a keen sense of how the sufferings of Christ continue in one whose life is embedded in the mystery of Christ.

Texts such as these, as well as the Gospel passion narratives, must have been the foundation for the conviction of later martyrs that their sufferings were not their own, but those of Christ present and suffering in them. While no explicit reference to these Pauline passages is present in the martyr texts that we will examine, a similar consciousness can be seen in the narratives, and we are left to wonder whether these Pauline texts or passages like them underlie the convictions of their authors.

The reasons for pre-Decian persecutions (before the imperial persecution of Decius, 249–251 CE) are not fully known, and much study for many years has never really clarified the issue. An additional puzzling factor that is clear in many of these accounts is that not all Christians were arrested in the sweeps that occurred. In some cases, it was only or mostly leaders who were targeted, as in the case of

Polycarp, who was arrested in a presumably Christian household that sheltered him, with seemingly no consequences for those who gave him hospitality. In other cases, witnesses lived to write about the events. In still others, family and friends visited those arrested in prison and were not bothered.

Other unofficial religions were at times persecuted as well, as suspicion arose that they were involved in clandestine rites that might undermine the Roman imperium. At the core, however, it was the refusal of Christians to honor civic religion that put them in a precarious position. Unlike the Jews (who similarly refused), Christians were particularly vulnerable because they did not have exemption from civic sacrifice, something the Jews had since the days of Julius Caesar. They and the Jews were considered atheists because they did not acknowledge the other gods upon whom Rome and its people depended.

I will focus on the three most popular early martyr accounts: the *Martyrdom of Polycarp* (ca. 165 CE), the account of the martyrs of Lyon and Vienne (177 CE) as related by Eusebius in *Ecclesiastical History*, and the *Acts of Perpetua and Felicitas* (203 CE).[1] In the first two of these accounts, it would seem that popular animosity, not government authority, was the prime mover toward persecution of Christians.

POLYCARP

Polycarp, bishop of Smyrna, known by Irenaeus in his youth, died in the amphitheater of Smyrna, present-day Izmir in Turkey, sometime in the middle of the second century. The range of possible dates accepted by scholars is 155–167 CE. The *Martyrdom of Polycarp* was known and mostly reproduced by Eusebius (*Hist. eccl.* 4.15.3–45),

---

1. These are some of the earliest accounts, though not the only ones. The events of the deaths of Ptolemaeus and Lucius reported by Justin Martyr must have taken place before 165 CE, the year Justin himself was put to death. The deaths of the Scillitan martyrs occurred in July, 180 CE, and those of Pionius and Apollonius around the same time. For texts and introductions of the accounts discussed here, as well as of the texts to be discussed below, see Herbert J. Musurillo, ed., *The Acts of the Christian Martyrs: Introduction, Texts, and Translations* (Oxford Early Christian Texts; Oxford: Clarendon, 1972).

and also survives in six medieval manuscripts. It does not have the suc-
cinctness of some other martyr acts that seem to resemble court tran-
scripts, like the *Acts of Justin* or those of the Scillitan martyrs. In its
received form, it is already a carefully composed theological account
in the guise of a historical report. What is significant for our purposes
is that every possible similarity to the passion of Jesus is brought out.

When the persecution breaks out, others are arrested. Some are
killed, though the narrative is vague on this point. It mentions one
Germanicus who dies bravely, and another, Quintus from Phrygia,
who is at first enthusiastic about giving himself up, but in the end
apostatizes by offering sacrifice.[2] Upon the advice of friends, Polycarp
first leaves the city for a country estate, then goes to another before he
is betrayed by two arrested and tortured slaves who know his where-
abouts; thus he is handed over by trusted members of the household.
The chief of the soldiers who arrest him is named Herod. Polycarp
becomes *Christou koinōnos*, a "sharer with Christ," so that his betray-
ers might receive the punishment of Judas (*Mart. Pol.* 6.2). When the
soldiers arrive where he is, it is Friday at dinner time. They come
armed "as though against a bandit"—an explicit reference to Matt
26:55. Urged to flee again, he refuses, saying: "Let the will of God be
done," quoting Paul when he faced arrest in Acts 21:14 (*Mart. Pol.*
7.1). He is brought immediately into the amphitheater, where a hostile crowd awaits. He is commanded to abjure his faith by saying "away
with the atheists," that is, the Christians. In an ironic turn, he gestures
instead to the crowds, saying: "Away with the atheists!" (*Mart. Pol.* 9).
This piece of irony enrages them all the more.

In an unexpected departure from christological typology,
Polycarp is not nailed to the stake where he will be burnt, but only
tied. When he is bound to the stake, he offers a prayer of thanksgiving
that he has been found worthy to be counted among the martyrs. By
this time the word *martyr*, originally meaning "witness," has acquired
in Christian literature the specific sense of one killed for refusal to

---

2. Since Phrygia was the origin of the charismatic movement known as Montanism,
which encouraged martyrdom, it is possible that this is what is meant by calling
Quintus a "Phrygian."

abjure the faith. He gives thanks that he has been found worthy to share in the cup (*potērion*) of Christ, an allusion to the cup that Christ, while praying in the garden, asks to be removed as he approaches his death, yet nevertheless ultimately accepts (Matt 26:39; Mark 14:36; Luke 22:42) (*Mart. Pol.* 14.2). Finally, once he has died in the fire, one of the executioners plunges a small sword into his body and an abundance of blood flows out, reminiscent of John 19:34 (*Mart. Pol.* 16).

These elements of conformity to the Gospel passion narratives are carefully constructed, grounded no doubt on a historical account that is then theologically embellished. They portray the old bishop of eighty-six years as accepting his death in quiet gratitude for its alignment with the suffering and death of Jesus.

THE MARTYRS OF LYON

The stirring account of the group of martyrs in Lyon (Lugdunum) in Gaul in the summer of 177 CE survives solely as preserved by Eusebius (*Hist. eccl.* 5.1.3–2.8). Its genre is a circular letter from the churches of Lyon and Vienne to those of the Roman provinces of Asia and Phrygia. Though it originated in Gaul and reflects interrogations conducted in Latin, its language is Greek in keeping with that of its recipients and the likelihood that the author and most of those involved were Greek-speaking immigrants to Gaul from Asia Minor. Indeed, their immigrant status may have been a factor in their being singled out for persecution, though a few of the names are Latin, which may suggest that some involved were locals. In an unusual turn, one of the immigrant Christians, Attalus from Pergamon, after having first been tortured, is remanded because he is believed to be a Roman citizen. An inquiry is sent to the emperor Marcus Aurelius, and an answer comes back that the Christians who are Roman citizens are to be beheaded, while the others are condemned *ad bestias*, to be killed by wild animals. Attalus's claim to

Roman citizenship, however, is not honored, and he dies in the amphitheater with the others.

According to Eusebius, Irenaeus was a member of that immigrant church in Gaul, but was away in Rome at the time of the persecution. Upon his return, he was elected bishop to replace the martyred bishop Pothinus (*Hist. eccl.* 5.5.6). Trouble with Roman authorities seems to have dissipated in Gaul after that.

The martyrdom text in Eusebius contains fewer miraculous elements than that of the *Martyrdom of Polycarp*, yet it is obvious that some theological embellishment occurred when the account was composed as a letter to other churches. As with the situation around Polycarp, here it is hostile crowds who demand the torture and death of these practitioners of what is perceived to be a strange and subversive religion, and the magistrates seem to think they have to go along with the crowd's demands. However, there is the conviction in the text that the real adversary is not the crowd or magistrates but Satan, the power of evil, who strategizes to defeat them. Throughout the story runs the countertheme of the noble athlete who endures all, even to the point of a noble death, thus winning the contest against Satan. Accounts of believers' great suffering under torture enhance this theme.[3]

One of the accusations against the Lyon Christians was the familiar one of insidious and licentious secret rites, such as the sacrifice of a child, incest, and sexual licentiousness in the dark. These accusations surface regularly in early Christian literature (see, e.g., Minucius Felix, *Octavius* 9.5–7). According to the account in Eusebius, slaves of some of their households, under torture and at the urging of the interrogators, make false accusations of "Oedipean marriages and Thyestean dinners" (*Hist. eccl.* 5.1.14). One of those arrested, a woman named Biblis, first apostatizes, then under torture regains her courage and when asked to

---

3. For the themes of resistance and of the noble death, see David Seeley, *The Noble Death: Graeco-Roman Martyrology and Paul's Concept of Salvation* (JSNTSup 28; Sheffield: JSOT Press, 1990); Arthur Droge and James Tabor, *A Noble Death: Suicide and Martyrdom among Christians and Jews in Antiquity* (San Francisco: HarperSanFrancisco, 1992); and James A. Kelhoffer, *Persecution, Persuasion and Power: Readiness to Withstand Hardship as a Corroboration of Legitimacy in the New Testament* (Tübingen: Mohr Siebeck, 2010).

ratify the accusations rejects them instead, arguing that Christians could not possibly eat children when they do not even eat the blood of animals (*Hist. eccl.* 5.1.26; an allusion to the following of Jewish food laws by some Christians—cf. Acts 15:20).

Three times in this long narrative there are explicit references to Christ suffering in or in place of the martyr. The deacon Sanctus from Vienne does not respond under torture to questions about his name or place of origin or legal status. To all questions, he answers in Latin, "I am a Christian," thus enraging his interrogators all the more. When red-hot plates are pressed to his side, he finds refreshment in the spring of living water flowing from the side of Christ (cf. John 7:38; 19:34). When his body is disfigured, *Christ suffering in him* is glorified and strengthened and conquers the adversary, the power of evil against whom it is understood that they are really contending (*Hist. eccl.* 5.1.20–23).

The narrator relates that many who were arrested died in prison, some by strangulation, others by torture. Among the tortured were some of the younger members who could not endure, and some of the oldest, among them Pothinus, entrusted with the *diakonia tēs episkopēs*, "the episcopal ministry," in Lugdunum. The bishop, over ninety years old and physically infirm, is nevertheless determined to attain martyrdom. He is dragged along by soldiers and a mob, who kick and beat him, shouting insults at him *as though he were Christ himself.* He is thrown in prison where he dies two days later as the result of his injuries and infirmities (*Hist. eccl.* 5.1.27–31).

The third and best known of the martyrs in the account of events at Lyon is Blandina, a central character in the narrative, a slave of uncertain age, whose mistress is also one of those arrested. Though the narrative suggests a large and indefinite number of Christians arrested, the force of antipathy falls on three men and one woman: Sanctus, a local deacon; the newly-baptized Maturus; Attalus, an immigrant from Pergamon; and Blandina. Through her, the text says, Christ shows that what is humanly judged to be ordinary and worthy of scorn is glorious before God. Through her love for Christ, she shows not only the appearance of fidelity but also demonstrates it in deed.

Blandina's mistress is among those arrested, but nothing more is said about her, except that she was worried for Blandina's endurance, due to her bodily weakness, which could suggest either youth or old age, or the usual stereotype of the slave as lacking in nobility and strength of character. But Blandina, to everyone's surprise, becomes the strongest in enduring torture. The torturers admit that there is nothing more they can do to her and, for the time being, allow her to live. Indeed, she seems to gain strength in her confession of faith, like a "noble athlete." As was the case with the interrogation of Biblis described above, the questioning seems to have centered around rumors of immoral behavior. After insisting that she is Christian, Blandina asserts that they do nothing shameful (*Hist. eccl.* 5.1.17–19).

Blandina appears for a second time in the narrative at the point at which she most typifies the notion of Christ suffering in the martyr. This passage has become a classic in women's studies and in the imaging of women in early Christian literature, often juxtaposed to later theories of women's incapacity to image Christ. After various and prolonged tortures in prison, some of the martyrs are brought out in public in the amphitheater at the beginning of the gladiatorial games. It was usual that the execution of condemned criminals by torture was carried on during the low midday period at the games, during the "lunch break," as it were.

Here Blandina is hanged on a stake and wild animals are let loose to attack her, but none of them would. This refusal of animals to attack was apparently not that unusual, perhaps because of the animals' confusion at the sights and sounds of the crowd. Since they would not touch her, she is taken down to face another ordeal on another day. This is a central moment in the narrative, however. The other Christians who are present see their sister Blandina hanging in the form of a cross, and see in her "the one who was crucified for them." Through her endurance, she demonstrates that those who are small, weak, and unimportant have put on Christ, himself the great and unconquered "athlete" who overcomes the adversary (*Hist. eccl.* 5.1.41–42). Blandina becomes the presence of Christ suffering in and among them.

Several days of the games follow, with various ordeals for the arrested Christians and many deaths. Finally, on the last day of the games, only two are left. Blandina is brought out again with Ponticus, a fifteen-year-old boy, two images of weakness: an adolescent boy and a female slave. Here another biblical motif is applied to Blandina. In an allusion to the mother of the seven sons in 2 Macc 7, she urges him on like a noble mother until his death. Blandina is the last to die, after incredible tortures, so that bystanders admit that they have never seen a woman suffer so much (*Hist. eccl.* 5.1.53–55).

The memory of Blandina as the rallying point for the martyrs of Lyon and Vienne has become one of the major accounts of the heroism of women martyrs. Her story dashes the stereotypes of female—and especially servile female—weakness, and provides supporting arguments for the presence of the Holy Spirit in the early Christian community, proving that nothing is impossible with God. The belief that Christ is present in the suffering martyr is a strong piece of the argument.

PERPETUA AND FELICITAS

Twenty-six years later in North Africa, another famous event of martyrdom took place that enhanced the convictions of the heroism of martyrs, and of women in particular. Another female slave became a rallying image for her companions. Herbert Musurillo writes of this account that it is "the archetype of all later Acts of the Christian Martyrs: for it is not only an account of the trial and sufferings of the African martyrs, but it is also an apocalypse in its own right, reminiscent of the book of Revelation and the *Shepherd* of Hermas."[4] The location is Carthage, the date accepted by most scholars is 203 CE. The text is preserved in nine Latin manuscripts as well as one Greek manuscript, which is thought to be an early translation of the Latin original.

The undoubted focal point in this story is not the slave Felicitas,

---

4. Musurillo, *Acts of the Christian Martyrs*, xxv. See also Joyce E. Salisbury, *Perpetua's Passion: The Death and Memory of a Young Roman Woman* (New York: Routledge, 1997); and Thomas J. Heffernan, *The Passion of Perpetua and Felicity* (New York: Oxford University Press, 2012), for text, translation, and extensive commentary.

but the twenty-two-year-old Roman matron Perpetua. She is the dominant personality both because of her social status—well born, solidly educated, respectably married (*honeste nata, liberaliter instituta, matronaliter nupta*)—which was probably higher than any of the others arrested with her, and because of her courageous behavior as leader. It is she who reproaches the guards who are treating the prisoners too harshly (*Acts Per. Fel.* 16), and who stops the procession to the amphitheater because the condemned have been forced to wear costumes of pagan gods against their will (*Acts Per. Fel.* 18). At her insistence, the magistrate relents and allows the condemned to wear their own clothes. Even as she is to be killed she is in control: the young gladiator is unskilled in his task of cutting throats. She puts the sword in the correct place on her throat (*Acts Per. Fel.* 21.9). This kind of initiative on her part is indicative of a forceful character, but also of the expectation that, as the one of highest social status, she takes the lead, which is necessary given the absence of equal-status males in the group. Another aspect of her leadership is the function of her dreams in the movement of the story. The narrative can be said to participate in the genre of apocalypse, as noted above by Musurillo, because of the revelatory content and interpretation of her dreams and those of Saturus. Though Perpetua is nursing a male baby, oddly her husband is never mentioned.[5]

In contrast to the wide sweep of those arrested at Lyon, here the group is limited to five young catechumens: two slaves, Revocatus and Felicitas; two other males, Saturninus and Secondulus; and Vibia Perpetua. Later, another man, Saturus, described as their moral support, who was not present at the time of their arrest, gives himself up to join them (*Acts Per. Fel.* 2, 5). This would suggest that he was their instructor in the faith.

The leading figures whose dreams set the direction of the story and the martyrs' fate are Perpetua and Saturus. It is therefore surprising that the name of the account seems to have always carried only the names of Perpetua and the slave Felicitas. The story was tremendously

---

5. I have argued elsewhere that Saturus could be that husband. See Carolyn Osiek, "Perpetua's Husband," *JECS* 10 (2002): 287–90.

popular in the North Africa of Tertullian, Cyprian, and Augustine. Its popularity carried it to Rome as well, and Perpetua's and Felicitas's names appear in the Roman Canon, a rare feature in lists that are otherwise almost exclusively biblical or Italian. Their story remains tremendously popular today, especially among women. A common popular assumption is that Felicitas was the slave of Perpetua, perhaps because at the end they face their final ordeal together. But there is no indication in this story that this was in fact the case, and Felicitas's owner is unknown.[6] Their association is, perhaps, due to the memory of Blandina whose unnamed "earthly mistress" was arrested with her.

Little else is known about Felicitas, not even her age. She is eight months pregnant at the time of arrest, and as in the case of Perpetua, the father of her child never appears. Perpetua, we are told, is in a legal Roman marriage (*matronaliter nupta*). Felicitas, on the other hand, could not contract a legal marriage because she was a slave. Slaves were subject to the sexual whims of their owners and those to whom their owners gave permission. In addition, it is true that promiscuity among slave populations existed, and children born of slave unions were subject to separation from their parents and to being sold. Nevertheless, there is good evidence of stable marital relationships among slaves in circumstances that allowed them, and sometimes the terminology of legal marriage for spouses was used in connection with them.[7]

Felicitas's golden moment arrives while the group is still in prison. They are all distressed that she will not be able to suffer and die with them, since it was against the law to execute a pregnant woman. She would be remanded and executed later and alone. The whole group prays intensely, and she begins labor pains. When she cries out in pain in the delivery, one of the guards mocks her, saying that if she thought

---

6. Surprisingly, even Musurillo refers to Felicitas in the introduction as Perpetua's "personal slave-girl"; see *Acts of the Christian Martyrs*, xxvi.

7. See, for example, Dale B. Martin, "Slave Families and Slaves in Families," in *Early Christian Families in Context: An Interdisciplinary Dialogue* (ed. D. L. Balch and C. Osiek; Grand Rapids: Eerdmans, 2003), 207–30; and Henrik Mouritsen, "The Families of Roman Slaves and Freedmen," in *A Companion to Families in the Greek and Roman Worlds* (ed. B. Rawson; Blackwell Companions to the Ancient World; Chichester, UK: Blackwell, 2011), 129–44.

this was suffering, being tossed by wild animals will be far worse. Felicitas replies boldly—the only time she speaks—that the suffering she now has is hers, but then another will be inside her suffering for her as she does for him (*Acts Per. Fel.* 15). She gives birth to a girl, who is taken home by a "sister," that is, by a member of the Christian community, and raised as her own daughter. Birth and death are brought together here: the one who gives life to another becomes the one who surrenders her own life to the dying of Christ within her.

When the day finally arrives, Felicitas and Perpetua appear together in the amphitheater. Both are tossed by a wild heifer. Perpetua lifts Felicitas to her feet and, for one moment, they stand together (*ambae pariter steterunt*), the noble woman and the slave woman (*Acts Per. Fel.* 20). It is the last we hear of Felicitas, who is taken back with the others to be finished off by having their throats cut with the sword. But Perpetua once again is singled out in the narrative. The inexperienced young gladiator who cuts her throat misses. She screams out in pain and then guides the sword to her throat, as if, the narrator notes, such a strong woman could not be killed without her consent (*Acts Per. Fel.* 10).

CONCLUSION

The early stories of the deaths of martyrs were a source of inspiration in the centuries that followed. The number of accounts and of martyrs increased in the early fourth century in the wider persecutions under Diocletian and Galerius. The stories of these later martyrs also acquired more legendary traits. The earlier accounts are not without some theological editing. Conformity to the suffering and death of Christ was a crucial motif in the narratives and in the consciousness of the martyrs themselves. It gave motivation and encouragement to those in a similar situation, who were prepared to die for what they believed in the face of mob violence or official persecution, following in the footsteps of Christ to whom they had pledged their life and their death.

Index of Sources

57	187n47	49:35	49
57:3	261n11	49:36	92
57:14	180	50:20	64
58	187n47	51:7–8 [LXX 28:7–8]	260
58:1 — 59:18	180	51:12 [LXX 28:13]	260
58:2	48n28	51:13 [LXX 28:13]	260
59	7		
59:8	174	**Lamentations**	
59:8–9	175	1:6	25n10
63	7	1:15	25
63:3	7	2:1	25n10
63:10	172	2:11–12	24
63:16	5	2:13	25
64:1	172	2:20	24
64:7 [E 8]	5	4:4	25
66:3	14	4:10	25
66:9, 13	10n15	4:21	28
66:18	172	4:21–2	27–28
66:24	173, 186		
		Ezekiel	
Jeremiah		1:26	6, 11
1:8	5	1:26–28	258
2	5	1:27	13
3:3	261n11	4:4–8	61
3:4	5	16	5
3:19	5	16:30	261n11
7	5, 8	16:31	261n11
7:11	186–87	16:35	261n11
27:3	27	17:22	48n27
27:5–7	91	17:23	52n41
27:6–7	26	20:31	52
27:9 — 28:17	27n12	20:33–34	43n11
29	27n12	23	5
31:9	5	23:28–29	265–66
31:20	4n2	23:43	261n11
34:22	267	23:44	261n11
44	5, 8	26:19	266
48:29	44	28:16–18	262n16
49:7–22	28, 35–36	31:3	48n27
49:10	35	32:2	93
49:12	28	33:18	238n6
49:16	36		

DEAD SEA SCROLLS

1:2b	173
1:2–3	172–73, 175, 189
1:3	172–73, 187
1:3a	173
1:3b	173
1:4	176
1:7	172
1:10	172
1:10–11	188
1:11	172, 283
1:14	172, 176, 183–84
1:15	176
1:21	214, 216
1:41	282–83
2:1 – 3:6	215
2:5–10	83
2:23	174
2:28	83
3:13–19	216
4	184, 216
4:4	174
4:10–12	170, 176, 179–84
4:11	182
4:11–12	176
4:11b–12	181n27
4:12	173, 193, 194n11, 196n25
4:15	174, 183
6:8	174
7	186
7:1	184
7:5	184
7:6–7	173, 184
7:6–8	184–86
7:8	185
7:17–23	186
8:3	174
8:17–18	188
8:22 – 10:52	189
8:27	174
8:30–32	217
8:31	172

9:31	172
9:33–34	174
9:33–37	216–17
9:38–40	186
9:42–47	217
9:42–48	186
9:48	173, 186
10:2–12	281
10:17	174
10:29	182n31
10:32	174
10:33–34	172
10:41–45	188n48
10:45	188n49
10:46	174
10:52	174
11 – 12	216, 218
11:8	174
11:17	172–73, 186
11:18	187
12:1	187
12:6–8	187
12:14	174
12:32	173
13	83, 216, 218
13:9–13	182n31
13:24	173, 187
13:25	173
14:22–26	232n23
14:36	293
15:34	281–82
15:39	172
16:1–8	213
16:9–20	280
16:17–18	280
Luke	
1 – 2	199
2:32	199
7:5	199
8:10	194n11, 196n25
12:41–46	218

RABBINIC LITERATURE